THE
UNKNOWN
WARRIOR

THE
UNKNOWN
WARRIOR

AN ARCHAEOLOGY OF THE COMMON SOLDIER

RICHARD OSGOOD

First published in the United Kingdom in 2005 by
Sutton Publishing Limited · Phoenix Mill
Thrupp · Stroud · Gloucestershire · GL5 2BU

British Library Cataloguing in Publication Data
A catalogue record for this book is available from the British Library.

ISBN 0-7509-3810-2

Typeset in 10.5/15pt Photina MT.
Typesetting and origination by
Sutton Publishing Limited.
Printed and bound in England by
J.H. Haynes & Co. Ltd, Sparkford.

For Katherine Freya

Contents

List of Illustrations

Acknowledgements

First, I acknowledge the great help that has been given to me by my friend and archaeological colleague Martin Brown, during the preparation of this work. Secondly, I would like to extend my thanks to the following individuals and groups for their assistance:

Bronze Age Britain Professor Mike Parker Pearson, for discussions on this topic over the years; Gail Boyle, of Bristol Museum, for helping with Tormarton; Ruth Pelling, for archaeobotanical information; Professor John Evans, for his kind donation of the Stonehenge images.

Early Roman Period Dr Eberhard Sauer, for information on his work at Alchester; Dr Simon James, for advice on matters pertaining to Dura Europos; Dr Susanne Wilbers-Rost and Kalkriese Museum, for information on the site of the demise of the Varus Legions; Professor Mark Robinson, for information on diet; Oxford Archaeology and English Heritage for Carlisle artefacts; Dr Martin Henig on matters religious.

Anglo-Saxon and Viking Era Dr Chris Knüsel and the Late Sonia Chadwick-Hawkes, for details of the Eccles skeletons; Dr Paul Budd, for information on the scientific studies of the Riccall burials; Professor Martin Biddle, for help with Repton; Dr Andrew Reynolds for matters Saxon.

Medieval Period Dr Chris Knüsel, for information on the work at Towton; all those connected with Visby, including Professor Ebba During and Marie Flemström; Siv Falk and Annica Ewing of the Statens Historiska Museum; the Royal College of Physicians, Edinburgh, for providing details of Soutra; Martin Brown and Lucy Sibun, for discussing the Lewes burials; Chris Daniell, for work on the Fishergate bodies.

Tudor and Stuart Ages Dave Allen and Alan Turton, for discussing the Basing House skull with me many moons ago; Glenn Foard, for comments made at a conference at the National Army Museum.

Nineteenth Century Tony Pollard, Ian Knight and Adrian Greaves, for their information on archaeological work in connection with the Zulu War; Phil Freeman, who gave me important information about his work in the Crimea; Professors Rimantas Jankauskas (burials of the Grand Armeé, Vilnius) and Barry Cunliffe (prisoner-of-war camp, Portchester), who provided assistance with matters Napoleonic; Mario Espinola, whose work on Centreville was vital to my understanding of aspects of the American Civil War – to him I also extend my thanks in pointing out other resources, both of excavation information and relevant literature.

First World War Information on the archaeology of the First World War was obtained from several sources, including discussions at conferences, emails and telephone calls. Alastair Fraser and Andy Robertshaw provided details about their excavations at Auchonvillers; Alain Jacques provided similar knowledge about Arras. Aurel Sercu afforded me information about The Diggers work in Flanders, assisted by Paul Reed and John Hayes Fisher; Rob Janaway discussed the findings of Belgian material with me. Evidence for practice trenches was provided by Paul Sidebottom and Peter Beckett; Bob Moore helped with evidence about prisoners of war. Martin Brown was always generous in keeping me abreast of his exciting work at Serre and of practice trenches on Defence Estates that lay outside Salisbury Plain. Richard Petty was kind enough to let me photograph his family's collection of trench art. Using the Internet, I was able to ask many people questions about First World War archaeology – Nils Fabiansson and members of the Great War Forum were especially helpful.

Introduction

The principal results we obtain from the whole of these considerations are:

1. That infantry is the chief arm, to which the other two are subordinate.
2. That by the exercise of great skill and energy in command, the want of the two subordinate arms may in some measure be compensated for, provided we are much stronger in infantry; and the better the infantry the easier this may be done.

(Von Clausewitz, *On War*)

As I write this, apart from the obvious bustle of the office – of colleagues, computers, printers and photocopiers – the only sounds I can hear are the sounds from the open window: the shrill warbling of a skylark. That is apart from the occasional whistle as a shell passes overhead and thuds into the earth some miles away with the resulting percussion rattling the same window. To my untuned ear I could not tell you whether this is the twenty-first-century equivalent of a 'Jack Johnson', a 'Minnie' or a 'Whizz-bang' and I marvel at the infantrymen who, within a short space of time, were able to distinguish such variances; an ability that could be life-saving.

I have just returned from a site visit to a set of Australian practice trenches from the First World War. Though these were backfilled in the 1920s, elements of the material that filled them are still being brought to the surface by burrowing animals. Hence, pieces of rusting metal, Bovril jars, Camp coffee bottles and an Anzora bottle now adorn my desk, much to the bewilderment of several workmates. Yet this is the fabric of humanity that fascinates me – the residue of life (anthropology if you like); for, where books will inform the reader of the outcome of a selected battle, the history of particular regiments or the lives of great generals, little time is dedicated to the average fighting soldier – the 'Poor Bloody Infantry'.

This, I believe, is where archaeology is invaluable, for it can inform us of the lives of those who did the fighting. How much has ever been written on what was eaten by men when training, or on the replication of conditions they could have expected to experience? Archaeology informs us of the lives of these men and women involved in combat, with the main bias being survival conditions. It can tell us about the actual weapons that were used in fighting, rather than those simply depicted in paintings or in an ideal inventory of weaponry of the age. It can tell us of the diseases suffered by these people, their living conditions and the assistance they could hope for when wounded. Survey and excavation can show us how footsoldiers passed their time when not fighting and can perhaps reinforce our impression that, even centuries ago, their acts were not so very different from those of troops today. Soldiers throughout history have, for example, left a trace of their presence; they have carved their names and messages into buildings and monuments. Perhaps the very fact that their lives are lived closer to death than many other people's renders a desire to leave a physical trace that much stronger. Even today, soldiers will add their names, or those of their regiments, to the walls of barracks and training facilities.

Traces of warfare in the archaeological record seem to have become a much-examined subject in recent years – the topic of many conferences, journal titles, monographs, television programmes and archaeological research designs. There is a profusion of Internet sites dedicated to this sphere alone. As a consequence, I have been fortunate to draw upon the splendid work of a wide range of people when assembling this book.

I have decided to concentrate on the fighting soldiers – the infantrymen – as they are the ones who are vital in any combat to take land and hold it. Wherever possible I have avoided recourse to historical references as it is the archaeology I wish to examine – after all, who is to say that written histories are unbiased? At least the archaeological resource favours no side or individual, and I hope that the work will illuminate the rich resource we can turn to when we question events that occurred many years ago. The only writings I want to dwell on in this study will be either the graffiti of the troops or the physical writings (and writing equipment) present in archaeological deposits. The amount of information available will vary from chapter to chapter – after all, there is nothing by way of epigraphic source for the Bronze Age, whereas there is much for the First World War – and thus the chapters differ in length.

I would also not be so foolish to claim that this work is all-encompassing. For each chapter I have tried to provide a flavour of the evidence available within the time period rather than to collate everything relevant to each epoch. Furthermore, one will also be aware that most of the chapters have a distinctly 'British-Isles-centric' feel to them, or at least to wars in which Britain had an interest. This seems sensible to me, as it would at least give an idea of evolution of tactic and of equipment within a country that has been engaged in much warfare from prehistoric times to the present day. That being said, we are still able to draw in examples from North America, Western and Northern Europe, South Africa and Syria, so, hopefully, the work does not prove to be too insular.

In the following chapters, we will examine the Bronze Age warrior in Britain, the legionary of the early Roman Empire, the Anglo-Saxon warrior and his Viking counterpart, the regular and peasant forces of the Medieval era, footsoldiers of the Tudor and Civil War period of Britain, those who fought in the Napoleonic and Victorian eras and the American Civil War and, finally, the infantrymen of the First World War.

> With this generous and noble spirit of union in a line of veteran troops, covered with scars and thoroughly inured to war, we must not compare the self-esteem and vanity of a standing army, held together merely by the glue of service-regulations and a drill book; a certain plodding earnestness and strict discipline may keep up military virtue for a long time, but can never create it; these things therefore have a certain value, but must not be overrated. (Von Clausewitz, 1997: 157)

New work seems constantly to be emerging on the subject of the archaeology of war and hopefully this will enable us better to understand the gamut of emotions felt by infanteers from training to combat. We all feel we know about various wars as a result, perhaps, of poetry, writings, paintings and even films. Archaeology, far from being a mere handmaiden of history, can actually add new tones to the canvas or even redesign the painting, providing aspects of detail unavailable to the historian. In discussing this subject with friends and colleagues, I have had many stimulating debates with serving soldiers, archaeologists and historians and feel that we are able to say far more through archaeology than simply 'soldiers smoked and drank' (something suggested to me by a historian friend) (see Plate 1). We have access to the life of the building blocks of the army. We can see how the soldiers lived, how and where they prayed for life, how they fought, what weapons were used, how they adapted their tools, how they strayed from the military manuals of the age as they realised such dictates were unrealistic, how they aspired to pass their free time and how they actually spent these hours.

Without wishing to sound trite, the following chapters also reveal the horrors suffered by many in combat, from the Bronze Age to the First World War. I hope I have avoided a mawkish or voyeuristic feel to this book, but I have included combat victims in each chapter as they reinforce the fundamental aim of warfare: to defeat, and often to kill, one's enemy. Combat victims reveal so much of the warfare of each period – wounds and diseases suffered, medical treatment, weapons used, armour worn, deities worshipped – that to write a book without recourse to such an assemblage would be foolish. These people were all human beings, who died probably in pain and great fear and thus they reveal the full horror of warfare far more eloquently than I can. Although archaeological work has enabled names to be established for some of those found on the battlefields of the First World War (Brown, 2005), all the people included in this volume are unknown – be they a regular soldier or a peasant fighting for their town against a foreign army. The fact that they are 'unknown' does not make their testimony more important, but perhaps adds to the poignancy.

The final example, Unknown Warrior 14 (see Chapter 7), does not involve archaeology, but cannot be excluded, because he is the inspiration for the work and title of this book – he is the 'Unknown Warrior' killed on the Western Front and buried now in Westminster Abbey, London. He says a great deal about our psyche and desire to commemorate and is essential on an emotional level rather than for what his death and burial can tell us in an archaeological sense.

Richard Osgood
Army Training Estate
Salisbury Plain

ONE

The Dawning of the Arms Race:
Bronze Age Warriors

The greatnesse and numeroussnesse of the Barrows (the beds of Honour where now so many Heroes lie buried in Oblivion) doe speak plainly to us, that Death and Slaughter once rag'd here and there were scenes, where terrible Battles were fought . . .

(John Aubrey, 'Monumenta Britannica')

Warfare was not something that came with the Roman legions, interrupting the otherwise peaceful lives of folk in the British Isles. There is evidence of combat in earlier periods – the Neolithic, for example, saw attacks on Crickley Hill in Gloucestershire, and Hambledon Hill in Dorset (Mercer, 1999). But it was the European Bronze Age that saw the Continent's first arms race: the rise of a panoply of deadly arms, prestigious pieces of armour and competition surrounding the movements of goods. It is from this point that I began looking at the archaeology of combat, and for that reason, and to illustrate the long history of warfare in Britain, I have included this chapter on part of the prehistoric sequence of the development of the British Isles. It also serves as an introduction to the elements we shall look at from the historic periods in later chapters.

Traces of the Bronze Age arms race can be seen alongside the burials of those who, in death, wished to be portrayed as warriors, and also those who had suffered from this weapon technology in life. Fortified centres, the precursors of many of the well-known Iron Age hill forts, were created, and the archaeological record also shows the possible modes of transport of the infantry. This was a period of infantry – horses did not appear in any numbers in the British Isles until probably the end of the Late Bronze Age, but when they did, their presence was significant and they were revered. A recent Optical Stimulated Luminescence (OSL) date obtained from the chalk hill carving of the horse at Uffington in Oxfordshire was Late Bronze Age. Furthermore, decorative pieces of horse gear were made in the Late Bronze

Age, around 700 BC, with some examples from Britain having been destroyed by weapons, as part of a votive act, in a similar fashion to the destruction of Late Bronze Age swords (Osgood, 1995). If, by the close of the period, the infantry was able to use the horse to add to its mobility, even if fighting was on foot, its other major means of transport was the boat.

Movement of war bands by boat was along the same riverine routes as trade goods and these boats enabled people to travel long distances. Bronze Age boats have been found at places such as Dover, Kent, and North Ferriby, Humberside. Rock carvings in Denmark from this period depict warriors, sometimes fighting, on board large vessels (Osgood and Monks, 2000: 31). Another example of the possible depiction of a Late Bronze Age to Early Iron Age raiding party using a boat to bring the warriors to their point of fighting was found at Roos Carr in Humberside. A wooden model of a number of warriors with round shields, clubs and phalluses was found here (Osgood, 1999b; Osgood and Monks, 2000: 34–5).

It seems that warfare was the preserve of those at the upper end of society, who had access to such prestige goods as bronze shields, helmets and weapons. Fighting at the start of the period, using the rapier, was specialised and probably accomplished only by champions; later, war bands and raiding parties would fight. It is possible that the archaeological record holds evidence for the more 'showy' elements of the arms of these warriors and that clubs and staves have not survived. Although such raiding was undertaken by a specialised group, other Bronze Age people would have had to fight if their settlement was raided or attacked. What we are seeing is perhaps only a sample of material related to combat, and the so-called common soldier was probably a member of an important class of society. In this chapter I shall avoid too much analysis of the typologies of weaponry as other scholars have dedicated large works to this subject and our study is, among other things, to look at the types of weaponry available to the warrior in this period.

WEAPONRY

With the Bronze Age in the British Isles spanning 1,500 years, it is not surprising that weaponry and its use changed over this time. At the start of the period, the bow and arrow was probably the main weapon of choice. Arrowheads and archer's wristguards were essential elements of the Beaker Culture burial package, and there is evidence of the effectiveness of flint arrowheads. Daggers are present in many burial contexts, but it was not until the emergence in the Middle Bronze Age of the rapier – a long, slender, stabbing bronze weapon – that we see the introduction of the hand weapon proper. Rapiers required precision and training was necessary; they were the weapon of 'champions'. Tears in the handle rivets of such objects indicate that a slashing motion was more natural and show how occasionally the rapier was used incorrectly.

Swords appear in the Late Bronze Age and have been found throughout the British Isles. Bridgford (1997) has examined large numbers of Irish examples and noted that the edge damage displayed is consistent with the swords having been used in combat. By the end of the Bronze Age, a type of sword had emerged that employed the classic leaf-shaped sword's slashing attributes with a tapering end more useful for stabbing (the rapier's strong point). The 'Carp's Tongue' sword has been found along the Atlantic fringe of northern Europe, including the British Isles (Cunliffe, 2001: 280–1). To date, swords have not been associated with any palaeopathological evidence of violence, but it seems safe to assume that these objects, although of great value, prestige and beauty, also had a functional aspect and would have been used in violent raids. Their importance within a votive setting has been demonstrated by Pryor (1991: fig. 11), whose work at Flag Fen, near Peterborough, has shown that they were deposited, along with other weapons and bronzes, in the water as religious offerings. Swords deposited in such a manner could be broken prior to their sacrifice, perhaps symbolising the 'killing' of an object imbued with power.

In addition to the sword and its predecessor, the rapier, the spear was present for much of the Bronze Age. This is not the place to discuss the many varieties of spear and the huge range in sizes, shapes and methods of fixing the spearhead to the shaft. Suffice it to say that the spear, along with the flint arrowhead, is the main weapon for which we have evidence for its use in combat. A Bronze Age shield from Long Wittenham in Oxfordshire had been stabbed by such a weapon and there are two sites that have yielded examples of skeletons with spear wounds, which we shall discuss below, both of which were subject to violent stabs with the weapon. In an earlier work (Osgood, 1998), I tried to evaluate whether one could distinguish between the throwing and thrusting types of spear and came to the conclusion that, although some were better suited as javelins and others for stabbing, the weapon would have been used for whatever purpose it was required. If the warrior had had a javelin-sized weapon in close combat, he would still have tried to use it to stab his opponent. Some spears were for show rather than practical use; the Wandle Park spear was over 80cm long (Osgood and Monks, 2000: 25).

One particular spear, found at North Ferriby, Humberside, was broad-bladed and had pegs at the base of the blade, on the spear shaft, to fix it in place. Bartlett and Hawkes believed that this might have acted as some form of harpoon with the shaft breaking from the spear when it hit its target. The heavy shaft was attached only by a thread and thus encumbered the warrior whose shield it had struck. If, indeed, this was how it was used, the spear employed tactics that the Romans would find successful with the *pilum* centuries later (Bartlett and Hawkes, 1965: 372–3).

Axes were present throughout the Bronze Age, from the early flat axes carved onto one of the trilithons of Stonehenge to the socketed axes and palstaves from the end of the period. The latter were sometimes found in substantial hoards (Cunliffe, 2001: 289). Axes were important items of equipment, but how far were they weapons? I believe that, rather like the daggers of the period, the warrior would use them if they were the only tool to hand. The rapier, sword and spear are the weapons for which we have physical evidence of their use in fighting and, while the axe was certainly an important object, we have no definite evidence of its use in combat.

A final note on the weaponry of the period must include a comment on the objects which might have been used, but which do not survive in the archaeological record. It is likely that wooden clubs and staffs or staves would have been used in fighting. As these are made of organic material rather than precious metals, we do not find them preserved in the soil – the fact that the raw materials for such weapons were readily available would have meant that anyone needing to defend a hut or village would have owned such an object. No elements of prestige were involved with their ownership and thus they would not have been solely the reserve of the Bronze Age warrior, though they could have been quite functional.

ARMOUR

In France, several breastplates of thin, beaten bronze sheet have been found. The Marmesse cuirass is a wonderful piece of workmanship although, with no evidence for any backing of, say, tough leather, it is unlikely to have provided much protection to its wearer (Osgood and Monks, 2000: 28–9). To date, no such corselet has been recovered in Britain and our evidence of armoured protection used by the warrior is limited to the find of a few studs and the crest of what would have been a couple of helmets from Flag Fen (Pryor, 1991: 115).

Many Bronze Age shields have been recovered from the British Isles, such as those from the River Trent, Nottinghamshire, and Coveney Fen, Cambridgeshire. Some of these seem to have been for purely ceremonial purpose; the 'Yetholm' type shield from South Cadbury, for example (Coles *et al.*, 1999), was so thin that it could have been punched through with a fist. Indeed, it seems to have been ritually destroyed or 'killed' by being stabbed when on the floor. Did this act and the shield's deposition at this hill fort represent the defeat of its owner in combat? This shield would have served little practical use unless it was part of a ploy to cow one's enemies into submission as a result of facing a warrior of great prestige. Some of the metal shields had been used for fighting at some point. The 'Nipperwiese' type shield from Long Wittenham, Oxfordshire, *c.* 396mm diameter and 1–1.25mm thick, had a number of perforations caused by spearheads that left tell-tale traces through their lozenge-shaped cross-sections (see Plate 2). This shield also seems to have been hammered flat in another area to beat out the damage of a separate engagement (Needham, 1979).

Occasionally, survival conditions permit the presence of materials that would otherwise decay. Examples of this come from waterlogged contexts in Ireland. Here we have some important evidence pertaining to shields. At Kilmahamogue, County Antrim, a wooden mould for a leather shield has been found – a radiocarbon date for this object of 1950–1540 BC (Early to Middle Bronze Age) was obtained. Wooden shields have been found in Ireland, too, at Annandale and Cloonlara (from the eighth century BC), and a leather example from Clonbrin. This latter Irish example is 50cm in diameter and 5–6mm thick, with the handle stitched onto the back of the shield, the warrior's hand fitting under a raised part of the shield that acted as the boss (for these shields, see Coles, 1962).

In a now famous piece of experimental work, John Coles replicated both a metal and a leather Bronze Age shield and examined the efficacy of their defence against the blows struck by a replica Late Bronze Age sword. The metal shield was cut almost in half by the sword's blow, whereas the leather shield was found to possess far better defensive properties (Coles, 1962:

184–5; Harding, 1999a: 89). As the Long Wittenham shield shows, metal shields were used on occasion, but, for practical warfare, the Bronze Age warrior was likely to have been equipped with wooden or leather shield – the bronze examples being used more for display.

PRACTICE AND DISCIPLINE

We have no remains that relate to anything resembling a training camp or training feature in the Bronze Age, nonetheless the weaponry used will have required a modicum of experience; the rapier is a weapon that needs practice if it is to be used effectively. Furthermore, anyone who has picked up a Bronze Age sword would probably be surprised at how small the handles seem – the way of holding such a weapon was to have some of the fingers on the handle, but others closer to the blade of the sword, on the small 'ricasso' notch just below the handle. This is something that would take some getting used to if one was to wield a sword to the desired effect.

THE LIFE OF THE SOLDIER

In the following chapters we shall look at elements of the soldier's life – his pastimes, religion, the food he ate, the availability of alcoholic drink and its significance, and his enjoyment of tobacco. Unfortunately, this is not possible within the context of the Bronze Age, as it is rare to find conclusive evidence of military settlement or of those engaged in combat. Evidence of warfare is often isolated. We might find food traces in a Late Bronze Age midden (such as Chisenbury on Salisbury Plain), or within the confines of a defended settlement, but this is not the same as, say, a latrine in a fort. We cannot be sure of the diet being specifically martial. Further work also needs to be done to analyse human bones, as the information such analysis can provide on diets could be applied to those we think are combat victims.

Drinking

If we are indeed looking at an elite form of warfare in the Early Bronze Age, followed by warriors collected in loose war bands, can we see any parallels in succeeding chapters for obligations that would ensure alliance? In the Saxon and Norse eras there is constant literary evidence for warriors being provided with hospitality and rewards by their leaders and rulers in return for their service. Those who were at the top were known by such terms as 'ring-givers' and we see throughout the epic poem *Beowulf* references to drink being taken in the great halls. By building up ties and obligation, so one could ensure service. Gift-giving and reciprocity is well known in the anthropological record and there is a possibility that this is what we are seeing occasionally in the archaeological record.

To this end, the Beaker Culture 'package' is especially interesting. Decorated ceramic drinking vessels – the 'Beaker' – are often found in burial assemblages within barrows associated with items of warrior paraphernalia, such as arrowheads and archers' wristguards. Occasionally, a site such as Barrow Hills (Barclay and Halpin, 1999) produces elements such as gold 'basket earrings' (or hair decorations), and very occasionally a fabulously rich burial is found, such as the Amesbury Archer excavated by Wessex Archaeology, with all of the above items and more, including a bronze dagger (see Wessex Archaeology, 2004b).

There is also the possibility that the inhumed were accompanied by leather jerkins and ornamental belts as part of the warrior's costume, such as those depicted on stelae in Switzerland (Osgood and Monks, 2000: 84). Why would a ceramic vessel be included in the same package as items reflecting a martial character – the arrowheads, wristguard, dagger – or of great wealth in gold and bronze?

Although a new type of vessel, the technology behind the ceramic beaker was not new. It is possible that we are seeing the ceramic vessel as part of the martial package – the symbol of obligation, feasting and bonding through drinking, like the warriors depicted in the Saxon chronicles, epic poems and Norse sagas. Strong liquor does indeed seem to have been part of a status assemblage: 'Some of the interments in Scottish graves appear to have been accompanied by vessels containing fermented drinks, as indicated by the analysis of scrapings taken from a beaker found at Methilhill, Ashgrove, Fife, and a food vessel from North Mains, Strathallan, Perthshire' (Clarke *et al.*, 1985: 201).

Sherratt (1994: 253) thinks that bell-beakers began as a variant of corded ware drinking vessels, as the latter tradition in northern Europe saw an assemblage accompanied with stone battle axes, as opposed to the archery equipment of the Beaker package. He writes: 'These vessels suggest individual hospitality rather than the great communal ceremonies at gathering places, which had hitherto dominated the ritual life of Western Europe.' Such hospitality could still be used to reinforce ties and bonds between warriors in local elites – perhaps the alcoholic drinks would also provide a form of Dutch courage to warriors, too.

Writings

In the following chapters we shall see many interesting facets connected to writing and the infantry: inscriptions – often of the owner's name – on weaponry, graffiti scratched by soldiers in buildings, and letters describing conditions found at fortress sites. In Bronze Age Britain there is no such resource. Carvings have been found that reflect the importance of weaponry or 'prestige goods', such as the extensive carvings of axes on one of the Stonehenge trilithons recently highlighted by a programme of laser-scanning. Unfortunately we have no writings – it is probably safe to suggest that the warrior of the British Bronze Age was illiterate.

Although there are no writings, there are depictions of warriors and the panoply of arms, which are as expressive. These are present throughout northern Europe – with many examples in Scandinavia. Here, spears, shields, swords and helmets are all depicted and there are images of combat on ships. In Britain there are possible rock carvings of shields in Ireland – Harrison (2004) has recently examined these carvings in depth.

Accommodation

As we have no regimental system in the Bronze Age and as those that did the fighting in this period would have used the same style of huts and enclosures as other members of society, it is next to impossible to differentiate something approximating a 'barracks' in the archaeological record. Bronze Age huts have been found, sometimes in walled enclosures like those from Grimspound on Dartmoor, Devon, and sometimes with fences such as Blackpatch, Sussex, and Trethellen Farm, Cornwall, but the main areas worth looking at are the large fortified centres or 'hill forts' of Bronze Age date.

In earlier publications (Osgood, 1998: 55–67; Osgood and Monks, 2000: 10–15) I have summarised some of the evidence for the emergence of these structures in Britain and Ireland. Many early hill forts were sited to dominate passes and to protect trading routes, primarily rivers, and areas of production

– Dinorben in Wales controlled the routes to Ireland and the region's gold industry. The ramparts of these fortified sites could be elaborate affairs. The various phases of timber palisades and ditches at Rams Hill, Berkshire, for example, date from 1410–1047 BC (Bradley and Ellison, 1975). Although these forts had substantial defences, the size of the population within would have been too small to garrison the entire perimeter. Perhaps this indicates that, in turn, raiding parties would have been too small to mount any form of siege and that the fortifications were more than adequate to provide protection to a tribal grouping when threatened. Perhaps warfare was so formalised that the gateway was generally the focus of the attack. At some point, the Late Bronze Age warrior is likely to have resided, even if only for a very short time, in one of these fortifications.

The competition for trade routes and prestige goods could lead to conflict between societies and individuals, particularly when added to the claims for land through division of the landscape that occurred from the Middle Bronze Age onwards with the cutting of huge linear ditches. These could run for many kilometres – like those on Quarley Hill, Hampshire, and the massive ditches that survive on Salisbury Plain, Wiltshire. Some ditches are still impressively deep, such as the double-ditches running up to Sidbury Hill and the example that skirts the huge longbarrow, known as 'Old Ditch longbarrow', close to Tilshead on Salisbury Plain. Digging these ditches, without recourse to metal tools, would have been a huge task in terms of the organisation of labour and must have been undertaken for major reasons, not simply to provide cattle ranches. These ditches are an important statement in the soil – an expression of land ownership and power, and thus territory. The ownership of territory is a source of dispute and thus potential conflict.

MEMORIAL AND BURIAL

The most visible elements of memorial in the Bronze Age are the burial mounds, the tumuli or round barrows that we see from the earlier part of the period. These mounds are often located by an early Beaker burial mound with a grouping or 'cemetery' of barrows then being created. Some of the more dramatic of these cemeteries are to be found on Salisbury Plain, close to Stonehenge. Silk Hill, Snail Down, King's Barrow Ridge and Normanton Down all have collections of round barrows and, from what we can glean from the excavation notes of the antiquarians who dug into them, many contained elements of weaponry. Some have been given names evoking the burial package of those inhumed, such as the Hunter's Barrow at Snail Down. As we shall see in Chapter 3, these barrows were often the focus for burials carried out by later societies, particularly in the Anglo-Saxon period, and were where people with weaponry were interred.

Despite the fact that we get weaponry from these burial mounds, prestige goods and an expression of a possible martial character of the deceased, it is rare to find proof positive of their involvement in warfare. As far as the commemoration of an individual warrior is concerned, the barrows are our most likely source of evidence, but must remain inconclusive. Unfortunately, John Aubrey's comments in the introduction to this chapter are thus impossible to corroborate.

After burials in barrows, there was a period of cremation. Cemeteries of urns have been found across Europe, but they are disastrous in terms of our chances of finding pathology to indicate combat. By the Late Bronze Age, burials were rarer still. We might find the odd body as a chance discovery following the individual's burial outside the normal realm of a cemetery – such as at Tormarton, see pages 13–15 – but these are rare. Were bodies excarnated and their bones deposited in rivers or lakes as water became an important religious context (as Flag Fen has shown)? Several skulls of probable Bronze Age date recovered from the River Thames in London might hint that this is the case.

THE FALLEN

Despite the changes in modes of burial in this period, there are burials from the Early Bronze Age through to the Late Bronze Age that bear testament to violence. One must be careful to remember that weapon injuries might have been the result of a myriad of actions and may not even have been inflicted while the individual was alive (Stead, 1991); nevertheless, combat is probably the best explanation for the causes of death for the people described below and in the following pages.

Excavations by Oxford Archaeology at the site of Barrow Hills, Radley, Oxfordshire, produced a fine Beaker assemblage from a crouched inhumation in the central grave, F203. The skeleton was accompanied by many grave goods – a drinking vessel or 'beaker' from which the package gets its name, a bone awl, a fragment of iron pyrites, a bronze awl, an antler spatula, several flint flakes and scrapers, and five barbed and tanged arrowheads near the foot of the burial, perhaps once within a quiver (Barclay and Halpin, 1999: 140–1). A further flint arrowhead was discovered lying in the ribcage, next to the vertebrae of the man who was buried here, with both of the barbs broken, and there was an impact fracture at the tip of the weapon. The authors believed that its presence in this location suggested the cause of the individual's death (*ibid.*: 140).

Another discovery in Oxfordshire gives evidence of fighting in the later Bronze Age. Work at Queenford Farm, Dorchester-on-Thames, in 1901, uncovered parts of a human skeleton – the frontal bones of the skull, and parts of a pelvis. The latter had been pierced by a triangular-bladed, basal looped spearhead, which had broken off in the wound when the attacker tried to recover his precious spear. The force of the stabbing and attempt to recover the weapon had not only broken the spear, but seems also to have twisted the metal. A radiocarbon date from this pelvis of 1260–990 BC was obtained – Late Bronze Age (Osgood, 1998: 21).

UNKNOWN WARRIOR 1

As we have seen at Barrow Hills, the Beaker burial assemblage proclaiming the individual to have some martial prowess or function is at times linked to actual evidence of weapon trauma. Excavations by John Evans in 1978 at the icon of British prehistory, Stonehenge, were carried out to examine the palaeoenvironmental potential of the site. As with many archaeological digs, the penultimate day provided important results. On this day the collapse of the ditch section revealed the bones of a human burial some 1–1.2m below the surface, in the ditch silts (O'Connor in Evans *et al.*, 1984: 13). On full excavation this body was seen to be a classic Beaker burial, from the start of the Bronze Age, with some elements of the package of archery grave goods. The body was complete, although partially disturbed by the actions of a burrowing animal, hence the feet were missing and the right shoulder was displaced.

The skeleton was sexed as being male, from elements such as the pelvic sciatic notch and mastoid process on the skull. An examination of the bones and teeth seemed to indicate that he was between 25 and 30 years old when he died, was muscular and of general good health before death. What made the burial so interesting was its pathology. Three of his ribs bear witness to penetration injuries; the fourth left rib has cracks on its surface and a small hole containing the tip of a flint arrowhead (see Plate 3), the rest of which was found lying by the right arm. The eleventh (left) and ninth (right) ribs also have cut grooves in them, probably resulting from a sharp projectile passing through the ribcage, and the back of the mesosternum had an embedded flint arrowhead tip. Overall, the evidence seems to suggest that 'the man was probably shot at close range as none of the injuries show the penetration downwards that would be expected from an arrow falling in an arc' (Evans *et al.*, 1984: 17). A radiocarbon date (BM–1582) was obtained from the left femur of the man, a result of 2170 ± 110 BC being obtained (*ibid.*: 22).

A further question arises from this burial. Stonehenge was still an important monument in the Early Bronze Age, as demonstrated by satellite pictures showing the profusion of round barrows in the vicinity. Was this man, provided with rich burial goods, of high importance to the society that buried him – after all, he was within the bounds of the great ceremonial site, something that had not been achieved even by the 'Bush Barrow Chieftain', who had been buried close to Stonehenge, accompanied by lavish grave goods?

A stone archer's wristguard or 'bracer', 110mm by 28mm, was found with the burial, with a circular perforation at either end to allow the item to be strapped to the arm or affixed to a leather backing. Three largely complete barbed and tanged flint arrowheads were also retrieved – the tip of one embedded in a rib, as we have seen. It is tempting to suggest that all three arrowheads were fired into the individual prior to death, with two of them causing soft tissue injuries hence they were lying loose on excavation. This seems especially pertinent given the presence of the other (fourth) arrow tip in the sternum. If we assume that all the arrows were embedded in the victim, he would only have been provided with a wristguard in burial. He would not have been given arrowheads, a copper dagger, gold items, or even the eponymous Beaker, and would thus have been quite poorly apparelled for someone buried in what was presumably a prestigious location. Was the fact that this man appears to have been killed in combat significant, and that his burial was one of a warrior hero in a sacred location to which his deposition might have added even more power, and was the wristguard worn by him in the fatal engagement? This is, of course, speculation, but it is a tempting scenario.

UNKNOWN WARRIOR 1

The Beaker burial from Stonehenge in Wiltshire

This is the body of a young man shot several times from behind by flint arrowheads. There is no evidence to suggest that the man was executed; he was either murdered or died in combat. His presence in a burial at Stonehenge might suggest the latter – a further indication of a martial nature being his wristguard. The man was killed at the start of the Bronze Age when representation in death as a warrior was of great importance.

UNKNOWN WARRIOR 2

In 1968 a gas pipeline was cut through fields in Tormarton, South Gloucestershire, uncovering a series of human bones. On closer examination these bones were thought to represent the remains of three individuals and were seen to have weapon injuries, including the presence of bronze spears transfixing some of the skeletal elements:

Skeleton No. 1 has in the pelvis a hole made by a lozenge-sectioned spearhead which must have been driven into the body by an attacker from the right side when the victim was either falling or had already fallen . . .

Skeleton No. 2, about a foot away, and in the same ditch or pit, exhibits features of even greater interest. Two of the lumbar vertebrae are stained blue-green by contact with a small Bronze Age spearhead, the blade of which was found, but the end containing the socket had broken off at the point of weakness behind the blade. This spear had pierced the spinal cord and would have caused immediate and permanent paralysis in the legs . . . The skull has a hole perhaps caused by a blow or wound. (R.W. Knight *et al.*, 1972: 14)

In 1999 and 2000, the author, along with the archaeologist Dr Tyler Bell (Osgood and Bell, forthcoming), returned to this site to establish the context for these burials and to examine whether more material was present. Initial site work soon revealed that the gas pipe had, in fact, truncated a segment of a V-shaped Bronze Age linear ditch, into which the bodies had been thrown (see Plate 4). The ditch was around 2.2m wide at the top and around 1.4–1.5m deep, of a type found in many areas of southern England in the

Middle and Late Bronze Age. A great deal of skeletal material was recovered and, when combined with the collection recovered in 1968, was examined by the palaeopathologist Dr Joy Langston. She concluded that there were now at least four, and probably five, individuals represented by this sample. All were male and their ages ranged from around 11 years to late 30s.

Table 1.1. *Details of the Tormarton skeletons*

Site number of skeleton	Age	Height	Wound
1	Mid–late 30s	175–176cm	Pelvis pierced
2	Mid-20s	178–181cm	Pelvis pierced (spear in situ), spine pierced (spear in situ), skull pierced
3	Mid–late 20s– early 30s	168cm	None visible
4	Early teens	–	None visible

A radiocarbon date of 1315–1050 BC was obtained from the humerus of the oldest male; the interface of the Middle and Late Bronze Age. An interesting point is that only two of the bodies displayed weapon trauma although they were presumably all thrown into the ditch at the same time. An analysis of the mollusca within the ditch indicated that the ditch had been initially cut through recently cleared woodland and was promptly backfilled.

The weapons used for this attack were clear, as parts of them are still embedded in their victims. A spearhead (the cross-section of which appears in the pelvis of Skeleton 1) was used to stab Skeleton 1 from behind. Another weapon was used on Skeleton 2; this man had again been speared from behind with such force that the spear passed straight through his pelvis, and snapped off when the assailant tried to remove the weapon, leaving it within the body (see Plate 5). A spear thrust to the same man's back had the same result with the weapon piercing the spinal column, a wound that would have resulted in the instant paralysis of the individual, and then becoming stuck – breaking off when the spear shaft was pulled to remove the weapon (see Colour Plate 4). If this was not enough, when this young man then fell to the ground as a result of his wounds, he was dealt a sharp blow to the side of his skull that would have killed him. It is possible that this was administered with the shaft butt (or ferrule) of the broken spear as the wound is circular (see Plate 6).

In both cases the wounds were inflicted from behind in a savage attack although others that may have left no trace on the skeleton might also have occurred – after all, the other individuals had no clear signs of weapon trauma. Why, though, were they attacked? It is my belief that the context is of great significance. The bodies were found in a linear ditch of a type that marked out territories and parcels of land in the Bronze Age, claiming areas for different groupings. The fact that these men were thrown into such a construction, which was then backfilled so soon after its cutting, may suggest that they were killed as part of a territorial dispute. One group had claimed the land and this claim had been disputed in the most violent of fashions.

One final note is that Dr Peter Northover's analysis of the metallurgy of the spear that ended up embedded in the back of Skeleton 2 pointed to the fact that the allotting of the tin and copper to form the bronze had originally taken place somewhere in the Alps. The spear itself was formed from this metal once the alloy had arrived in Britain. As such, it serves to indicate the long-distance trading of precious materials in this phase of prehistory (Northover, in Osgood and Bell, forthcoming).

UNKNOWN WARRIOR 2

The body of a man killed in a territorial dispute at Tormarton

This man had suffered a brutal attack, probably in a territorial dispute, in the Middle to Late Bronze Age. He had been speared in the back and pelvis with such ferocity that on each occasion the spear had broken off and remained in the bone. Once the man had fallen to the ground, he was finally killed by a blow to the head. The man was in his mid-20s when he died and was quite tall, being some 178–81cm in height. Analysis of his skeleton showed that the lowest lumbar vertebra had fused to the top of the sacrum although the man would have been unaware of this ailment. His skeleton also bore traces of Schmorl's nodes indicative of him having lived a fairly active life. No dental disease was noted on this man. Skeleton 2 from Tormarton is to date the most unequivocal evidence for combat in the Bronze Age of the British Isles.

TWO

Under the Eagle's Wings:
In the Service of the Roman Legions

The Romans were faced with very grave difficulties. The size of the ships
made it impossible to run them aground except in fairly deep water; and
soldiers, unfamiliar with the ground, with their hands full, and weighed
down by the heavy burden of their arms, had at the same time to jump
down from the ships, get a footing in the waves, and fight the enemy . . .

(Caesar, *The Conquest of Gaul*, IV, 3: The First Invasion of Britain, 55 BC)

One could write a huge volume on a particular type of Roman armour, on
weaponry of the legionary, on graffiti found on pottery within a military
context. I am simply trying to draw together some of the strands of evidence.
Archaeology is only one source of information on the Roman soldier. I shall,
however, stick to archaeology as far as possible when examining the life of
the legionary – be it finds from military battle sites, or fragments of writings
uncovered on excavation sites. Thus, while it is possible to draw information
from written sources on elements such as the pay of the Roman soldier, I
shall not be doing so. The Roman Empire spanned several centuries, but here
I shall focus on the Roman soldier of the first couple of centuries AD, on the
legionary soldier rather than the auxiliary – the latter without citizen status.
Many of the examples are drawn from Britannia, the most far-flung post of
the Empire.

These caveats in place, a large amount can still be said about the
unknown Roman soldier, those citizen soldiers of the Roman Empire. The
Roman army was a formidable piece of organisation and much has found its
way into the archaeological record; the huge numbers involved in the army
and it logistics rendering this more or less inevitable. Britain was one of the
most garrisoned of all of the provinces, de la Bédoyère (2001: 17) putting a
figure of some 16,000 legionaries and the same or more of auxiliary troops
in Britannia.

According to Brewer (2000: 32), legionary life included many military chores – patrols, escorts, sentries – and also those connected with the day-to-day running of the camp, such as stoking furnaces, cleaning latrines, sweeping barracks and maintaining armour: 'A surviving duty-roster from Egypt, for ten days in October 87, reveals a varied existence for an ordinary legionary. One of the men listed worked in the armoury, the quarries, the baths and on the artillery, as well as doing other general duties on different days over that period.' The soldier would have to construct forts, camps and roads.

WEAPONRY

Our examination of Roman weaponry is devoted to the legionary and excludes archery and artillery. It is based on a summary of some of the material taken from the sites of forts, encampments, battlefields and a small number of stray locations. Weaponry can also be seen depicted on tombstones, sculptures and triumphal arches, and it has been recovered from sealed stratigraphic deposits.

Blade Weapons

The Roman infantryman used both dagger (*pugio*) and sword (*gladius*) against his enemies. The latter was not just a short stabbing weapon, it could be used effectively in a slashing motion, with blades of the early – up to *c.* 20 BC – *gladius Hispaniensis* varying between 64cm and 69cm long and 4–5.5cm wide (Cowan, 2003a: 28). This type was replaced in popularity by the Mainz/Fulham type which was, on average, some 20cm shorter, and by the second half of the first century AD, by the parallel-edged, Pompeii-style *gladius*, which had a short triangular point (*ibid.*: 29).

A longer sword, the *spatha*, emerges in the late second century (Feugère, 2002: 115). These longer iron swords have been assigned a 'Barbarian' origin by such authors as Feugère (*ibid.*) and were, on average, some 75–85cm long. The *spatha* made use of impressive pattern-welding technologies with a high degree of craftsmanship (Cowan, 2003b: 60). This type of sword also has a wide distribution, being found on the northern limits of Empire in Scotland (for example, the *spatha* from Newstead; Goldsworthy, 2003: 133). Although more popular in the period beyond the scope of this study, third-century wooden scabbards for these swords have been found in peat bogs in Denmark, at Vimose (Feugère, 2002: 121).

Roman swords have been recovered from varying contexts. From the battlefield site of Kalkriese, near Osnabrück in Germany, our evidence is only fragmentary, presumably as Roman weapons would have been very useful and would have been collected by the victorious German tribespeople who had destroyed Varus and his legions in AD 9. What has been found to date includes bronze and silver mountings of a sword sheath, and 'the tip-binding for a sword scabbard, sword sheath-brackets, sheet metal at the sheath mouths, and guards . . .' (Schlüter, 1999: 138–9). These fittings would have enabled the *gladius* to have been worn by the Roman legionary on his right side and still be unsheathed quickly. Feugère (2002: 110) has detailed a number of the many sword finds throughout the Roman Empire. Handles of the *gladius* were also made from wood, and had bronze covers; a wooden pommel has been found at Vindonissa with a possible guard for this in similar material. The Royal Armouries, Leeds, has a first-century Roman sword blade that originated in Germany. This sword, which was ornately decorated with figures – perhaps the god Mars – was probably carried by a Roman infantryman, although its quality may hint at it being the belonging of someone with more wealth. Its owner also had his name engraved on the sword – Caius Valerius Primus.

As far as Britain is concerned, excavations at the fort of the II Legion at Caerleon, Wales, have produced numerous sword fittings. These include a bone-ribbed *gladius* handle. This piece, some 86mm long, though broken, was believed to have come from a Hadrianic–Antonine context – the early to mid-second century AD. Bone scabbard chapes were also found on this site (Greep, 1992: 188–9). Another Welsh site yielded a *gladius*; the iron sword from Caernarvon, some 46cm long, had a badly corroded blade and cracked bone grip (de la Bédoyère, 2001: 28). A bone *gladius* handle was uncovered from a first-century ditch at Aldgate in London (*ibid.*: 28).

The military dagger or *pugio* was not only a front-line weapon, but also a tool of campaign, used perhaps for cutting food as well as opponents. Suspended from the left side of the legionary's belt, the dagger ranged in size from *c.* 20 to 35cm (Goldsworthy, 2003: 134) with a scabbard that could be richly decorated. By the second century AD, the dagger had become less common as a weapon, so much so that it is not depicted on Trajan's Column in Rome (*ibid.*: 134). Having said this, the weapon still appears on tombstones of this period and the discovery of a military workshop at Künzing, Germany, the stock of which was buried in the third century AD, revealed some fifty-nine dagger blades and twenty-nine sheaths (Feugère, 2002: 128). In addition to the sword fragments discussed above, the remnants of the defeated Roman force at Kalkriese also included dagger parts: bronze rivets from the hilt of a weapon as well as a fragmentary iron blade. Iron daggers and their sheaths have been found in Britain, too – from Copthall Court, London (de la Bédoyère, 2001: 213; Feugère, 2002: 128) and from Exeter (I.R. Scott, 1991: 263 and fig. 120). Rarer, perhaps, was the beautifully decorated sheath that was found with the body of a Roman at Velsen in the Netherlands, discussed in detail below.

In addition to blade weapons, the Roman soldier used projectiles to deadly effect. Following the reforms of their commander, Marius, in the later years of the second century BC, infantrymen were each provided with a heavy throwing spear or *pilum*, The 2m-long *pilum* was formed from a heavy wooden shaft into which a long thin iron spear tang with sharp point was attached. A pointed iron ferule completed the weapon. Two methods of attaching the iron head to the wooden shaft were used: 'Some of the iron heads ended in a socket, the joint reinforced by an iron collet fitting over the top of the wooden shaft, but the majority had a wide rectangular tang which slid into a groove in the wood and was fastened into place by two rivets' (Goldsworthy, 2003: 132). By all accounts, the metal tang of the *pilum* was designed to bend on impact rendering the weapon useless and either preventing the enemy from throwing it back or encumbering him should it stick in his shield. This weapon was in use until the third century AD and had, according to Goldsworthy, a range of *c.* 15m requiring close discipline in its use (*ibid.*: 132). Smaller spears could also be used to provide a lethal barrage.

Archaeologically, it is only fragments of these *pila* that have been recovered. A *pilum* head and a couple of collets have been found at Kalkriese (Schlüter, 1999: 138; Cowan, 2003a: 25–6) in addition to several other iron spears. Feugère points to a number of other *pilum* finds from elsewhere in the Empire, including several shafts from the valley of the Saône in France, and others from Oberaden, Germany, with collets recovered from Hod Hill in Dorset (Feugère, 2002: 130). A socketed iron *pilum* head, 241mm long, was also part of the assemblage in the hoard from Corbridge discussed below (Allason-Jones and Bishop, 1988: 9). Forty-six throwing spears were also present in this hoard, many of which had been bound together and were fused when excavated, as were three catapult bolts and several ferrules and sockets illustrating the throwing arsenal available to the legionary (*ibid.*: 10–17). As with other pieces of the infantryman's equipment, spears were sometimes inscribed by their owners and thus we have traces of names of those who fought to maintain the Roman Empire. One first-century example from Bucklersbury House, London, proclaimed it was the '(property) of Victor in the century of Verus' (Collingwood and Wright, 1991: 51).

Although not part of the standard legionary equipment, slings were used effectively in sieges and add colour to the picture of Roman warfare. The shot from these was often of baked clay or lead and some Roman examples from the second and first centuries BC, like their Greek predecessors, bore inscriptions. This subset includes invective aimed at the enemy – for example, the sardonic *avale* or 'swallow this' (Feugère, 2002: 160). Under battle conditions, sling shot could be manufactured with relative ease. At Velsen, in the Netherlands, a soldier poked his finger into local sand to provide a simple mould for the lead that would make the shot. In so doing, a cast of his finger, complete with nail, was preserved. These lead projectiles (*glandes plumbeae*) were also among the weapons available to the ill-fated soldiers at Kalkriese in AD 9 (Schlüter, 1999: 138).

ARMOUR

In addition to countless portrayals on gravestones, triumphal arches and sculptures, fragments of Roman armour have been recovered from a multitude of sites – one of the most important of recent years being the battle site of Kalkriese, Germany. This site, dating to AD 9 has yielded a large quantity of equipment discarded by or hacked from the bodies of legionaries defeated by German adversaries. Some of this material is fragmentary and may simply be elements of the armour neither taken as booty, nor set up as a trophy by the victors. Elements of two types of body armour have been found, namely of mail (*lorica hamata*) and of articulated plate armour (*lorica segmentata*). Of the former (probably, as Goldsworthy (2003: 126) states, the most common early body protection), a fine fastening hook was excavated with a human face depicted upon it and ending in an animal's head terminal, while the latter is attested by hinges, buckles and a part of a breastplate made of both iron and bronze, some 18.8cm in length (Schlüter, 1999: 136–7;

Patscher and Moosbauer, 2003). Roman soldiers were also provided with an apron to protect the groin – parts of the silver and bronze fittings of such protection having been found.

London also produced a piece of *segmentata*, which may have been damaged in conflict: a fragment of breastplate from the Bank of England seems to have suffered a blow just below one of its hinges (Bishop, 2002: 83).

One should remember that, although very similar, Roman equipment was not totally uniform – certain pieces would vary and would have been adapted or handed down. Armour was worn over, or stitched onto a leather tunic, as without it the legionary would have found the protection far too uncomfortable to wear.

Articulated plate armour has been found on many fortress sites, too. Exeter has produced a series of the essential fittings for this armour – buckles, hinges and rivets – although, as the authors point out, 'they do not, unfortunately, add up to much more than would be required for one shoulder' (Holbrook and Bidwell, 1991: 244).

One of the most sensational finds of Roman armour came from the fortress site of Corbridge, northern England. Uncovered in July 1964, a hoard of Roman equipment in the remains of a wooden chest was excavated. This chest had been placed in a rectangular pit, which had been dug through destruction layers of an earlier building. Archaeologists were able to date the deposition of this hoard to around AD 122–138. As well as the projectiles mentioned above, various tools were present, including an iron pick axe, chisel, bow or frame-saw, knives, pulley block, hinges, nails, lamp and bracket, and the remains of a sword scabbard and writing tablets (Allason-Jones and Bishop, 1988: 53–60). The armour was probably the most important part of the collection, enabling the reconstruction of the full layout of one pattern of Roman armour. Many elements of *segmentata* were present, including breastplates (up to 90mm wide and 95mm deep), shoulder guards and collar plates. The breastplates even held traces of the mineralised remains of internal leather straps and textiles (*ibid.*: 23–51 and fig. 53).

Mail alongside a probable armour plate with a hinge, a buckle and a rivet was found in the excavations of the Roman Gates at Caerleon, Wales (Evans and Metcalf, 1992: 166). Verulamium (St Albans), Kingsholm (Gloucester), London and Richborough, Kent, also produced elements of *segmentata* fittings.

Sauer (2000) discusses its presence in the early Imperial fortresses of Vindonissa (Germania Superior) and Oescus (Moesia Inferior) among others –

including his own excavations at Alchester in Oxfordshire. *Lorica segmentata* seems to have gone out of fashion in the third century (Goldsworthy, 2003: 128), though as it has been found at Kalkriese, AD 9, this type of protection was in vogue for more than 200 years.

One must be careful not to assume that finds of armour in a fort or barracks represent the presence of an armoury; it may have been left either as some type of votive deposit or, in some cases, of clearing away material no longer required. This is the interpretation given to the armourers' hoard found at Corbridge. Many of the objects were damaged and either awaiting repair or scrapping and were abandoned along with the fort (Allason-Jones and Bishop, 1988: 109).

In addition to segmented armour hinges, Alchester produced segments of scale armour (*lorica squamata*), which was a form of protection for which we also have iconographic evidence (Sauer, 2000: 25). A further British example of scale armour, along with mail, was found at the fort of the II Legion at Caerleon (Brewer, 2000: 30; de la Bédoyère, 2001: 98). In terms of finds of scale armour, perhaps the most important discovery has come from Carpow in Scotland. Here, not only were scales (each *c.* 1.3cm wide by 1.5cm long) uncovered in a pit within the Severan fortress, but also the textile backing and leather binding, which had been preserved as a result of corrosion products from the bronze scales. The scales were fastened by means of a cord running over a pair of holes on each scale, with linen yarn passing through these holes and affixing an underlying cloth (Wild, 1981; Dore and Wilkes, 1999). Large numbers of late first-century protective scales were recovered from the excavations at Newstead in Scotland (Goldsworthy, 2003: 128). Carlisle has also yielded some splendid examples of scale armour. Research on this material is under way, but already conservation analysis has revealed that, although 'the armour is mainly iron, copper alloy coatings and wire have been found on the scale armour, and copper alloy rivets on some of the laminated limb defences' (Jones and Watson, 2003: 11) (see Colour Plates 2 and 3).

Fragments of intact mail have been found on Roman sites on the European mainland, too. In addition to the segments from Kalkriese, Feugère (2002: 100) points out examples of links and attachments from Chassenard, France, and Künzing, Bavaria, and compares them with the depiction of such a protective coat on Vachère's statue of a Gallic nobleman (Goldsworthy, 2003: 30).

Leather armour was almost certainly worn by the early Roman soldier, but our archaeological understanding is dictated by preservation of such organic remains. Waterlogged or desiccated conditions are required if such materials are to survive. Out of the scope of this study, as it is from the third century, the fortress site of Dura Europos in Syria retained leather limb armour (James, 2004: 122–4).

With all the choices of protection available to the Roman legionary, it may come as a surprise that, as Cowan highlights, some front-line infantrymen fought without armour. 'Casear made use of such legionaries to fight as *antesignani*, that is lightly equipped legionaries (*expediti*), who probably skirmished with light missiles in front of the main battle line or reinforced the cavalry . . . A relief from the legionary headquarters building (*principia*) at Mainz shows two legionaries fighting in close order, equipped with *scuta* and *pila*, but apparently without body armour, suggesting that even the 'heavy' legionaries could fight *expediti*' (Cowan, 2003a: 31).

Shields

The shield (*scutum*) that protected the early Roman infantryman was composed of laminated wood and hide with metal facings and shield boss. An example of this first-century BC type was recovered from Fayum in Egypt and was 128cm long and 63.5cm wide, 1–1.2cm thick and around 10kg in weight (Cowan 2003a: 27; Goldsworthy, 2003: 31). These shields were curved and oval in form.

A later, Augustan variant was more in the shape of a curved rectangle and had the great advantage of being lighter. This curved shape covered the majority of the soldier's torso and, when linked together, could cover a group of infantrymen from attacks from the side, in front and above. This 'tortoise' formation is depicted on Trajan's Column in Rome. The only complete example of one of these sub-cylindrical shields was found at Dura Europos and many reconstructions are based on this example. The Dura shield from Tower 19, *c.* AD 250, was formed from plywood around 5mm thick and 5.5kg in weight. Neither shield boss nor its associated rivets survived, but, incredibly, its stunning painted decorations did (James, 2004: 176–9).

Infantrymen were carrying shields on the ill-fated mission at Kalkriese in Germany. When wet and heavy, this equipment may actually have been more of a hindrance than help as it encumbered the legionary. Shield fragments –

the metal fittings – have been recovered from this site, including a shield boss (*umbo*), shield grip (*ansa*) and edge-binding (Schlüter, 1999: 136). The former could sometimes be included in a list of offensive weapons used by Roman infantrymen, as part of their tactical panoply was to use this part of the shield to drive into their opponents.

On the move, or in periods of inactivity, shields were provided with leather covers to protect them from the elements and wear and tear (Goldsworthy, 2003: 122). Feugère (2002: 88) cites a number of these covers found at Valkenburg, in the Netherlands, and Vindonissa, Switzerland, the latter with clear markings of the XI Legion. These covers had rounded corners similar to the shield from Dura Europos. The mark of an organised army is, perhaps, its propensity to inspection. Shield covers would thus be a vital tool in the quest to keep one's kit clean and escape the scorn of the NCO and subsequent punishments. The maintenance of the infantryman's arms was essential to afford the maximum effectiveness of the weaponry.

Shields were important pieces of an infantryman's defensive panoply and, as such, those who made them as well as those who bore them were justly proud. A splendid shield boss found in the River Tyne in northern England had depictions of the four seasons, of the god Mars and the bull, the symbol of the VIII Legion. If one was in any doubt of the symbolic significance of the latter image, an inscription proclaims that it was used by a member of the VIII Legion Augusta. The legionary was named: '(property) of Iunius Dubitatus in the century of Iulius Magnus' – possibly in the reign of Hadrian (Collingwood and Wright, 1991: 48–9). A further bronze circular shield boss from London, some 192mm in diameter, proclaimed 'Cocillus made (this)' (*ibid.*: 51).

Helmets

As with armour, the iron helmets of the early Roman legionary changed through time, but always afforded good protection to the wearer. A frequently used early-pattern helmet, the 'Monteforino' (third to first century BC) was superseded in popularity by a type known as the 'Coolus' in the late first century BC to early first century AD. This helmet made use of a metal cap with reinforced peek and guards for the cheeks and neck, often with a spike or ball at the top. By the middle to end of the first century AD the 'Imperial Gallic' and later 'Imperial Italic' (early second century AD) helmets were available, which broadened and strengthened the protective parts of the helmet.

Bronze variants of these helmets were also present and emphasised protection at the front and back of the soldier while leaving the ears and face open, thus enabling him to hear orders and to have good all-round vision (Goldsworthy, 2003: 121–6). As with body armour, helmets would have required a fabric lining to facilitate their fitting and to provide a degree of comfort for the wearer.

The fact that these helmets were retained for long time periods, stored and repaired or handed down to comrades, is attested to by several examples that have the names of their users stamped onto the neck-guards. One first-century coolus-type helmet from London had four different soldiers' names on it:

(Property) of Lucius Dulcius in the century of Marcus Valerius Ursus
In the century of Martialis, Lucius Postumus
(Property) of Rufus in the century of Scribonius
(Property) of Aulus Saufeius in the century of Martialis
(Collingwood and Wright, 1991: 44–5)

Another British example was recovered from Verulamium (St Albans). Again a coolus-type helmet of the first century, this one proclaimed that it was the '(property) of [.] Papirius (in the century) of the *primus pilus*' (*ibid.*: 45).

Mainland Europe also retains traces of the names of infantrymen on helmets, a further inscription being on an Imperial Gallic helmet from Mainz. The name of its owner was shown as 'L. Lucretius Celeris' and his unit, I Legion, was included (H. Robinson, 1975: 60–1; Feugère, 2002: 205).

As with armour, helmets are depicted on carvings such as those of the Mainz *principia* and Trajan's Column and, although archaeological finds of complete helmets are not unknown (the iron example from Brigetio in Hungary (see Brewer, 2000: 29) and the Gallic helmet from the vicinity of the Augustan fort at Nijmegen in Holland (see Cowan 2003a: 42–3)), it is far more common to find fragments that were one part of the composite element of the helmet.

Excavations at Alchester have recovered helmet parts that include a crest-holder and a carrying handle (Sauer, 2000: 37). Work at the fortress of the II Legion at Caerleon also yielded helmet fragments such as a bronze segment of an Imperial Gallic helmet (from just in front of the ear cut-out), which also had an iron hinge for the cheek piece and a number of rivets along with a helmet crest support of a type similar to another example found close by at Usk (Evans and Metcalf, 1992: 113–14).

Table 2.1. *The weight of the burden borne by the Augustan legionary*

Piece of equipment	Weight (kg)
Monteforino helmet	2
Mail shirt	12
Cross belts	1.2
Oval *scutum*	10
Mainz *gladius* and scabbard	2.2
Dagger and scabbard	1.1
Pilum	1.9
TOTAL	30.4

Source: as calculated by Cowan (2003a: 43).

This was a large load, but such encumbrance was not something suffered only by infantrymen of the Ancient world. Soldiers making the early attacks on 1 July 1916, the first day of the Battle of the Somme, were known to have carried a weight of up to 30kg. This may seem extraordinary for surely quick attacks by lightly armed troops were far more likely to succeed? Not necessarily – once troops arrived at their objectives, they needed equipment to defeat their opponent (often well-protected adversaries) and then to refortify the area taken to favour the troops who had captured it.

In addition to their armour, the legionary had other elements of clothing, as itemised on tablets recovered from the fort of Vindolanda on Hadrian's Wall: twenty pairs of socks, two pairs of sandals and two pairs of underpants (Bowman, 2003: 74). Those who have experienced some of the harsher weather conditions along Hadrian's Wall will appreciate the need for as many warm comforts as possible.

PRACTICE AND DISCIPLINE

We see no other explanation for the conquest of the world by the Roman People than their military training, camp discipline and practice in warfare.

(Vegetius, *Epitome*, 1.1)

Discipline and unit cohesion were essential attributes of the Roman legions and this could only be attained through practice. This practice could be gruelling and was enforced by centurions and training officers. Cowan (2003a: 11) states that legionaries were trained on a daily basis for four months and were expected to be able to march '29km in five hours at the regular step, and 35km in five hours at the faster step, loaded with a pack of about 20.5kg in weight'. The infantryman was expected to be able to perform a series of complicated tasks that would help to ensure his survival on campaign, from the construction of protected marching camps to the formation known as the *testudo* (tortoise) depicted on Trajan's Column in Rome, whereby a unit of troops would surround themselves with their shields – both to the side and above. Such a manoeuvre could only be accomplished if the unit had been drilled.

Soldiers kept their fitness up and their skills honed by the building of practice camps and by training on parade grounds. Traces of practice encampments – of banks and ditches – have been located at a number of places. Perhaps the best examples in the British Isles – and possibly the largest group of practice camps in the Roman Empire (Daniels and Jones, 1969: 132) – are those at Llandrindod Common, Wales, where eighteen practice camps have been found. Other training camps include Blaenos and Trawsfynydd in Wales (Frere *et al.*, 1984: 267; see also Nash-Williams, 1969) and at Gilnockie in Scotland. In an interesting palimpsest of military training, there are six marching camps in very close proximity to one another alongside the Roman road of Dere Street on the current British Army training estate at Otterburn in Northumbria (see Hammond, 2004).

To have these earthworks so close together makes no military sense – it seems most likely that they were practice works, probably of the garrison of the nearby fortlet of Rochester.

In recent years, archaeological fieldwork has been undertaken at Alchester, Oxfordshire. This has not only uncovered a vexillation fortress and marching camp, but has also revealed the presence of what the excavators believe to be a military training ground, although there is some debate as to whether this training area was for cavalry training alongside its infantry counterpart (Sauer, 2000: 32). Artefacts from this site included five three-winged arrowheads, which Sauer believes indicate that those trained within its boundaries were practising to counter mounted threats (*ibid.*: 33).

On the subject of the training of the legionary, Adrian Goldsworthy wrote: 'They were taught how to use their personal weapons by practising thrusts and cuts against a 1.8m post fixed into the ground. At first they used wooden swords and wicker shields of twice the weight of the normal issue to strengthen their arms. On at least one occasion these wooden practice swords were used as batons by troops quelling a riot' (Goldsworthy, 2002: 132).

Excavations at the Flavian timber fort at Carlisle, northern England, have yielded one complete wooden practice sword and the handles of two others. The complete example, some 571mm in length, was a replica of the soldier's stabbing sword, the *gladius*. Carauna (1991: 11–12) debated the possibility that this sword might have been a child's toy, but decided that the context of the artefact, the west gate tower of the fort, probably meant that it was more likely to have been a practice weapon for soldiers. Extensive training in the use of all the individual weapons in their panoply of arms was essential. An ox skull from Vindolanda displays a series of square perforations, the result of light ballista impacts, perhaps indicative of troops training with this weapon (Goldsworthy, 2003: 81).

THE LIFE OF THE SOLDIER

Drinking

Alcoholic drinks were certainly available to the Roman legionary – indeed, the supply was deemed essential to Roman forts. Traces of the vessels used to transport alcohol, the amphorae, have been found in many military contexts, some with evidence for the individual units to whom it was supplied still evident. 'A "Rhodian" amphora from Caerleon, with an internal resin coating, has LEG.II.AVG painted on it. The resin is thought to suggest liquid contents, perhaps wine or honey. The type is associated with raisin wine shipped in from the Aegean area, and bought either for the legion or by an individual soldier' (de la Bédoyère, 2001: 131). Within Barrack Block B (Phase II) at Caerleon, a bronze tankard handle was also found (Evans and Metcalf, 1992: 152).

A Welsh fort, Segontium (Caernarfon), also yielded amphorae fragments, although not in huge quantities. Dressel type 2–4 amphorae brought wine to the site in the first to mid-second centuries AD, although it seems as though only Gallic wine was imported after the mid-second century. Whether this was a result of taste, fashion or availability is unclear. Barrels of larch wood and silver fir have also been found, the excavators suggesting that these too might have been used to bring Gallic wine to the fort (Casey, *et al.*, 1993: 77–8). Richborough also yielded an amphora which had graffiti on its neck attesting the presence of wine; this referred to LYMP(A) – 'this wine came from Mount Vesuvius and presumably was produced before AD 79' (Davies, 1971: 131). Wine was also consumed on campaign, a fact attested to by the wine strainer at Kalkriese (Wells, 2003: 53).

One of the Vindolanda writing tablets from the fort on Hadrian's Wall examines supplies coming into the Roman camp around AD 111: 'the items accounted for include *cervesa* (Celtic beer) and *clavi caligares* (nails for boots)' (Bowman, 2003: 34). Much of the garrison was of an auxiliary nature, composed of Batavians and Tungrians who fought with the Romans. The tablets seem to reveal that, 'Although wine was clearly available, the staple drink is much more likely to have been beer, which we find in several of the accounts and which was urgently requested for a detachment of soldiers in a letter to Cerialis from one of the decurions of his unit' (*ibid.*: 73). Perhaps the stereotypical image of northern Europeans drinking beer and those in more southerly climes opting for wine held true from a very early stage. Up on the forts in Scotland, too, there were possible traces of the consumption of wine – an amphora with the inscription VIN on its handle being found (Curle, 1911: 268).

Eating

In addition to buildings constructed for the storage of foodstuffs in Roman forts, the ubiquitous granaries (*horrea*), artefactual evidence also provides useful details as to the diet of the legionary.

Spanish consumable products seemed well represented at legionary sites in Britain. In Exeter, for example, finds have included Spanish amphorae bearing fish sauces and Dressel type 20 amphorae carrying olive oil to the soldiers of the fort (Holbrook and Bidwell, 1991: 17). The legionary fortress of Wroxeter also revealed amphorae (Rhodian types and from Gaul), some of which had brought olive oil to the Romans (Webster, 2002: 182). Usk, too, has many fragments of these storage vessels, some of which had contained *garum*, a fish sauce from Spain (Camulodunum Type 185A; see Manning *et al.*, 1995: 87). In addition, fragments of two Camulodunum 189 type amphorae are thought to have held fruit brought in from North Africa (*ibid.*: 87).

Pork, as Goldsworthy records, was an important element of the diet: '. . . pig bones turn up far more frequently in the excavation of legionary fortresses than auxiliary forts, especially in northern Europe, which suggests that citizen soldiers had a greater fondness for this meat. They are especially common in early legionary bases, such as Nijmegen in Holland' (Goldsworthy, 2003: 98).

At the fort of Segontium (Caernarfon), the assemblage of animal bones gave indicators of other elements of the soldiers' diet. The bulk of the bone was of cattle, as it was at Wroxeter, with animals seemingly arriving on the hoof to be butchered within the fort's defences. Mutton consumption tended to decline on this site after the second century AD, yet pork was still popular. Birds were also consumed, with the bones of mallard, geese, plover, woodcock and wood pigeon all being found alongside domestic fowl – although the latter formed 75 per cent of the bird bones on site. Fish and shellfish, too, were eaten, with oyster and winkle shells being found (Casey *et al.*, 1993: 76–7).

> ratio frumenti em[ensi ex quo
> ipse dedi in cupam [
> mihi ad panem . . .

> ad turtas tibi   m(odii) ii
> Crescenti   m(odii) ix
> Militibus legionaribus . . .

(Bowman, 2003: 104–5)

Although mostly relating to auxiliary troops, the astonishing written texts recovered from Vindolanda give further information on foodstuffs available to the soldier – one such text, from AD 111, discusses the dispensation of salt, pork and goat-meat (Bowman, 2003: 34). A 'long account of dispensation of over 300 *modii of frumentum* (wheat) to various individuals includes a group of legionary soldiers . . . other [entries] suggest that it is being used for baking bread and twisted loaves (*turtas*) [see above] . . . Another account records a fairly large quantity of lard (*lardum*)' (*ibid.*: 73). Further accounts of foodstuffs include spices, pepper, roe-deer, ham, young pig, venison, honey, beans and emmer wheat (*ibid.*: 118–19). The Vindolanda tablets thus show the importance of wheat as a staple – especially for bread. One fascinating artefact associated with this activity has been found in a military context in excavations at Caerleon. Lead bread stamps have been excavated, marked out as being the provisions of the century of Quintinius Aquila of the II Legion (Brewer, 2000: 32). Cheese presses have also been discovered on military sites, and the excavations of the incredible site of Dura Europos in Syria revealed traces of graffiti in a pantry which recorded 'payment for new cheeses and another type of cheese' (Davies, 1971: 132).

A further strand of information on dietary condiments available to the Roman soldier was found at Carlisle in northern England. Excavations at the Roman fort retrieved part of a Roman amphora which contained tunny fish paste. This was found outside the commanding officer's house, in rubbish assigned a late first-century AD date. 'Clay panels on it proclaimed its superior quality to the discerning Roman palate. The translation of the Latin words, written in ink, reads: "Tunny fish relish from Tangiers, old", "for the larder", "excellent", "top quality". It is believed that the reference to Tangiers was to the style of the sauce rather than its true place of origin – as a modern sauce could be described as "Italian" but in fact made in the UK' (Roman Hideout, 2002). The authors of this report took the paste as being the property of an officer, but, nevertheless, this serves to indicate that exotic foodstuffs were making their way to the legionary fortresses in far-flung outposts. Another amphora, found at the fort of Vindonissa in Switzerland, bore the inscription 'THUNNI' and thus would also once have contained this paste, while another had OLIVA NIGR EX. DE. FR inscribed upon it (Curle, 1911: 268).

Spanish fish sauce was also present in Pannonia. At Carnuntum an inscription on an amphora read . . . O . . . D|Q ACONI VERI| PRI LEG XV APO, which Bezeczky takes to mean 'Perhaps ". . . [c]o[r]d(ula)?| Q(uinti) Aconi(i) Veri| pri(ncipis) leg(ionis) XV Apo(llinaris)"; "young ink-fish sauce, (property) of Quintus Aconius Verus, *princes* (centurion) of Legion XV Appolinaris"' (Bezeczky, 1996: 329).

Fish was a popular foodstuff even when not in sauce form and their bones have been noted by excavators on sites throughout the Roman world: 'Pike was eaten at Butzbach, perch at Chester, sturgeon at Saalburg, and cod at Hod Hill . . . [Valkenburg at the mouth of the Rhine] also produced evidence for the common porpoise and whale, and also the cuttlefish, a great delicacy' (Davies, 1971: 129–30).

As those who have had a bad experience after eating shellfish will know, there is always a risk to the consumption of these foodstuffs: 'In the early second century Terentianus, a legionary stationed at Alexandria, wrote to apologise to his father for not meeting him and explained why: "for it was at that time that so violent and dreadful an attack of fish poisoning made me ill, and for five days I was unable to drop you a line, not to speak of going to meet you. Not one of us was even able to leave the camp gate"' (*ibid.*: 130). Shellfish fragments, including oysters, mussles, limpets, whelk and cockle, have been discovered on fort sites from Caerleon to Chester (*ibid.*: 129).

Barrels might also have be used for transporting food to the legions, in barracks or hospital. One example, from Aquincum in Pannonia, bears a Latin legend Expac NTR VAL LEG II ADI (possibly Expac(to) n[u]tr(imento) val(etudinari) leg(ionis) II adi(utricis)) branded onto the staves, which Bezeczky (1996: 335) believes to mean 'food on contract for the hospital of Legion II Adiutrix'.

In terms of cooking equipment, the Roman legion took bronze kettles with it on campaign (Wells, 2003: 97). A number of these kettles have been recovered from military contexts, including the ditch around the fort. Seven such kettles have been found at Newstead (Curle, 1911: 273–4). These are battered and have been repaired on several occasions, having been dented on the march; one kettle had a centurial mark upon it, another TVRMA CRISPI NIGRI (*ibid.*: 274).

Food was not just available as rations within the barracks or on campaign, the infantryman could also purchase items when he had any spare time – for example, when relaxing at the baths. At Caerleon, there is a great deal of evidence for the presence of Roman 'fast-food' sales at the legionary fortress baths. Many mutton chops were recovered from the drains of the baths, along with chicken joints and ribs and trotters of pigs. Further finds from this context included wildfowl bones, shellfish, a hazelnut shell and even an olive stone (Zienkiewicz, 1986b: 20). The latter is especially interesting, and Zienkiewicz noted another discovery of olives – 'an amphora containing olive stones of the first century AD has been found off Pan Sands, Whitstable, Kent. Davies notes that black olives preserved in wine must were eaten by legionaries' (*ibid.*: 224).

Archaeobotanical studies also give us good information about the diets of Roman troops. Samples from the sewage-filled ditch at the Beasden fort in Scotland were taken by J. Dickson during David Breeze's excavations in the 1970s; the bulk of the organic material found was of bran fragments, either of rye or wheat type (grain weevils also being found), the cholesterol levels perhaps indicating a bran-based diet. In addition, 'the first discoveries were of great interest; they were fig pips. It seemed clear that they represented some of the food issued to the soldiers. Other unusual seeds were found: Coriander, Dill and Wild Celery' (Dickson and Dickson, 2000: 118). Similar seed assemblages have been found at a Roman fort at Carlisle, in a sewer next to a legionary bathhouse at York (both northern England) and at a fort in Welzheim (south-east Germany) (*ibid.*: 123). Seed coats of beans and lentils were found, as were seeds of the opium poppy – perhaps used on bread (*ibid.*: 118). Further traces of food found in the sewage included raspberry, bramble, bilberry, wild strawberry and some hazelnut shells' (*ibid.*: 122).

Waterlogged cereal bran, probably residue of the sewage produced by the garrison, dating to the middle or later 40s AD, was excavated from the inner ditch at the fortress of Alchester. The outer ditch contained evidence for crop processing – spelt wheat, and also a coriander seed (M. Robinson, 2000: 64).

Toilet

One image that is perhaps more enduring than most when it comes to the life of the Roman legionary is his toilet habits. The latrines at Housesteads fort on Hadrian's Wall would indicate that the men sat and performed bodily functions together, anathema to many modern sensibilities. Tradition decrees that sponges were used by the Roman soldier for his ablutions, but these were not always available, particularly in colder northerly climes, and a substitute had to be sought. Excavations of the sewage (which also contained parasites in the form of human whipworm and roundworm) in the ditch at the Bearsden fort might perhaps suggest an alternative: 'the presence of weft-forming mosses in the ditch strongly suggested that these had been gathered as a substitute' (Dickson and Dickson, 2000: 120).

Some of the articles that soldiers would have taken on campaign have been excavated at the site of the encounter at Kalkriese, Germany. Here, the archaeologists have retrieved toilet articles (or at least fragments of some): 'in particular a bronze carrying ring for *strigiles* (skin scrapers), a small pair of iron scissors (*forfex*) and the bronze handle of a razor (*novacula*)' (Schlüter, 1999: 104). Further nail cleaners were recovered from a garrison context of Exeter fort (Holbrook and Bidwell, 1991: 257–9). *Sebum* (or tallow), which was probably used as soap by Roman soldiers, was one of the items on the list of purchases made by the troops at Vindolanda and recorded on the tablets, and there is also a reference to *sudaria*, napkins or towels which might also serve to illustrate the fastidiousness of the Roman soldier (Bowman, 2003: 35).

Bathing was indeed important to the infantryman – testament to this lying in the various bathing buildings at military establishments throughout the Roman Empire. In Britain, one only has to look at the forts of Exeter (Bidwell, 1979) and Caerleon (Zienkiewicz, 1986a) to confirm this. Furthermore, the great bathing establishment at Bath was frequented by the military, with soldiers also able to perform their religious duties in a visit to this health centre. There are five military tombstones at Bath; through these, we know of Marcus Valerius Latinus and Antigonus of the XX Legion. Neither of these has the title *Valeria Victrix* awarded to the legion after its crushing defeat of Boudica, thus they were perhaps sculpted before the revolt (Cunliffe, 1984: 183–4). An armourer of the XX Legion, Julius Vitalis, was also commemorated here, having died at the age of 29 after nine years' service with the legion – he was recruited in Gallia Belgica and had belonged 'to a craft guild, equivalent now to a friendly society. When he died his colleagues paid for his cremation and tombstone, carefully recording on it "with funeral at the cost of the Guild of Armourers". Even a young soldier could be assured of a decent burial if he belonged to a guild' (*ibid.*: 185).

The II Legion was also represented in the tombstones at Bath – Gaius Murrius Modestus of the Second Adiutrix Legion, from Forum Julii in southern France, died at the age of 25 and had perhaps been visiting Bath in the forlorn hope of curing his wounds (*ibid.*: 185). Bathing was not simply an activity connected to cleanliness – it was a social activity. As we have seen above it was a place where soldiers would meet off-duty, they could buy food, they could also gamble.

Gaming

As we know, fighting was a relatively small part of the life of a legionary. Martial practice was important, as were other physical activities – often constructional. However, pastimes were essential for those moments not taken up by the orders of the centurion, and the Roman legionary liked to gamble. This, as we shall see in succeeding chapters, is something that the 'squadie' of all periods has enjoyed.

Glass and bone gaming counters have been found from several phases at the fort of the II Legion Augusta at Caerleon in Wales, some unstratified, but

others in the barrack blocks themselves (Barrack Block B). In addition, a die
to aid the progress of the game was found (Barrack Block B) (Evans and
Metcalf, 1992: 161–2, 184). It was not only the barracks that yielded gaming
counters – at the fortress baths several small finds, particularly from a drain
running from the baths, pointed to elements of gambling by the troops. Here
30 coins were recovered: 'We may presume that money was brought to the
baths not only to pay for refreshments, and for such services as were available
there (the massage, bath-oil, depilatory and dental services, etc) but also to
gamble. Large numbers of counters (of pottery, bone, samian, glass, stone,
shell and lead, on decreasing order of frequency) and dice of bone and bronze
indicate that gaming formed an important function at the baths' (Zienkiewicz,
1986b: 20).

A similar story seems to be applicable at another legionary fortress in
Wales, at Usk, where eighty-seven glass discs were found and, as Manning
wrote, these 'clearly . . . had a function in life in the Fortress, and this is most
likely to have been in some of the many "board" games which the Romans
played. Such games will have helped to alleviate the boredom which was an
inevitable part of the legionary's life, and, no doubt, there was the added
spice of gambling' (Manning et al.: 1995: 87). These counters were less
frequent in later layers within the fortress and the excavators speculated that
this might mean that gaming was not so popular with native Britons now on
site who did not have the 'Mediterranean cultural background' of the first-
century legionary soldier (ibid.: 87). In northern Britain, the same story is
true – one finds gaming counters at the fort of Newstead in Scotland (Curle,
1911: 338–9) and even a probable gaming board from Corbridge in
Northumberland, constructed from stone and with an incised square with
lines demarcating fifty-six internal squares (ibid.: fig. 50). Dice and counters
were also present on this site.

One can picture the bored legionary trying to pass the hours in the
barracks by gaming, but the pursuit may also have taken place in quieter
moments on campaign – for example, when camp was struck. The Kalkriese
excavations have recovered glass gaming counters (latrunculi) (Schlüter,
1999: 148).

Gambling by the Roman infantryman might not have been restricted to
board games. Placing money on animal fights might be attested to by the
large number of leg bones of fighting cocks still with spurs in place at
Caerleon, in what was, perhaps, a cock-fighting pit (Zienkiewicz, 1986b: 20).

Certainly this would not be a surprise given the occurrence of amphitheatres at some of these military sites, Caerleon being a case in point. Not only would legionaries have been able to watch combat in these amphitheatres, it seems likely that they would have used these sites for training.

Writings

Although I have been concentrating, insofar as is possible, simply on archaeological evidence rather than evidence provided by the classical authors, certain archaeological finds have important written elements. As we have seen, inscriptions on objects have provided clues as to the lives of the common soldier and tantalising evidence as to their names, thus deviating from the 'unknown' soldier of this work. We also see a degree of literacy among some of the soldiers – indeed a stylus for writing was found on the site of the barrack block of the II Legion at Caerleon, though this may not have been the property of a legionary (Evans and Metcalf, 1992: 169).

The work of the archaeologists Professor Robin, Andrew and Eric Birley at Vindolanda, on Hadrian's Wall, has resulted in some of the most important finds relating to life in the Roman legions. The Vindolanda writings are a series of texts, including letters and military documents, which were written on wooden tablets preserved in the waterlogged levels of the fort and retrieved by archaeologists. They are mostly between 1mm and 3mm thick and were discarded in a short period of time in the area of the *praetorium* and later barrack block workshop (Bowman, 2003: 30). As stated above, some of these tablets discuss the provisions of the troops, but they also provide the names of those who served: in this case generally of men of two auxiliary cohorts – the Ninth Cohort of Batavians, and the First Cohort of Tungrians – from AD 90 to 125. 'Some of the names are conspicuously Germanic (though several are not elsewhere attested) and we are certainly dealing with the ordinary rankers here: Tagarminis (or perhaps Tgarannis), Gambax son of Tappo, Ammius, Messor, Hue . . . (a version of Vettius?), Tullio, Butimas' (*ibid.*: 35).

The troops corresponded with one another – surely as a way of passing dull hours – and if no reply was forthcoming would rebuke the recipient for their rudeness. One such writer was Chrauttius, who admonishes his brother (comrade) and former messmate Veldeius for not writing back to him (*ibid.*: 107). Tablet 131 again reproaches a soldier for not returning correspondence, this, 'from a man called Collemnis to his "brother", i.e. comrade, Paris, opens with a half-joking but obviously seriously meant complaint that Paris had not written to him: "So that you may know that I am in good health, which I hope you are in turn, you most irreligious fellow, who haven't even sent me a single letter – but I think I am behaving in a more civilised way by writing to you!"' (*ibid.*: 106). As a soldier, perhaps one was expected to make use of one's literacy by fellow messmates, peer pressure within the fighting unit helping to alleviate boring moments.

Other written elements, known as Military Diplomas, recovered from the archaeological record give us details on the auxiliary troops serving alongside the legions. These diplomas were issued to auxiliary soldiers on their completion of twenty-five years' service and act as a token of proof of the granting of citizenship (Denison, 2003: 7). Some of these diplomas relate to Legio I and Legio II Adiutrix, legions that were unusual in accepting non-citizen soldiers. A number of writing tablets (*cerae*) were recovered from the great wooden chest that held the hoard at Corbridge (Allason-Jones and Bishop, 1988: 83).

In addition to inscriptions on weaponry and armour discussed above, written evidence for the presence of particular troops is also to be found on tile stamps located at the bases of particular units. In Britain, for example, there are many tiles that proclaim to be the property of the II Legion (stamped 'LEG.II.AVG') at their fort of Caerleon. These were probably made in the legionary kilns, which made use of the clays of the River Severn and its tributaries, such as the Usk (Brewer, 2000: 20–1). These tiles can also be seen in situ at the legionary fortress baths, alongside others which have the mark of the bottom of a hobnailed boot (having been walked on when the tile was still wet). Sea Mills, close to Bristol on the other side of the Severn, also has similar tiles and bricks, illustrating the legion's presence and movement (Ellis, 1987: 94). South Shields fort incorporated a stone with LEG VI carved into it in the front wall of the headquarters (de la Bédoyère, 2001: 71). Throughout the rest of the Empire we can see the presence of certain legions through their graffiti inscribed, for example, on their projectiles, such as an iron catapult head from Oberammegau (Wiegels, 1997: 8). In addition to the ability of contemporary logisticians to link material to particular units, was this, perhaps in some way, also a message of delivery in the same manner that armourers often scrawl messages on ordnance delivered to targets by bomber aircraft?

Accommodation

The Roman army built large forts in the lands they occupied to provide bases
for their legions.

Table 2.2. *The size of Roman forts*

Fort	Metres	Hectares	
Usk	475 × 410	19.5	
Colchester	c. 490 × 420	20.5	
Exeter	440 × 350	15.4	
Gloucester	440 × 348	15.3	
Lincoln	375 × 448	16.8	
Inchtuthil	460 × 472	21.7	
Caerleon	490 × 418	20.5	
Chester	595 × 412	24.3	
York	485 × 418	20.3	
Neuss	570 × 432	24.7	
Bonn	528 × 524	27.7	
Vindonissa	Irregular	c. 22.2	
Lauriacum	539 × 398	21.5	
Carnuntum	500 × 400	20.0	
Lambaesis	500 × 420	21.0	
Haltern	490 × 370	18.1	
Oberaden	Polygonal	54.0	(double legionary fortress)
Vetera I	902 × 621	56.0	(double legionary fortress)

Source: from Manning (1989: 161).

Within these forts, individual barrack blocks were laid out to house the
soldiers. Several Roman barracks have been excavated and their layout is
quite familiar to archaeologists. Indeed, extant barracks are still to be found
at Caerleon, base of the II Legion Augusta. These bases were built by the
military and depictions of men wearing *lorica segmentata* (articulated plate
armour) undertaking this task are to be found on Trajan's Column (Feugère,
2002: 211). Timber in vast quantities was required for the first phases of a

fort's construction. This was yet another task of the Roman infantryman, a fact revealed by the excavation of a wooden writing tablet at Caerleon, which referred to guards being sent to fetch pay, and also of parties collecting building timber (Brewer, 2000: 16).

The size of individual barrack room cells for the Roman infantrymen were far from huge, some of the best examples being at Caerleon (see Plate 7). Here, within the Prysg Field, lie the remains of barrack blocks – one for each century. The blocks are narrow, L-shaped buildings, which have twelve pairs of rooms fronted by a veranda. 'Each century was divided into ten mess units (contubernia), each of eight men, who shared a pair of rooms in the barracks or on campaign. In theory, only ten pairs of rooms should be needed for the 80 men in the century, but there are often extra rooms and these were probably needed for storage, or new recruits, or the junior officers' (Brewer, 2000: 35). Caerleon's barrack buildings seem to have been timber constructions in their earlier phases, with more substantial stone-built structures following later. These clay-floored dwellings would have housed between 5,000 and 6,000 soldiers (Evans and Metcalf, 1992: 2). In the first phase of this fort (first century AD), the average internal room sizes in this barrack block were 4.2m × 3.4m (Block A) and 4.4m × 3.4m (Block B) – hardly palatial (Evans and Metcalf, 1992: 79).

Fragments of military tents have been recovered from Birdoswald (Wilmott, 1997: 114, 340–1), Carlisle and Vindolanda (Haines et al., 2000: 121–2), and these would have been used in the field when the army was on campaign – indeed, the term *sub pellibus* (under tenting) was used to mean 'on campaign' (de la Bédoyère, 2001: 45).

Excavations within the Roman fort at the Carlisle Millennium site (1999–2001) yielded the remains of a leather tent (Jones and Watson, 2003: 12) from Carlisle stamped SDV. This was found in a partially waterlogged trench and is thought to date from late first to second centuries AD. Tents must have been fairly large as they had to accommodate a *contubernium* – a unit of men who shared rooms at barracks at base, or tents on campaign (Wells, 2003: 95–6).

Early twentieth-century excavations of the Roman fort at Newstead in Scotland also discovered elements relating to tents used by the Roman infantryman. On this site a large number of tent pegs were recovered from the ditch of the early fort. 'They were made of oak, and varied in length from 10 inches to 20 inches. They were triangular in section, and pointed at both ends, and had a well-defined notch for the attachment of the ropes. The same type has been found at the Saalburg, and also at the fort of Coelbren in Wales' (Curle, 1911: 210).

Curle believed that the subdivision of long barrack blocks showed that the 'tent tradition', as he called it, survived (ibid.: 74). Wooden tent pegs have been found in a well at Velsen (Morel and Bosman, 1989: 174) and at Annetwell Street fort in Carlisle and Melandra Castle, Derbyshire (P. Robinson, 2001: 80).

Initially a series of circular holes within the Roman Marching Camp at Rey Cross, in the North Pennines, were thought, perhaps, to be the remnants of tent peg holes demarcating the layout within the camp. However, as the authors discussed, the fact that these holes were circular rather than triangular would suggest that the features are in fact something else (ibid.: 80). This marching camp was located in an area with such little soil above the bedrock that most of the protecting rampart was created from turfs (ibid.: 83). On this site there was no evidence of the wooden stakes carried by the legionaries and taken by some as being lashed into large wooden caltrops and forming a barrier at the top of marching camp banks. One of these stakes has been recovered from an excavation at Welzheim (Feugère, 2002: 44, fig. 27). In many ways, a similar arrangement existed for Roman soldiers besieging sites. At Masada in Judea troops built huts with low stone walls to be roofed with their tents. In some locations there were, perhaps, even storage rooms for their equipment 'similar to the pairs of rooms occupied in a permanent barrack block' (Goldsworthy, 2003: 172).

Religion

There was no state requirement for the Roman legionary to follow a single, set religion. Artefacts excavated at military sites attest the presence of some variety in those of the pantheon of gods favoured by soldiers. At Caerleon, for example, an inscription records the restoration of the temple of Diana (Brewer, 2000: 40), while an altar to Salus, goddess of health (ibid.: 41), and a bust of Mars, the god of war and thus most suitable for the legionary, were also found (Evans, 1988: 27).

A number of the eighty-eight gems dating from the first to early third centuries AD, found dropped into the drains of the fortress baths at Caerleon, also portray a variety of divinities: Mercury, Minerva, Roma and others

(Brewer, 2000: 42–3). In the later levels of the barrack block at Caerleon, a small statuette or *Genius Paterfamilias* – traditionally associated with the head of a household – was found, perhaps forming part of the shrine of a late-Roman soldier. Evans (1988: 23) believes that this might even indicate the later incorporation of married quarters for the ordinary soldier within the fortified area.

As we shall see below, a figure of Victory was found with a presumed legionary cremation by the fortress at Exeter. Rather unsurprisingly, Victory and Mars feature in statuary and carvings recovered from many military sites, as with Caerleon (de la Bédoyère, 2001: 20, 80, 146).

Perhaps the best known of the religious cults associated with the army was that of Mithraism. This secret cult, originating in Iran, had seven ranks for its devotees, including that of *miles* or soldier (Sumner, 2003: 46), and often cave-like places of worship beneath the ground. At the cult's core was a promise of an afterlife, of the triumph of light over darkness. Evidence for legionary involvement in the cult is present on sites throughout the Empire, from Carnuntum in Pannonia (Clauss, 2001: 34) north to Carrawburgh on Hadrian's Wall (Goldsworthy, 2003: 112). Carvings of Mithras wearing a phrygian cap and slaying a bull are some of the most enduring images from these temples. Furthermore, one of the Mithraic carvings at London identifies the man responsible for its commissioning, Ulpius Silvanus, a veteran of the II Legion Augusta (de la Bédoyère, 2001: 147).

Caerleon also appears to have had a temple to Mithras outside the fort, according to inscriptions excavated at the site (Brewer, 2000: 42). Dedications at one of the temples to Mithras in Poetovia, Slovenia, included entire groups of soldiers from the Legio V Macedonica, and Legio XIII Gemina although here, as on other Mithraic sites, dedications by officers were more frequent than by ordinary legionaries (Clauss, 2001: 34, 36).

Medicine

In addition to the widely known assemblage of medical equipment from civilian sites of the Roman Empire (Jackson, 1990), medical tools are also found in differing military contexts – from forts to battle sites. At Exeter instruments used to probe the wounds of infantrymen or to mix medicines have been recovered (Holbrook and Bidwell, 1991: 257–9). Forts were provided with hospitals to treat wounded and sick soldiers (*valetudinarium*).

People with medical skills would also be taken on campaign with the legions to work with battle-injured soldiers. Among the finds at Kalkriese were a bone elevator (*elevatorium*) and the bronze handle of a medical knife (Schlüter, 1999: 147). A field-dressing station during a battle in the Dacian campaigns is depicted on Trajan's Column (Goldsworthy, 2000: 128).

Perhaps some of the archaeobotanical evidence derived from the Bearsden fort ditch might also hint at medicinal treatments. Here, some barley was found that resembled pearl barley that had been rubbed with a pestle and mortar – Pliny wrote of the use of this in medicines (Dickson and Dickson, 2000: 124). The fragments of linseed located in the same context might have been used in a poultice of some form (*ibid.*: 122).

We have already mentioned the presence of human whipworm and roundworm in the sewage in the Bearsden fort, but Roman legionaries were afflicted with other parasites, too. A soldier's comb was recently excavated from waterlogged levels at the fort at Carlisle (Luguvalium), which still retained an intact 3mm-long head louse. This was recovered from levels within the fort dating to *c.* AD 72–3 (see BBC News, 2004a). The misery caused by lice is more readily associated with the infantryman of the First World War, but parasites are something with which the infantryman from the ancient past was also familiar.

One of the writing tablets from Vindolanda details the sickness suffered by the legionaries. Of those present at the base, some thirty-one were listed as being unfit for service (inv. no. 88.841), this figure being made up of: sick 15, wounded 6, and 10 suffering from inflammation of the eyes (Bowman, 2003: 16). A further tablet mentions a hospital for the soldiers (inv. no. 195, 198).

THE PRISONER

In the past we have been almost totally dependent on the classical authors for evidence about prisoners of war and their camps in the Roman period. Such gems as Tacitus' line in the *Agricola* when, in reference to the Emperor Domitian, he wrote, 'He was conscious of the ridicule that his sham triumph over Germany had excited when he had bought slaves in the market to have their dress and hair made up to look like prisoners of war' (Tacitus, 1970: 91), confirm our thoughts that prisoners of war were used in victory parades. Roman prisoners were also kept, for example, 'In the mid 170s Marcus Aurelius made a peace settlement with a tribe called the Iazyges on

the Danube frontier. The deal included a return of Roman prisoners . . .'
(de la Bédoyère, 2001: 74). We also have recourse to several contemporary
monuments that are relevant, for example: the depictions of Dacian prisoners
of war being presented to the Emperor on Trajan's Column in Rome; defeated
Gauls chained to a victory monument on the triumphal arch at Carpentras
(Carpentorate) (King, 1990: 42); and barbarian prisoners being lead away by
Roman soldiers on the *Tropaeum Traiani* at Adamklissi in Romania (Dorutju,
1961).

In addition to carvings of prisoners taken by the Roman legions, there are
also depictions of prisoners of war and associated trophies of captured
military hardware on coins of the era – for example, an issue of *denarius* of
Julius Caesar (*c.* 46–45 BC) shows such a collection of victory elements and
the legend CAESAR beneath (Wiegels, 2000: 8).

In recent years several authors have suggested that perhaps we do have
archaeological evidence for these camps and for the incarceration of
prisoners before they were enslaved, used in triumphal processions or in the
arena. The excavation of the fort of Vindolanda on Hadrian's Wall in
northern Britain is a case in point. The work of the Birleys here is
fascinating: 'In the early third century something very curious happened at
Vindolanda. The entire fort was levelled and dozens of circular, stone huts
were erected, in neat rows. They were clearly not to house Roman troops.
It had something to do with Severus' expedition. He was in Britain from
208–11 with a vast expeditionary force, intending to re-conquer all north
Britain – a return to the policy of Agricola (or Domitian). Native Britons
were surely quartered at Vindolanda: hostages from Caledonia . . .' (Birley,
2002: 159). These circular buildings might hold up to 2,000 people and are
unlike structures at any other fort in the empire. Little more evidence was
obtained from them as they had been kept clean in antiquity. Is it possible
that circular houses at a fort equate, necessarily, with prisoners, can they not
be Roman? It is true to say that they are unusual and that barracks and
similar structures of Roman use are generally rectangular, but it is not
impossible that they are Roman. Furthermore, circular stone dwelling
structures of Roman vintage are known on other sites in Britain, at
Ironmongers Piece in Marshfield, South Gloucestershire, for example.

De la Bédoyère has also suggested that the massive 'Saxon Shore' forts on
the south-east coast of England, and mentioned in the late Roman record of
military dispositions – the 'Notitia Dignitatum' – might have been used as a

holding camp for prisoners: 'Under Probus (276–82), "Bergundian" and "Vanda" prisoners-of-war seized in continental wars were reputedly despatched to Britain to keep them out of the mainland empire, later serving as imperial allies' (de la Bédoyère, 2001: 104).

All our evidence for prisoner-of-war camps thus relates to Roman captives rather than captive Romans – perhaps it is simply a weakness in the archaeological record that traces of Romans captured by Britons, Germans, or Gauls have not, as yet, been found. Not all combat was quite so final as the defeat of the Varus legions in AD 9 by Arminius, when the taking of Roman prisoners was perhaps not high on the agenda of the Cherusci – after all, we have the account of prisoner exchange, above. Roman carvings of the torture of their men by female Dacian captors (using a flaming torch) could perhaps be taken as propaganda to confirm the barbarity of Rome's enemies.

MEMORIALS AND BURIALS

For many men, burial on the battlefield was probably generally in a mass-grave – a mode of deposition that we shall see in all subsequent chapters – although, by the end of the nineteenth century, a greater effort was made to name the individual soldier on monuments, and to provide single graves. Despite the fact that commemorations of victories with trophies and triumphal arches were far more likely within the Roman Empire, it is not true to say that individual soldiers were not remembered. Perhaps one of the most intriguing monuments is the fragmentary altar, the *Tropaeum Traiani*, found at Adamklissi in Romania. This once had walls 11.67m long by 6m high with the names of legionary and auxiliary soldiers who had fallen fighting for the Roman Republic in Dacia (Dorutju, 1961; Hope, 2003: 91–2).

Those legionaries who survived to live a long retirement were also given burials that noted their lives in the army. Many Roman military tombstones have been recovered from sites across the Empire, frequently in close proximity to the fort in which the soldier was based, and often depicting him with all the accoutrements of soldiery. The information on these tombstones often relates to the unit in which the individual served, length of service, age and tribe. Part of a soldier's wage was taken at source to pay for membership of a 'burial club' so that, in the event of his death, sufficient funds would be in place for the funeral. As Hope (2003: 93) states: 'For the soldier, basic, anonymous, and communal burial must have been the common expectation during war. Peacetime could present a very different scenario, with the soldier receiving individual burial, often in a marked grave.'

One unusual relief, probably a tombstone, from Croy Hill in Scotland (and now in Edinburgh Museum), is thought to date to the mid-second century AD. Although there are no inscriptions to assist in identifying the individuals depicted, the stone shows three people. Their panoply of arms includes helmets, cylindrical shields (*scuta*) and heavy throwing spears (*pila*). The three men are shown wearing military cloaks (*paennla*) and the figure on the left has padded armour. Cowan (2003b: 59) has speculated that this carving may represent a father and his two sons.

The heirs of a deceased soldier could also be responsible for constructing his memorial, one example being that of Caius Valerius Vales, now in the Museum of Archaeology in Corinth. This translation of the inscription on the tombstone reads:

Caius Valerius Vales, son of Caius, of the voting tribe Quirina, of the Camunni, soldier of Legio VIII Augusta, of the centuria of Senucio, 35 years of age, served 14 years, [lies here]. His heir set this up according to his will.

(The relief depicts the soldier with his *gladius*; see Kos, 1978.)

The costume and accoutrements of third-century soldiers are depicted on a number of tombstones. One example, from Istanbul, Turkey, portrays a soldier of the 'humble Numerus Divitensium' – Aprilius Spicatus (Sumner, 2003: 7). Another, that of Aurelius Lustinus, a soldier of Legio II Italica, shows a man with weighted *pilum* and an oval shield. Lustinus was killed in a campaign against the Dacians (Cowan, 2003b: 7).

Despite the provision of often elaborate mausolea and tombstones, burial was far from being the only mode for treating the remains of the dead. Cremation was also popular – an example of this that might relate to the remains of Roman legionaries is to be found at Exeter, the site of a legionary fortress from *c*. AD 55 to 75 almost certainly for the Legio II Augusta (Salvatore, 2001: 125). Excavations, appropriately enough on the site of the former 'Valiant Soldier' public house, revealed at least three Roman military buildings containing three broadly contemporary cremation pits. These pits lay on high ground some 200m outside the south gate of the fortress and thus meeting Roman burial customs of burial outside the settlement boundary (*ibid*.: 126). All the cremations were given grave goods that one might expect of the everyday soldier – pottery vessels, gaming counters, drinking beakers and a small religious figurine associated with the army.

These pits contained many bones, representing at least two and possibly three individuals who could have served with the legionary garrison. Pit VS356 (0.82m wide by 1m long and surviving to 0.54m deep) held an almost complete beaker, a near-complete glass funnel, fortress wares and charred bones (*ibid.*: 129). Pit VS368 (1.5sq m and 1.14m deep) had a complete south-east Dorset Ware pedestalled bowl or urn, a south Gaulish decorated samian vessel and an incomplete bronze lamp (*ibid.*: 133).

The cremation and its associated artefacts in Pit VS362 (some 3m by 2m wide and 0.5m deep) were perhaps the greatest indicators of a military funeral. The burnt bones in this deposit were accompanied by at least two flagons, one of which is of a fabric associated with army supply, three stamped samian vessels, fragments from four glass vessels, two gaming counters (one black, one white), a coin of Nero, and a small bronze figure of the goddess Victory (*ibid.*: 133). We must not assume that this was necessarily even the cremated body of a man, let alone a soldier; Cool (2005: 34) refers to the burning of two Roman adult women on a pyre at Brougham, Cumbria – these with the bodies of horses and with military equipment accompanying them.

For the purposes of our study, however, the information derived from excavations of the buried skeletons of soldiers is far more useful.

THE FALLEN

The remains of Roman soldiers (and possible Roman soldiers) have come from a number of varied contexts, their demise being equally disparate. Those who died after retirement could be afforded the pleasantries of a formal funeral, of the ceremonies associated with cremation or burial and the subsequent monuments of memorial. Those who were killed in battles in which the Roman army was defeated and did not hold the field afterwards were not so fortunate. Examples of burials of the martial dead are found throughout the Empire and include such unusual cases as the 'inhumation' of a body at Lugdunum (Lyon) in France – assumed to be hurried. The artefacts found with this man were deemed important as they included 'one of the first *spathae* [long swords] which can be associated with an infantryman . . . This discovery, which can perhaps be linked with the battle there in AD 197 (the soldier's purse contained twelve silver *denarii*, the latest being struck under

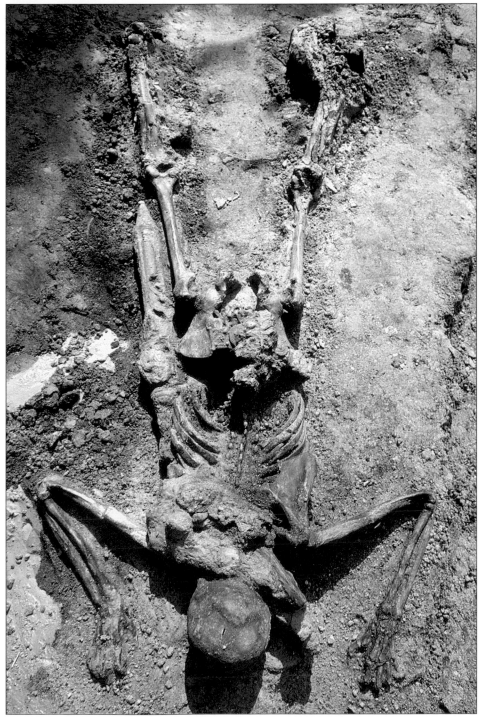

1. The skeleton from Herculaneum of a man killed by the eruption of Vesuvius in AD 79. The man is wearing a military belt with coins at his waist, and has a *gladius* (blade weapon) by his side and some tools slung on his back. *(Copyright Jonathan Blair/CORBIS)*

(i)

(ii)

2. Fragments of Roman armour recovered from excavations at Carlisle, Cumbria: (i) segmented arm guard; (ii) shoulder guard composed of scale armour with what could be decorative bronze fixings; (iii) Newstead-type iron breastplate armour with bronze fastenings. *(Copyright Oxford Archaeology North on behalf of Carlisle City Council)*

(iii)

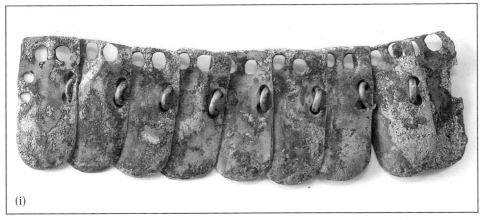

(i)

3. Fragments of Roman armour recovered from excavations at Carlisle, Cumbria:
(i) bronzed scale armour. *(Copyright Oxford Archaeology North on behalf of Carlisle City Council)* (ii) an iron greave. *(Copyright English Heritage)*

(ii)

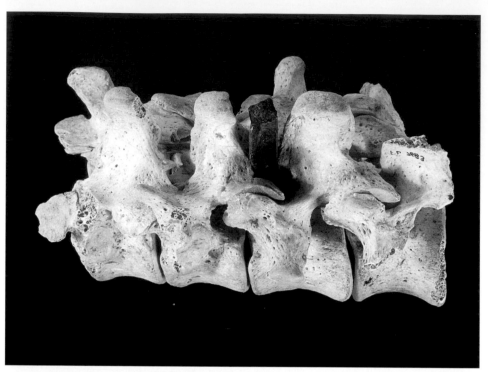

4. A Middle Bronze Age spear embedded in the spine of Unknown Warrior 2, Tormarton, South Gloucestershire. *(Photo by Ian Cartwright)*

5. The skull of Unknown Warrior 3, Kalkriese, Germany, showing a cleft made by a bladed weapon. *(Kalkriese Museum)*

6. Unknown Warrior 5, Repton, Derbyshire. Note the small Thor's Hammer just to the left of the jaw. *(Photo by Birthe Kjølbye-Biddle. Copyright The Repton Excavations)*

7. Unknown Warrior 6, an Anglo-Saxon combat victim at Eccles, Kent, with an iron projectile embedded in his spine. *(Copyright Bradford University)*

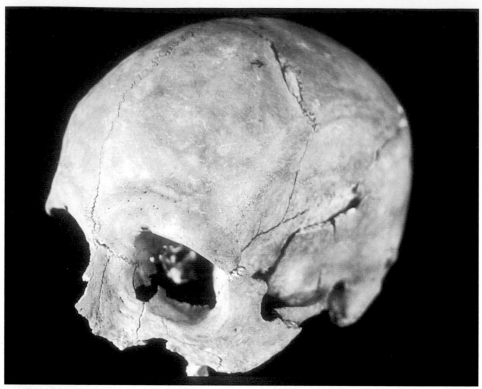

8. The skull of Unknown Warrior 7, Towton, North Yorkshire, showing head injuries. *(Copyright Bradford University)*

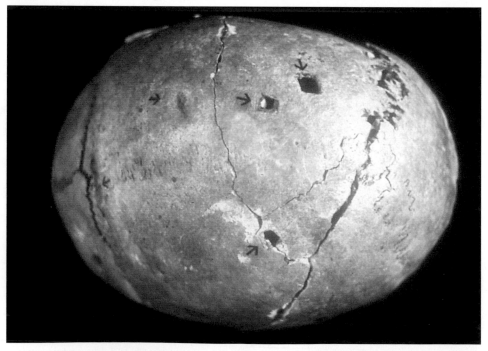

9. The skull of Unknown Warrior 7, Towton, North Yorkshire, showing head injuries. (Copyright Bradford University)

10. Unknown Warrior 8, Visby, Gotland. *(Historiska Museum, Gotland)*

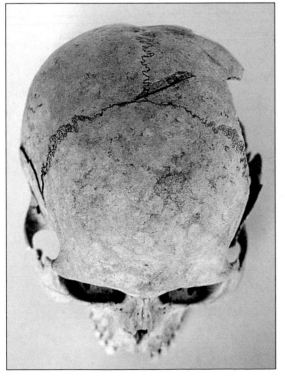

11. The skull of Unknown Warrior 10, Basing House, excavated from the Postern Gate. *(Hampshire County Museums and Archives Service)*

12. Skeleton of Unknown Warrior 13, Boezinge, Flanders. *(Photo courtesy of John Hayes-Fisher)*

Septimius Severus in AD 194), also gives us accurate information on the new method of hanging the *spatha*' (Feugère, 2002: 115–16). In addition to the sword and coins, artefacts such as a brooch and sword chape were found, as were belt fittings composed of letters spelling out 'Utere Felix' or 'use luckily' – perhaps somewhat ironic given the fate of its owner.

In AD 79 during the same eruption of Vesuvius that buried Pompeii, the city of Herculaneum was covered by lava and mud. Excavations of the city in the 1980s revealed not only buildings and artefacts, but also the skeletal remains of many of the inhabitants. Some of the most poignant of these were found in the seafront chambers (Gore, 1984: 570) and were of individuals trying desperately to escape. The human remains included those of an individual who was armed (see Colour Plate 1). This man – said to be around 37 years of age at death – was found face down with a dagger and a short sword (*gladius*), which was attached to the remains of a military-style belt (Guzzo, 2003: 74). He was accompanied in death by a series of carpentry tools, an adze and three chisels, that may have been in a bag on his back (Gore, 1984: 572–3). The pathology showed three missing front teeth and a lump in the femur, interpreted as resulting from a possible stab wound. So who was this man? De la Bédoyère (2001: 203–4) is in no doubt that if the body had been found in Britain, it would have been immediately taken as being the remains of a legionary. As there was no fort nearby, he suggested that the man was 'probably a soldier, but going about his business in a wealthy civilian settlement either in a private capacity or because he had an official post in the city connected with a public building project, security of policing . . . he is a reminder that the Roman world was not divided into clearly demarcated civilian and military zones' (*ibid.*: 204).

A further intriguing case is found at Dura Europos in Syria, where excavations revealed artefacts relating to a particular action during a siege. Some of the Roman defenders at 'Tower 19' had sunk a countermine beneath one of the siege-works of the attackers when it collapsed, killing attackers and the defenders. Sadly the bones that were found were not kept and it is impossible to reconstruct the associated artefact group with any confidence, although some sketch plans exist (James, 2004: 34–5). The deposits from this collapsed tower of the AD 250s included the skeleton of a man in a mail shirt (*ibid.*: fig. 52), a helmet, sword and shield umbo. The idea of mining beneath enemy defences and of the defenders countermining to prevent the assault would persist right up to the First World War.

In terms of formal depositions, burial with one's weapons was not the Roman way. There are burials that include Roman military equipment, which are generally interpreted as being of auxiliary troops. Feugère (2002: 32) highlighted a number of Gallic examples: at Berry-Boux, in the Cher department in France, a burial of *c.* 20 BC included a sword, lance and shield (although the author did not feel that this was enough to denote a soldier's grave), while a grave at Neuvy-Pailloux (*c.* AD 40–50) included a lance-head and two bronze face helmets – perhaps the interment of a cavalry auxiliary; an infantry example, albeit of an officer, was found in a burial of *c.* AD 40 at Chassenard and here the body was accompanied with a jug, cup and razors, four dies for striking coins, a sword, military belt, mail coat, a face helmet and torque – all possessions of a soldier, possibly a *decurion*. Our study is concerned with the infantryman and not his commanders. Although not conclusively legionaries, the remains of the 'unknown warriors', below, come from contexts with established Roman martial elements: from the disaster that befell the legions in the Teutoburg Forest, and from the Roman fort at Velsen in the Netherlands. Both individuals played their part in major engagements of the Roman legions and neither were placed in what one would call formal burials, although it is possible that both were interred within a formalised context.

UNKNOWN WARRIOR 3

An army unexcelled in bravery, the first of the Roman armies in discipline, energy and experience in the field, through negligence of its general, the treachery of the enemy and the unkindness of Fortune was surrounded, nor was as much opportunity as they had wished given to the soldiers either of fighting or of extricating themselves, except against heavy odds; indeed some were even chastised for using their weapon and showing the spirit of the Romans. Hemmed in by forest, marshes and ambuscade, it was destroyed almost to a man by the very enemy it has always slaughtered like cattle . . .

(*Velleius Paterculus*, 2/119; Cowan, 2003a: 14–15)

In the Teutoburg Forest in AD 9, one of the greatest reverses was suffered by the Roman Army: the defeat of three legions, the XVII, XVIII and XIX, under the command of Publius Quinctilius Varus. The legions were lured into an ambush by Arminius – a member of the Cherusci tribe and someone who had served with the legions – and, trapped between wooded forest, a turf wall and a marsh, were annihilated. Perhaps 20,000 soldiers were killed, along with camp followers and Varus himself. There were very few survivors.

As we have seen above, a contemporary legionary legate, Velleius Paterculus, gave a written account of elements of the battle (see page 48). Archaeologically, very little relating to this astonishing battle had been found until recently, a cenotaph commemorating one of the dead being a notable exception. This memorial to an officer, a centurion named Marcus Caelius, of the First Cohort of the XVIII Legion, shows a man decorated with phalerae and torcs for valour in battle and with a civic crown of oak leaves awarded for saving a fellow citizen's life. The monument was uncovered close to the legionary base at Xanten, Holland (Cowan, 2003a: 15). Caelius' body and those of the men who died alongside him were never recovered, although the subsequent campaigns of Germanicus (AD 14–16) visited the site of the Roman humiliation and found the bones of many of the slaughtered in groves in the forest; they buried as many as possible in pits on the site.

The site of Kalkriese, near Osnabrück, Germany, was initially discovered by a British army officer, Major Tony Clunn, with a detailed metal-detector survey (Clunn, 1999) and subsequently extensively excavated under the direction of Wolfgang Schlüter. As we have already seen, artefacts from the site included large quantities of Roman military material and of the paraphernalia associated with the movement of an army; its support teams, baggage and supplies. Some of the many coins that have been found were stamped with the letters VAR, interpreted, perhaps not unreasonably, as standing for 'Varus'. The excavations at Kalkriese revealed not only finds associated with the Roman legions, but also some important structural elements, in particular the remains of a turf wall c. 4.5m wide, on which sat a wooden fence (Schlüter, 1999: 130–1). This fortification helped to ensure that the Roman troops continued into the bottleneck and afforded some cover to the attacking tribes people; its construction also indicated that a large degree of planning had gone into the attack. The remains at Kalkriese have led most authorities, though not all, to believe that this was almost certainly the site of the *Varusschlacht*, the destruction of the three legions.

Over the course of the excavations, despite the sandy soils which are not conducive to the preservation of skeletal remains, large numbers of bones have also been recovered. Among them, beneath a collapsed section of the turf wall, was found the articulated body of a mule complete with a bell that had been stuffed with straw to prevent it ringing. In other areas, human and animal bones were jumbled up and displayed signs of weathering, having been left open to the elements prior to their deposition (Zylla and Tolksdorf-Lienemann, 2000).

Since 1994, five pits have been found in front of the turf wall on the Oberesch at Kalkriese (Wilbers-Rost, 2003b: 138). In 1994 a pit was uncovered which was half filled with bones. These, too, were weathered and non-articulated with several human skull fragments, representing a number of individuals. This picture might fit reports of Germanicus' men interring the remains of the dead legionaries in pits, years after their death. Some of the bones displayed cut-marks to suggest violence.

A further pit, excavated in 1999, was lined with limestone slabs and was packed with bones. Again the assemblage was composed both of human and animal bones with a human skull in the middle. On the base of the pit was a further skull, which displayed a sword cut. Apart from one isolated bone, it appears that the bones in this pit represented the remains of two individuals. Both were male, one around 30 and the other around 35 years of age, and c. 1.63m and 1.65–1.71m tall respectively (Wilbers-Rost 2003a: 34). Although

---

UNKNOWN WARRIOR 3

The remains of one of the victims at Kalkriese

This skull, found with other bones, may well represent one of the men of the lost XVII, XVIII, or XIX Legions. The fact that it was associated with a jumble of other bones also indicates that the man's remains had been left exposed to the elements for some time following his death prior to deposition in a pit. The interment may have occurred when Germanicus visited the site of the battle.

It is impossible to tell whether this male, who had suffered a sword cut, was an officer or a standard infantryman – all suffered a similar fate. As such, this is a perfect example of an 'unknown soldier' found during the course of an archaeological excavation; although we can infer a great deal about the events that surrounded his death from the stratigraphy (even without recourse to the classical texts), we shall never know his name, or even his unit.

the palaeopathological analysis of the site at Kalkriese is still under way, initial examinations suggest that 'the human skeletal remains must be classified exclusively as those of young or elderly adult males. Bones of female or sub-adult individuals are not present. Both the individual teeth found and sets of teeth verify that the humans were in good health. Two *calvae* (skull caps) give clear indications of fatal injuries inflicted by sharp or semi-sharp weapons [see Colour Plate 5]. Various indications suggest that the human and animal bones lay for a time on the surface' (Schlüter, 1999: 135–6). What is certain is that the site at Kalkriese was the location of a fairly important military engagement involving the Roman army – there are sufficient finds of Roman militaria and of human remains to demonstrate this. The majority of those who have examined the material are also firmly of the belief that all the evidence points to this being the major site of the *Varusschlacht*.

UNKNOWN WARRIOR 4

That same year the Frisii, a nation beyond the Rhine, cast off peace, more because of our rapacity than from their impatience of subjection . . . The soldiers appointed to collect the tribute were seized and gibbeted. Olennius anticipated their fury by flight, and found refuge in a fortress, named Flevum, where a by no means contemptible force of Romans and allies kept guard over the shores of the ocean . . .

(Tacitus, *Annals*, IV, 72)

The fort at Velsen I (*Flevum*) was the only one downstream from the Roman base at Vechten in the Netherlands and was thus of considerable strategic importance. In AD 28 it was attacked by the Frisians. It was held with some difficulty – detritus on the site, including a series of lead slingshots, attests to this. Excavations revealed a series of wells within the fortifications, several of which were found to contain human remains. One, in particular, was of interest, given that it held a virtually complete skeleton of a robust *c.* 25-year-old man, *c.* 1.90m in height, and with a dagger and sheath (Morel and Bosman, 1989: 167). The articulated body was supposedly found in a supine position (Constandse-Westermann, 1982: 139) (see Plate 8). Constandse-Westermann (*ibid.*: 158) examined the possibility that this man was of Mediterranean or more local origin – something to which his equipment did not give any enlightenment, and concluded that he was probably the body of a 'native, serving in the Roman army' mainly from an examination of comparative statures of known contemporary Roman skeletal assemblages.

The man's skull had a crack in the right frontal/parietal area and some chipped-off bone splinters, which might have been caused by a blow of ante- or post-mortal origin (Constandse-Westermann, 1982: 141, 146–7). This 'wound' might have rendered the victim unconscious – leading to subsequent drowning in the well – had it occurred prior to death and if it was not fatal. The pathology is certainly not enough for us to state whether the man had been killed in combat or in an accident, murdered, or simply expired from disease or illness – the 'wound' being a post-mortem event.

The well shaft in which the body was found was lined with a series of barrels with staves of spruce and silver fir. These might perhaps have held wine. Below the body, and present in the well prior to its decommissioning, were possible parts of the well-head equipment and bucket (Morel and Bosman, 1989: 168). The body and his accoutrements were then cast or placed in the well along with fragments of quernstone, a lamp, various amphorae and pot shards, a 'ballista ball', animal bones, shellfish and even a wooden tent peg. Following this, the well was filled with huge quantities of stone and refuse from the fort (*ibid.*: 168–70). The filling of this well in one quick phase was a deliberate act.

It is not known whether the placing of the body was a votive act to commemorate the abandonment of the fort or simply a convenient location to inter a body, almost in a way in which one would tidy up rubbish. The discovery of a complete pot with the body might perhaps indicate a provision of 'grave goods' for the afterlife and thus lessen the likelihood of the latter theory. It might also be taken to reveal that, if this man had died a violent death, he was probably buried by comrades rather than an enemy, who would have been more likely to loot the dagger had it been visible (*ibid.*: 168, 170). What is certain is that a body would not have been deposited in a well that was still in use and so this event has been taken to date to the abandonment of Velsen I in AD 28, the date of the Frisian rebellion.

As mentioned, the body was found to have several items about his person or in a stratigraphic sequence, which would suggest former association. An iron dagger (*pugio*) that was excavated survived to a length of 23.05cm and the bone or antler grip of the knife, still retaining three rivets, was also recovered (*ibid.*: 177). The sheath of this weapon was of fine craftsmanship with an iron plate decorated with silver, red, and yellow enamel and with designs of triangles, a temple, oak leaves and geometric motifs (*ibid.*: 177–86). Its very presence with the body would tend to suggest that, if the man was killed before being thrown into the well, then the motif would not be robbery.

While the sheath was a fine piece of equipment, other items were altogether more utilitarian. Eight belt-plates and a buckle of a military-style belt were located and these were essential for the attachment of the sheath and the dagger. The belt-plates were of worn copper alloy, which, along with the buckle, had once been silver-plated (*ibid.*: 180). The authors of the report on the burial thought that, together, these finds illustrated the fact that the soldier's equipment was far from standardised and that the quality of the belt would, perhaps, indicate that this was the body of a low-ranking soldier (*ibid.*: 187). The fact that other equipment of martial character was not present need not preclude this interpretation – it means simply that he was not in full battle apparel when deposited, the full panoply of armour and weaponry perhaps having been taken from the body (Constandse-Westermann, 1982: 139).

In terms of the man's clothing, one hobnailed shoe was found, along with twenty-one of the studs of the other, and a bronze fibula was also located. The man had an iron ring with a glass paste setting of a male head wearing a helmet, perhaps Mars or some other deity venerated by the military (Morel and Bosman, 1989: 170).

UNKNOWN WARRIOR 4

Roman soldier from the well of the fort at Velsen, Netherlands

This man, excavated in 1977 in Well Number II at Velsen I, was around 25 years of age at his death and about 1.90m tall. His pathology may indicate a blow to the head suffered at the time of his death. He was thrown into a well in the legionary fort c. AD 28 – perhaps as a result of the Frisian rebellion – and was possibly a Roman soldier of non-Mediterranean origin. He took a dagger, scabbard, belt, shoes and ring to his 'grave'.

THREE

Heroes of the Chronicles and Sagas: Anglo-Saxon and Viking Warriors

Their mail-shirts glinted,
hard and hand linked; the high-gloss iron
of their armour rang. So they duly arrived
in their grim war-graith and gear at the hall,
and, weary from the sea, stacked wide shields
of the toughest hardwood against the wall,
then collapsed on the benches; battle-dress
and weapons clashed. They collected their spears
in a seafarers' stook, a stand of greyish
tapering ash. And the trips themselves
were as good as their weapons.

(*Beowulf*, 321–30, in Heaney, 1999: 12)

Although there was no standing army in the Anglo-Saxon period, men were expected to provide military service to those in the upper levels of society. The stratification of Anglo-Saxon society gave specific roles to specific class ranks. For example, the *gesith* was a man, well-born in status, who had military obligations, and an *ealdorman* was a regional official. The war gear (*heriot*) of such men showed that the individual was offered the gift of weaponry by a lord to one entering his service – returnable on the man's death unless this was in battle (Reynolds, 2002a: 59). Reynolds (*ibid.*: 59) reveals the *heriot* of a tenth-century *ealdorman* as being 'four armlets of 300 mancuses of gold, and four swords and eight horses, four with trappings and four without, and four helmets and four coats-of-mail and eight spears and eight shields'.

The ordinary freeman (*ceorl*) was also expected to perform military duties. According to the epic poem 'The Battle of Maldon', one such *ceorl* was fighting as part of the retinue of the Saxon Earl Byrhtnoth against the Vikings in this battle in Essex in 991. Nicolle (1984: 14) believes that the role of the *ceorl* differed depending on where in the country they lived: 'The early role of the low class *ceorl* varied between Wessex, where he seems always to have been both farmer and fighter, and Northumbria, where he probably had no military obligation.'

Anglo-Saxon warriors seem to have been exclusively infantrymen, even though they possessed horses – these were used as a means of transport to the battle rather than a fighting platform. Norsemen, given the epic voyages they undertook, used ships as their major means of transport. A number of examples have survived and are displayed in museums, such as those from the fjord at Roskilde in Denmark, and the Oseberg, Gokst and Tune ships in Oslo, Norway.

It must be remembered that there were occasions when Vikings sought to avoid combat if they could, accepting payment (*Danegeld*) rather than fighting. Although much work has been done to dispel the 'rape and pillage' reputation of the Viking lifestyle, a martial element was nonetheless present in their lives and can be traced in the archaeological record. The raids and their effects might show up in the presence of weaponry, or bodies of those engaged in the fighting, or in particular layers of destruction. The effects might also be seen, as Reynolds's work (2002a: 93) suggests, in the presence of warning beacons to raise the alarm when a Viking raiding party was detected, one example being seen at Yatesbury, Wiltshire.

With all of the elements discussed below – armour, helmets, swords, spears and suchlike – as with most infantrymen, what made the Anglo-Saxon or indeed Viking warrior successful was the closeness or *esprit de corps* of the war band: 'For in the final analysis, men did not and do not fight for king or country but for the small group of men around them' (Underwood, 1999: 148).

WEAPONRY

In this period, Underwood (1999: 145) believes that, although there were some variations in usage, 'the basic weapons were enduring: spear and shield for the rank and file, sword, spear and shield for higher ranking warriors. Only the very richest wore a helmet or body armour.'

This period saw some major battles, including some which have become enshrined in the British psyche, such as the Battle of Hastings in 1066. It is thus probably surprising that so little has been recovered from battlefield sites, perhaps as a result of long-term scavenging. For example, the paucity of material from Hastings – only one iron axehead was supposedly recovered from the field – leaves a large gap in what we are actually able to say about the weapons used in combat and their method of employment. We have recourse to skeletal material that has weapon wounds and we have the finds of weapons in grave contexts, but there is nothing quite like Kalkriese (see Chapter 2). The Bayeux Tapestry portrays men with armour, such as footsoldiers and their formations, which may be useful for our study, but should, like a document, be treated with a degree of caution, as it was created by one side to celebrate its victory.

Iron spearheads are the most common type of weapon in Anglo-Saxon graves, comprising 85 per cent of all such examples found (Underwood, 1999: 39). The spear, with a wooden shaft up to 2m long, was used in conjunction with a round shield to form a very strong formation known as the shield wall or shield fortress (*scyldburh*). Spears were used both as throwing and thrusting weapons, as they had been in the Bronze Age (see Chapter 1). 'The Battle of Maldon' refers to an encounter in which a man finds his own spear being thrown back at him after his initial salvo. To avoid such an event, Anglo-Saxon technology continued the Roman *pilum* encumbrance principle: barbed spears, which could not easily be removed from shields they had hit and then be thrown back, have been found – a 52.5cm-long example having been uncovered in Abingdon, Berkshire (*ibid.*: 25). 'Slaves were denied the right to bear arms; consequently ownership of a spear defined a man as free and a warrior in Germanic Society' (*ibid.*: 39). Spears have been found on sites throughout Britain – recent work on the Bronze Age burial mound of Barrow Clump, on Salisbury Plain, being just one example (Jonathan Last, pers. comm.).

If spears were a relatively common weapon type, finds of swords are more unusual and thus they were probably used by senior warriors. At their most basic, Saxon swords were forged from several pieces of iron and were, correspondingly, weak. At the top of the range, pattern-welded blades were made by twisting together strips of mild steel and wrought iron during the forging process. The resulting blade had both a hard edge and a herringbone-patterned, lustrous appearance. These were works of art, as well as being intended for a deadly purpose, yet their efficacy is indisputable – the cut wounds to the skulls of the deceased at Eccles in Kent, which we shall discuss later, being a case in point. Examples of Anglo-Saxon swords have been found in several burials, including Barrow Clump, Buckland in Kent and Westgarth Gardens in Suffolk (Underwood, 1999: 52–5). Underwood (*ibid.*: 54) points to the fact that some swords bore runic inscriptions – a sixth-century example from Gilton, Kent, bears the legend EIC SIGIMER NEMDE ('Sigimer named this sword'). Such weapons were prestigious, precious items. Saxons also used a large knife (*seax*), both in hunting and everyday life, as well as, perhaps, in combat.

Vikings also had swords, as witnessed by the burial of the presumed warrior at Repton, examined below, and examples found in the River Thames in London. Although probably depicting Doomsday, the commemorative stone from Lindisfarne may well have been inspired by the terror of a Viking raid. The warriors portrayed on this carving were armed both with sword and axe (Cunliffe, 2001: 483). As with their Saxon counterparts, some of these Viking swords were also marked by their makers – inscriptions include INGELRII, from the River Thames (Peirce, 2002: 80–8), and ULFBERHT. The number of blades with the 'Ulfberht' inscription may mean that more than one individual was forging the swords (Oakeshott, in Peirce, 2002: 7). 'Viking craftsmen often added their own elaborately decorated hilts, and many swords were given names, such as leg-biter and gold-hilt' (see Ager, 2001). These swords had leather sheaths for protection, such as those found at York, Durham and Gloucester (Siddorn, 2000: 84).

Another Viking sword was excavated by Bersu from Jurby, Ballateare, on the Isle of Man, in 1946 (Richards, 2001: 104). This ninth-century example had been deliberately broken into three pieces by those who put it in the grave. As swords were given names and identities, so were they imbued with their own powers. This, perhaps, ended on the death of the warrior, or their owner and, as with Bronze Age examples (see Pryor's work on Flag Fen, 1991: fig. 11), they were destroyed on deposition. It was an important act, because swords were prestigious items. The sword from Ballateare was not a gift to the gods, but rather something that the person inhumed could take to the afterlife. The Viking practice of destroying swords is also found outside the British Isles – a late ninth- to tenth-century example from Vestre Berg in Norway being a case in point. Here, the sword had been bent into an 'S' shape and was interred in a grave along with two arrows, another small sword, an axe, two shield bosses and other items (Peirce, 2002: 87).

If the spear was the main Anglo-Saxon weapon, the battleaxe was the weapon of choice for the Viking warrior. An eleventh-century Anglo-Danish example of the war axe has been recovered from London (Nicolle, 1984: 20) and a further group of early eleventh-century iron spears and axeheads were recovered from the Thames near London Bridge (Gravett, 1999: 36). The axe was also used by Saxon forces, as depicted on the Bayeux Tapestry of the Battle of Hastings. Sixth- to seventh-century Saxon battleaxes have been found at Petersfinger and Howlett's in Kent (Nicolle, 1984: 20).

Although weapons found in burials – both Saxon and Viking – are a good source of information on the equipment available to the warrior, if not of pieces actually used in combat, it is possible that these graves do not belong to the men and women who fought in the battles, but that there is simply a martial portrayal in the burials. The rich grave goods given to the probable Saxon king in his burial at Sutton Hoo, Suffolk – a pattern-welded sword, mail coat, battleaxe, shield, spears and, most famously, a Scandinavian-style helmet – illustrate the panoply of arms, but their context is most unusual (Reynolds, 2002a: 55).

A further weakness of the archaeological record is the paucity of material relating to archery. We know from all manner of written sources, such as chronicles and epic poems ('The Battle of Maldon' for one), from pictorial representations, including the Franks Casket and Bayeux Tapestry, that the bow and arrow was a weapon used by Saxon infantry, yet there is little in terms of excavated material that would back this up; only 1 per cent of Anglo-Saxon graves holding arrowheads (Underwood, 1999: 26). A bone bracer or wristguard not too dissimilar to those of the Beaker package (see Chapter 1) was found at Lowbury, Berkshire (*ibid.*: 30), and arrowheads were found at sites such as Empingham, Rutland (*ibid.*: 33). This, perhaps, should serve as a cautionary tale that material gained from archaeological excavations may not give the full picture of the infantry at times.

ARMOUR

The most frequently occurring element of protective equipment from this period to be found in the archaeological record is the shield, or, at least, the metal shield boss. The shield and spear were essential accoutrements of the Saxon infantryman. According to Underwood (1999: 77), almost a quarter of Anglo-Saxon male burials contain evidence of a shield. Furthermore, there are a number of possible graves of females that also have shield parts. At Beckford A, Worcestershire, grave number A2 seemed to have a sharp weapon wound to the skull resulting from an oblique blow. This skeleton was initially thought to be female but, on discovery of the grave goods of spear and shield boss, was reassigned as male. Shepherd (1999: 232) points out the problems in assigning the sex of the individual purely on the basis of the perceived 'sex' of the grave goods. Grave B5 from Beckford B, some 550m away, also contained the body of a possible female along with spear and shield boss (*ibid.*: 237).

Shields were circular throughout much of this period, changing to the kite-shape, as depicted on the Bayeux Tapestry, in the eleventh century. These shields were composed of wooden boards and had a central iron boss. From impressions of burials in the soil, it seems that most Anglo-Saxon shields were 0.46–0.66m in diameter (Underwood, 1999: 79). We suspect that such shields were painted, but, as of yet, do not have the archaeological evidence to back this up.

Shield bosses, being metal, are the major surviving component of the shield and their form varies dramatically from the flattened cones of the fifth and sixth centuries to the dramatic 'sugar-loaf' bosses of the seventh century. Shield grips have been found on occasion, too, including the example from Morning Thorpe cemetery, Norfolk, where traces could be seen of the leather strips that covered the grip that in turn enclosed a wooden handle (*ibid.*: 87).

Shields not only provided protection against swords, axes and arrows, they also had an offensive role with the shield boss being used to smash into an opponent. There is only one surviving example of a wooden Viking shield, found on the buried warship at Gokst, Norway, *c.* 905. Discovered on the gunwales of the ship, the shield was made of 'seven or eight white pine planks of varying widths, and only 7mm thickness' (Siddorn, 2000: 40). As it was so thin and had a poor handgrip, this circular shield of 94cm diameter might well have been purely decorative for the ship.

In terms of body armour, some examples survive, such as at Vimose in Denmark, but as the only complete Anglo-Saxon example of a mail coat is the one from the Sutton Hoo ship burial, it is likely that the Saxon warrior of lower birth would not have worn body armour.

That is not to say that armour is unknown on archaeological sites from this period. Recent work at the prosperous eighth- to eleventh-century Viking town of Birka, Sweden, examined the headquarters of the royal garrison, including its longhouse. Material from the abandonment of this site in the eleventh century included arrowheads and armour, with the latter assemblage composed of items both of mail and of lamellar armour (Shaw, 2003). Although a royal retinue would perhaps be expected to have equipment of higher status than that available to the average footsoldier, it nonetheless indicates that such armour was in use at this time.

Several authors have suggested that tough leather and hide coats were used both by Saxon and Viking warriors as they provided good protection from blade weapons – something that infantrymen from the English Civil War would discover some 600 years later (see, e.g., Gravett, 1999: 46).

The archaeological record seems clear on one aspect in relation to body protection: although helmets were present in this period, probably the preserve of men of power and taking many forms, the horned helmet does not appear to be present. We have a seventh-century example that may have been an heirloom and based on late-Roman helmets, with visors portraying faces (Sutton Hoo), an eighth-century iron example with mail neck protection, brass decorations and anthropomorphic noseguard (Coppergate, York (see Nicolle, 1984: 18; Tweddle, 1992)), iron helmets with decorated crests in the shape of boars (Benty Grange (see Underwood, 1999: 100–2, figs. 16, 17); Wallaston (*ibid.*: 103–4, fig. 21)) and other variants, but nothing of Saxon or Viking design with horns. The only examples of helmets with horns from northern Europe known to the author date from the Bronze Age and come from Viksø in Denmark.

One find of a Viking helmet within a proper context is from Gjermundbu, Norway. This tenth-century helmet was discovered in a man's grave and comprised four sections of iron that were joined together to form a dome with a lateral and traverse crest. A visor, resembling a pair of spectacles, was cut from a further sheet of iron and joined to the front of the helmet to protect the upper part of the face. There are traces of metal rings to the lower edge of the helmet and it seems likely that it was originally provided with some form of mail neck guard (Gravett, 1999: 30).

In terms of Saxon examples, the helmet from Coppergate bears intriguing evidence as to its owner. Each crest has the same inscription:

INNOMINE·DNI·NOSTRI·IHV·SCS·SPS·DI·ET·
OMNIBVS·DECEMVS·AMEN·OSHERE·XPI

In the name of our Lord Jesus Christ, the Holy Spirit (and) God: and
To all we say Amen, Oshere

Oshere is an Anglo-Saxon name, most probably the owner of the helmet (Underwood, 1999: 103).

PRACTICE AND DISCIPLINE

Training would have been part of the lives of the Saxon and Viking warrior – attempts to draw up an effective shield wall and to maintain it against determined assault would have been futile without practice. Indeed, in 'The Battle of Maldon', the Saxon leader, Byrhtnoth, spent some time instructing his forces in this. There is little by way of archaeological evidence for this, however, and we would have to turn to chroniclers such as the Dane, Saxo, for evidence that the warrior practised swordsmanship even in periods of peace (Underwood, 1999: 121).

THE LIFE OF THE SOLDIER

Drinking

Then the due time arrived
For Halfdane's son to proceed to the hall.
The King himself would sit down to feast.
No Group ever gathered in greater numbers
or better order around their ring-giver.
The benches filled with famous men
who fell to with relish; round upon round
of mead was passed; those powerful kinsmen,
Hrothgar and Hrothulf, were in high spirits
in the raftered hall. Inside Heorot
there was nothing but friendship.
(Beowulf, 1007–17, in Heaney, 1999: 32)

Our image of the Saxon longhouse or Viking hall, with large retinues of men feasting and drinking, is perhaps influenced by films such as *The Vikings*, yet epic poems, including *Beowulf*, make large play on the reward of men with mead and wine for their service in battle. Drinking vessels were included in the ship burial at Sutton Hoo, perhaps reflecting the requirement of those in the upper echelons of society to provide hospitality in return for fighting service (Reynolds, 2002a: 55).

An expression of hospitality provided by those in power to their retinue and to the war band that helped these men to retain power was found in the phenomenal burial package at Prittlewell, Essex. Among the objects inhumed with the deceased were several glass beakers and the remains of a drinking horn (MOLAS, 2004: 24).

Another poem, 'Gododdin', recounts warfare in the sixth century during which a warlord named Mynydogg paid for the fighting services of his men through feasting and mead. These warriors were defeated at the battle of Cattraeth, Yorkshire, and found that 'they paid for their mead-feast with their lives' (Newark, 1993: 54).

Eating

Studies of the diet of Anglo-Saxon and Viking warriors are hampered by a lack of secure military contexts with excavated cesspit remains. Archaeobotanical evidence for the diet of the period does exist, but not from specifically martial sites. For instance, excavations within Norse houses at Drimore Machair, on South Uist, Orkney, revealed the presence of cattle, sheep and pig bones. Other food elements included bird bones (great black-backed gull, razorbill and duck) and fish bones (cod). Shellfish also seem to have been eaten with cockle, limpet, mussel, oyster, scallop, whelk and winkle all exploited (Dickson and Dickson, 2000: 172–3). As one might expect, Norse societies made use of all local food resources possible.

Fish formed an important part of the Viking diet. Barrett's excavations at Westray, Orkney, have examined a midden site. It seems as though there was a dramatic change in the material deposited in the rubbish dump in the ninth or tenth centuries. Beforehand, pig, cattle and sheep bones were common, but this seems to have been replaced by huge quantities of shellfish and fish bones. It has been suggested that this represents the arrival of the Vikings, who were salting fish to use on voyages or to export (Richards, 2001: 66–7).

Toilet

Although we have evidence of waterlogged latrine deposits on sites of Anglo-Saxon and Viking vintage, none of this can be directly associated with a military context.

Gaming

Much of the material relating to gaming as a pastime comes from a non-military context, but these elements are still important as being available to the warrior – after all, the first phases of Viking settlement often followed military action, perhaps including several of the later settlers in the war band.

The phenomenal discovery of what is almost certainly an Anglo-Saxon royal burial at Prittlewell, Essex, included some of the richest grave goods excavated since the ship burial at Sutton Hoo with which it is broadly contemporary (*c.* 630). Among other items inside this tomb were two pairs of glass jars (blue and green), a couple of gold foil Latin crosses, and a gold belt buckle, perhaps a reliquary, two cauldrons, two Merovingian coins and a probable sword and shield (Dawson, 2004: 70–1). This material was hanging on the walls of the tomb, in its original position. Further to these great finds were several bone gaming pieces and two antler dice provided for the royal afterlife (see also MOLAS, 2004: 37).

Gaming pieces have been recovered from archaeological contexts. A Viking boat burial from Scar (see Memorials and Burials, pages 69–70) held the remains of a man with a sword and twenty-two gaming pieces, perhaps for playing the Viking game *hnefatafl* (Dalland, 1992: 475); a gaming board was excavated from Balinderry, Ireland (Richards, 2001: 118). Discoveries during the excavations of Viking York also included gaming pieces and part of a wooden gaming board (see York Archaeological Trust, 2005). Although again not associated with a martial context of the Viking period, bone and antler dice have been recovered from Viking sites in Dublin, and a gaming piece supposedly of Viking age was found in one of the mass graves in Visby (formerly Wisby; see Chapter 4), on the Baltic island of Gotland. Here, among the mail-clad deceased, was a chessman made from a horse's tooth. The piece was 'square at the base, but spherical at the top, such as have been found in several places in male tombs from the Viking period' (Thordeman, 2001: 132–3). Had the mass grave accidentally disturbed an earlier Viking tomb, was the piece simply a residual artefact within the topsoil, or had it been held by one of the soldiers as a good-luck token, an heirloom? These are questions for which it is unlikely that we shall ever have an answer. Chess became popular in northern Europe from around the end of the eleventh century, after the First Crusade.

Another set of gaming pieces, known as the Lewis Chessmen, depict warriors of this period (see Plate 9). Probably once owned by someone with money, it is possible that they were made in Norway between 1150 and 1200 from whales' teeth and walrus ivory. Some mystery surrounds their discovery near Uig on the Isle of Lewis, but it is likely that they were found in a stone chamber that had been covered. The chessmen, up to around 10cm in height, depict not only kings and mounted knights, but also the footsoldier of the period; wearing a conical helmet and carrying a sword and a kite-shaped shield. There is the possibility that these footsoldiers represent a type of warrior known as a 'berserker', who would fight with frenzied ferocity in battle. Robinson (2004: 37) believes that 'the Beserkers, although irresistibly comic to a modern audience, were probably not conceived as figures of fun, but as serious fighting machines who embodied an heroic ideal'.

Admittedly much of this gaming material comes from wealthy contexts, but almost certainly those lower down in society would have had access to similar material, or would have adapted their own examples.

Writings

That there was a level of literacy among the Anglo-Saxons and Norse is beyond dispute with such elements as the *Anglo-Saxon Chronicles* surviving. What is less certain is the number of men in a Saxon shield-wall or a Viking longship who would have been able to write.

Harald set out for Orkney at Christmas with four ships and a hundred men. He lay for two days off Graemsay then put in at Hamna Voe on Mainland, and on the thirteenth day of Christmas they travelled on foot over to Firth. During a snowstorm they took shelter in Orkahaugr and there two of them went insane . . . (*The Orkneyinga Saga*, 93; see Ancient Sites Directory, 2005)

The subject of *The Orkneyinga Saga* is a crusade led in 1150 by Earl Rognvald of the island of Orkney to the Holy Land. Taking advantage of his absence, Harald Maddadarson landed on the island on 6 January 1153. He and his party of warriors broke into the Neolithic tomb of Maes Howe (Orkahaugr), using it as a shelter. On their return later in 1153, Rognvald and his men also entered this tomb. Both parties left their mark on the ancient burial chamber by carving graffiti throughout. Some of the carvings were of mythical animals, such as the supposed 'dragon', but much was in the form of writing. As these men, like so many on Orkney, were Vikings, the inscriptions they left on the stone walls of the tomb were in runes (see Plate 10).

These runes referred to the prowess of the warriors, their names, their lusts. Examples of the writings of the warriors included 'Ingigerth is the most beautiful of all women' (next to the image of a panting dog), 'Ingebjork the fair widow – many a woman has walked stooping in here a very showy person', signed by 'Erlingr', and, more crudely, 'Thorni fucked, Helgi carved' (the former being a woman's name).

Several Viking names are present: 'Haermund Hardaxe carved these runes', 'Ofram the son of Sigurd carved these runes' or others referring to carvings made 'with this axe owned by Gauk Trandilsson in the South land'. It is not uncommon for warriors to carve their names, images and more lascivious thoughts, but it also shows that there were those who were literate among the war band's ranks – this in the twelfth century (for all of these, see the work of Farrer, 1862, for the initial discovery).

Accommodation

In Ireland, an intensification of Viking raids from 830 onwards resulted in the creation of defended enclosures for warriors and ships, the so-called longphorts. These enabled the Vikings to remain in Ireland over winter prior to continuing their campaigning when the weather improved (Cunliffe, 2001: 505). Although the longphorts ultimately resulted in a more integrated sedentary lifestyle for many Vikings, their initial *raison d'être* was military. As with the attempts to study latrines, we have no direct martial evidence. Barracks were not in existence and, although we could examine the longhouse of the period as a place that provided hospitality to the warrior, or individual hut sites, none of these give direct evidence for the individual footsoldier.

Religion

The religious persuasion of Anglo-Saxon and Viking warriors changed over time. Burial practices indicate this with grave goods being provided for a pagan afterlife for Saxons at the start of the period, but a Christian burial style being prevalent by the end. The Vikings, too, had a changing outlook – the warrior found at Repton (see pages 74–5) was buried with a miniature version of Thor's hammer, unequivocally following the old gods. This was also an issue between the Saxon king, Alfred the Great, and the Viking Guthrun when, on the latter's defeat, the *Chronicles* proclaimed that Alfred ensured the Viking was baptised.

Rognvald's men, who set out from Orkney on the crusade to the Holy Land in 1150, referred to in *The Orkneyinga Saga* (see page 64), were Christian and, on their return, one of them appears to have carved a crucifix on one of the stone walls of the Neolithic tomb of Maes Howe to affirm this fact.

The religious beliefs of the Norsemen were not always as simple as being either Christian or following the pantheon of Norse gods. In the British Isles there are several carvings in which the two religions coexist comfortably. At Andreas, on the Isle of Man, there is a stone slab on which is carved a large cross; below one of the arms of the cross is the figure of Odin with one of his ravens perched on his shoulder and being attacked by the wolf Fenrir, as described in the Norse sagas. A cross in Gosforth, Cumbria, depicts the crucifixion alongside various scenes from Norse mythology (Page, 1990: 10–11). An artefact from the Coppergate excavations, York, also shows the juxtaposition of beliefs. A coin die from the 920s, for the 'reverse' side of the coin, bears the inscription 'St Peter's money', alongside an image of a great sword and Thor's hammer (Wood, 1986: 147).

Burials, too, show signs of religions coexisting. Viking graves found on the Isle of Rousay carefully avoided the earlier burials that were marked by boulders (Cunliffe, 2001: 502). The Norse burials at Cumwhitton in Cumbria were provided with grave goods as well as being aligned in a Christian fashion.

Medicine

A skull from Quentovic, northern France, a site dating from *c.* sixth–tenth centuries, shows a severe head wound caused by a sword or axe which had, at least, partially healed (Maude, 1987: 42). Surviving Anglo-Saxon medical texts, as Deegan and Rubin (1988) point out, suggest various herbal treatments – betony, for example – for such wounds. But is there archaeological evidence for treatments being carried out, rather than for wounds simply healing by chance?

Evaluation of some of the human bones from the site of Wharram Percy, Yorkshire, appears to indicate that treatment of weapon injuries was not unknown. This site, which was abandoned as a result of the ravages of the Black Death on the population, yielded the body of a 40-year-old man who displayed signs of surgery to a wound. The man's skull had suffered a near-fatal blow by a blunt weapon, causing a severe depressed fracture on the left side. This wound had been trepanned, that is to say that a 9cm by 10cm area of bone had been removed from the wounded area, supposedly to relieve the pressure that would have built up. The wound showed signs of healing and palaeopathologist Simon Mays stated that 'the skull is the best evidence we have that such surgery to treat skull fractures was being performed at this time . . . Violence at Wharram seemed to involve objects that were near at hand, like farming tools' (BBC News, 2004b). Even if this trauma was the result of local feuding, or simple violence, it illustrates that surgical techniques would have been available to the Saxon footsoldier.

The Vikings made use of plants in their medicinal repertoire. Some of the plant species found to this day on the more remote Scottish islands may have been introduced by the Norse as they moved westwards. For example, Kvann, the Norse for Garden Angelica, has anti-inflammatory properties and can also retard bacterial growth. It was grown in gardens in Shetland until 1973 and had probably been brought to this region and the Faroe Islands by the Vikings (Dickson and Dickson, 2000: 178).

THE PRISONER

We have no archaeological evidence for places where prisoners were held during this period, but it is possible that the burial of a man in Lejre, Denmark, reveals evidence for the killing or execution of prisoners. Here, around 49 graves from the Viking period were excavated between 1953 and 1968. Grave 55 contained two male skeletons 30–40 years of age. The upper of these bodies had no grave goods and appeared to have had both of his hands and feet tied when he went into the grave. His skull had been separated from his neck, having been cut from the body by a horizontal blow through the third cervical vertebra – an act that had also left a mark on his jaw. It appeared that he had been trussed up and then executed. This could, of course, simply have been an execution of a criminal, but there remains a possibility that he was a captive (Bennike, 1985: 108–9). Other Viking-period decapitations were recorded at Kalmergården, Denmark, where two such bodies were noted, dating to *c.* 1015 and 1040 (*ibid.*: 106–7).

In Britain, there may be further evidence for the Viking slaughter of captives or of those who opposed a raid. At Anglesey, north Wales, the bodies of five people – men, women and children – were found having been thrown into a ditch. Although no weapon trauma was visible on the skeletons, one of these bodies had seemingly had their hands tied behind the back before or at the time of killing. These bodies were inhumed some distance from the normal burial place and had not been afforded the normal burial rites of the period – they had simply been thrown into a ditch and stone had been cast on top (Richards, 2001: 96–9).

MEMORIALS AND BURIALS

A dreadful battle ensued in which many English fell. But for every one who fell three came in his place out of the country behind, and when the evening came on the loss of men turned against the Norsemen and many were killed.

('The Saga of Hakan the Good', in Wood, 1982: 183)

In his examination of the life of the tenth-century Viking King of York, Eric Bloodaxe, historian Michael Wood examined the stump of stone cross on the bleak site of Stainmore – the legendary siting of Eric's last battle and death, as the *Anglo-Saxon Chronicle* puts it, at a 'certain lonely place called Stainmore'. Was this cross, Wood (1982: 185) speculated, 'commissioned by sympathisers in York to commemorate their king' and hence their lost independence following their betrayal and defeat in battle here in 954? If so, it would indeed have been a strange Christian memorial to a pagan king. This monument, the 'Rey Cross' was moved to accommodate the A66 road and the chance was taken to see if it did indeed have any visible links to King Eric and his fallen warriors. Sadly, little of early medieval date was found and nothing to link the cross to commemoration of the dead of this battle (Vyner, 2001: 117–21).

In terms of memorials to Anglo-Saxon warfare, the best commemoration resides in the epic poetry of the era, such as the 'Battle of Maldon'. For physical commemoration of fields of conflict, Hastings has a stone marking the place where King Harold may have died, and another where his supposed grave is to be found. This, however, remembers the last Anglo-Saxon king rather than any of the 'housecarls' or common soldiers of the army. Folklore also suggests that one of the huge chalk horses carved into the hills of Wiltshire – the Westbury White Horse – although much later in its current appearance, was originally scoured to celebrate the victory of King Alfred the Great and his army over the Viking, Guthrun, at nearby Chippenham, but this is far from being proven.

Shepherd (1999: 242) makes some important points regarding the different grave goods packages found in Anglo-Saxon burials and suggests that 'weapon-bearing may well have had several different meanings in Anglo-Saxon society, including the representation of warrior occupation, special political or economic status or rank, the individual's functional role within the kin group, basic male identity, or other personal qualities unrelated to biological sex, but denoting courage and eagerness to defend family honour or inheritance'. In Shepherd's study, several graves with female skeletons and 'male' grave goods are discussed, including that of a 13–15-year-old girl at Empingham II, Leicestershire (Grave 106), which was provided solely with pottery and a spear beside the head – traces of its wooden shaft also survive, demonstrating that this was not a piece connected with weaving (*ibid.*: 241).

It is difficult to discern male skeletal remains simply from the assemblage of grave goods; it is even more difficult to state that the finding of weaponry in a grave means that the person inhumed was a warrior or ever even lifted a sword arm in anger. There are statements being made by the burying group about the person who was being buried, but this is probably as far as we should take it.

Norse burials can also be associated with weaponry, such as the Viking boat burial at Scar on the north coast of Sanday, Orkney. In addition to the *c.* 6.5m-long boat (traced through the position of the 300 or so iron rivets), the finds included the bodies of three people in a central chamber: a man, woman and child. Next to the male was an iron sword with a wooden scabbard – it was covered with several arrowheads. Fragments of an iron rod, sickle, a bone comb, a ninth-century Norwegian-type brooch, twenty-two gaming pieces and a pair of scissors were recovered, too, alongside a spindlewhorle, bone comb and a whalebone plaque with two carved horsehead terminals (Dalland, 1992).

We are left with the same questions as before with this inhumation assemblage: was this man provided with weapons because he was a warrior, or because this portrayal with martial aspects was essential for someone in his society? The grave goods may have been his belongings placed into the grave, or may have belonged to those attending the funeral, as offerings. If the latter, they speak more resonantly of the society that buried these people than of the three individuals themselves. It is, perhaps, worth noting that burials in ships or representations of a ship, such as at Scar and Sutton Hoo, were not a new entity in this period – there are burials of Bronze Age date in Gotland, Sweden, that are in cists shaped like stone boats. The sea as major trade and raid route was essential and thus vital to the perception of the individual in death (Osgood and Monks, 2000: 18).

Oxford Archaeology North has also recently excavated a series of six richly furnished Viking graves. Although almost no human bone survived the acid soils of the site at Cumwhitton, Cumbria, many of the grave goods were retrieved. These included swords, knives, spears and a shield boss. The graves, although provided with grave goods in the pagan fashion, were all aligned in a roughly east–west Christian fashion. Perhaps this is yet more evidence that the two belief systems were not necessarily mutually exclusive (see English Heritage, 2004).

Pyres were used to burn the bodies of warriors and the remnants of the fire were buried. At Ingleby, near Repton, a cluster of around 60 mounds were opened in the 1950s and several contained such cremation hearths. Pyre goods included swords, buckles and strap ends. Richards (2001: 150) believes that these may be a material remnant of the Viking Great Army of 873.

THE FALLEN

Context and dating are all important if our analysis of burials is to be of any use. A case in point is the so-called Neolithic skeleton excavated from a Neolithic longmound in Dorset by Sir Mortimer Wheeler in 1943. The skeleton had wounds from stone weapons and was touted as being evidence for cannibalism in this period. Brothwell (1971) examined the wounds and found eight separate cuts to the skull, in addition to wounds to both arms, the left collar bone, both legs and the right side of the pelvis – all inflicted with a sharp, probably blade weapon. A radiocarbon date of 1315 ± 80 BP, was obtained for the skeleton of *c.* AD 635 (*ibid.*: 240). Rather than Neolithic, this man was an Anglo-Saxon and was the subject of severe weapon trauma that probably caused his death (as opposed to wounds inflicted post-mortem).

Another cautionary tale comes from Wiltshire. Within an Early Bronze Age bell barrow at Sutton Veny lay the body of a man. The barrow was one of three in a cemetery common for this time period in the county. At the centre of the barrow, the body of the 28–35-year-old man had been placed in a wooden coffin, with a turf mound over it, and accompanied by a bronze dagger, a miniature accessory, so-called pygmy, vessel and a large pottery food vessel. A further cremation urn had been placed in the barrow and, more surprisingly, a secondary inhumation (Johnston, Powers and Wheeler, 1980). What was particularly interesting about this second body, of an adult male some 24–28 years of age, was that he was 'the victim of a particularly violent head wound, probably from a sword' (ibid.: 38).

As the authors pointed out at the time, swords did not appear in Britain until the later Bronze Age – around 1,000 years after the initial inhumation and, as a result, this burial must have been sometime later. But was a Late Bronze Age date the most likely for this man? Unfortunately, the skeleton has been lost, so it is not possible to apply dating techniques, such as Carbon 14. Yet it is possible to make some overall statements on secondary deposits within barrows.

Skeletons with sword wounds are exceptionally rare and, in Britain, Late Bronze Age examples are non-existent to date. Reynolds (2002b: 173) stated that secondary burial within a barrow was a relatively common form of inhumation in seventh-century Wessex (the south-western Saxon kingdom) and elsewhere. It is my belief that a Saxon date is far more likely for this individual's death. In a study in 1999 I saw that there were some eighteen secondary Saxon burials in Wiltshire round barrows. These could be quite extensive and rich burial cemeteries, as recent work at Barrow Clump on Salisbury Plain has established (Jonathan Last, pers. comm.). The blade wound to the Sutton Veny skull was very similar to Burial G at Eccles, Kent, being to the left of the skull, from behind, and was inflicted by sword or seax (Osgood, 1999a).

The man had suffered other wounds before death; a depressed fracture to the left malar bone that had removed the crown of an embedded left upper canine tooth and had damaged the left upper incisor at the same time. This was probably caused by a fairly major facial blow (Johnston et al., 1980: 47). In death, the man was provided with a grave good for the afterlife – a shark's tooth that might have been worn as some sort of amulet. The tooth may have come from a Mako shark, of up to 100kg weight, probably retrieved from a dead specimen that had washed up on the shore (*ibid.*: 38, 43). So we are left with an individual buried with a grave good in a round barrow with a sword cut to the head and older, healed wounds.

Therein lies a problem: though the man was killed with a sword, was he killed in battle, murdered, sacrificed or executed? Perhaps the Sutton Veny man was unlikely to have been an executed criminal given that he had a grave good, but it is impossible to be too dogmatic based on the surviving evidence and thus it is always important to bear in mind the possibility for differing scenarios for the final moments of those with weapon injuries when examining the archaeological record.

Executions also leave skeletons with weapon trauma and archaeologists must be careful to consider this when asking questions of wounds in the archaeological record. One such Anglo-Saxon skeleton, from Stonehenge, Wiltshire, is that of a 28–32-year-old man who had died between 600 and 690. He was probably around 1.65m in height and had been decapitated with a single blow delivered from the rear right (McKinley and Boylston, 2002: 136–7). There are several sites that seem to suggest judicial execution in this period (Reynolds, 2002a: 105–10).

Other Anglo-Saxon burials with trauma have been located in excavations in Britain. The body in Grave 1 at Puddlehill, Bedfordshire, was 'assumed to have been killed by a sword blow, as there were severe unhealed cranial injuries. The youth with a sugar-loaf shield-boss, spearhead and knife from Ewell, Surrey, had lost his left foot before death' (Lucy, 2000: 68) – but the latter case may not have been related to warfare. More convincing was a male skeleton from Harwell, Oxfordshire (Body G7), with a spear embedded in his left side (*ibid.*: 68–9) and a male from Letchworth, Bedfordshire, with a spearhead embedded in his chest (Kennett, 1973: 103). In addition to these, a large male skeleton with an iron javelin head transfixing his pelvis was excavated at Cross Hands, Compton, Berkshire (Peake, 1906: 279).

Excavations at St Andrew's Church, Fishergate, York, have also produced several burials that display combat wounds. Not all are contemporary and some, as we shall see in Chapter 4, have led at least one author to suggest that they may indicate the presence of 'trial by combat'. This being said, twelve males who were excavated from late eleventh-century contexts also had weapon injuries. Those from the middle to late eleventh century included three double graves from period 4b (Phase 110), and two double graves from period 4d (Phase 208). Within these double burials, skeletons number 1886 and 1873 displayed weapon wounds, as did 1902/1887, and 2351/2363; 1893 also had wounds though the inhumation with it, 1894, showed no traces of trauma, and a further pairing, 2371/2392, saw only the former with wounds.

As Daniell (2001: 222) has said: 'When the similar archaeological phasing, the weapon injuries and five double burials with weapon injuries are all taken together, there is a strong likelihood of a single violent event. The most likely documented event was the Battle of Fulford Gate fought in 1066 shortly before the Battle of Stamford.' Fulford Gate was one of three major battles fought in England in that fateful year, resulting in a Viking victory over Saxon armies. It was, however, indecisive and the main Anglo-Saxon army under King Harold was able to crush the Viking forces at Stamford Bridge prior to marching south to face William of Normandy at the fateful Battle of Hastings.

Table 3.1. *The location of wounds to the skeletons in the double graves at Fishergate*

Skeleton number	Wound locations
1886	Spine (thoracic vertebrae 1, 2, 3, 6, 11 and lumbar vertebrae 2 and 3), scapula, humerus, lower arm/hand (possibly an old injury), femur (a pointed weapon injury, perhaps old)
1873	Spine (lumbar vertebrae 2 and 3), ribs, pelvis (pointed weapon injury), femur (pointed weapon injury)
1893	Skull (two wounds), mandible, ribs
1902	Ribs
1887	Skull (one wound), ribs
2351	Skull (two wounds)
2363	Humerus, pelvis
2371	Ribs

Source: after Daniell (2001).

At Riccall, North Yorkshire, only a few miles from Stamford Bridge, the second of the 1066 battles, a burial ground was uncovered in the 1950s. Several skeletons were found and others were unearthed during flood-bank construction work in the 1980s (see Environment Agency, 2005). On analysis, the bones of a number of the skeletons bore traces of combat injuries – of edged-weapon and projectile wounds. Were these the bodies of fleeing Vikings from the battle? Initially this was thought to be the case (Richards, 2001, postscript). However, several of the skulls from the excavations were examined by Dr Paul Budd (pers. comm.) of Durham University, whose Oxygen Isotope analysis of the teeth concluded that the bodies were probably indigenous Anglo-Saxons who had died in the tenth or eleventh centuries.

If the work at Fishergate tends to indicate that the bodies were of those killed in the Battle of Fulford Gate, excavations at another site seem even more unequivocally connected to Viking warfare in this period – perhaps against Anglo-Saxon opponents once more, though almost 200 years earlier. In the churchyard of St Wystan's, in Repton, Derbyshire, the disarticulated remains of some 249 individuals were found in a burial chamber by Martin Biddle and Birthe Kjølbye-Biddle. According to the *Anglo-Saxon Chronicle*, the Viking 'Great Army' had its winter quarters here at Repton, at the site of the Anglo-Saxon monastery. Just to the north of the church of St Wystan's, and within the defensive ditch that the Vikings constructed, they buried numbers of their dead – perhaps a fitting place of repose as Repton was the chosen resting place for a number of the Mercian kings, including Æthelbald (716–57) (Biddle and Kjølbye-Biddle, 1992: 36). Among the burials, Number 511 was of particular interest, as the man had suffered weapon injuries and was, without doubt, a Viking.

UNKNOWN WARRIOR 5

Grave 511 was the burial of a man around 1.82m in height and at least 35–40, 'who had been killed by a massive cut into the head of the left femur. He lay with his hands together on the pelvis, and wore a necklace of two glass beads and a plain silver Thor's hammer [see Colour Plate 6] with a ?bronze fastening. A copper-alloy buckle with traces of textile and leather from a ?belt lay at the waist. By the left leg was an iron sword of Petersen Type M in a wooden scabbard lined with fleece and covered with leather' (*ibid.*: 40–1). In addition to these grave goods, which illustrated the pagan Norse nature of the inhumed, two iron knives were discovered as was an iron key. Between the thighs of the man was a jackdaw bone and a wild boar's tusk.

Further fascinating elements of this burial came to light when it emerged that the grave itself had been covered by a series of broken stones, which included the smashed remnants of an Anglo-Saxon cross shaft (*ibid.*: 41). Additional analysis of the man's pathology was undertaken by Bob Stoddard, of Manchester University, who believed that, rather than having one simple wound to the skull, this individual had several elements of trauma. The man had been stabbed in the head (with two probable spear wounds to the skull), jaw, arm and thigh; each of his toes and both his heels were split lengthways; and marks to his spine suggested he had probably been disembowelled (Leonard, 2001). Stoddard believes that such mutilation had a particular end in mind: 'The mutilation was clearly done by someone who knew how to do it. It suggests the Saxons were in the habit of doing this when they caught Vikings . . . Maybe they did it because they knew that Vikings believed they needed their bodies intact if they were going to go to Valhalla' (*ibid.*). It is also possible that the Viking's genitalia had been hacked off with an axe, resulting partly in the wound to the femur. This would perhaps explain the presence of the boar's tusk in this region of the skeleton; an attempt to make the man's body seem more complete.

If this scenario is close to the truth, one can imagine the rage of the man's comrades when his body was found and when they had to bury him. The smashing of the Christian cross, a symbol clearly connected to the beliefs of the people who had probably killed him, would have been an obvious act of retribution as the man was sent on his journey to the afterlife.

UNKNOWN WARRIOR 5

Grave 511, a Viking burial at Repton, Derbyshire

This is the body of a tall 35–40-year-old man, a Viking who worshipped the Norse gods as testified by his wearing of Thor's hammer. He was killed in a savage attack with multiple wounds, some of which seem to have been inflicted by spears. He was buried in preparation for entry to Valhalla and was given the broken remains of a Christian cross to cover his grave – the remnants of a conflicting belief set. Was the man killed in ambush, on the battlefield, or simply murdered? We do not know, but his body must have been in the hands of the perpetrators for some time for it to be mutilated before his friends had time to bury him.

UNKNOWN WARRIOR 6

A cemetery of Anglo-Saxons has produced evidence for the wounds inflicted in Anglo-Saxon combat. At Eccles, Kent, six male skeletons on the site bore the scars of edged-weapon wounds, which would have proved fatal. All of these skeletons had one wound to the head, with two of them having more than one such wound. Of those with multiple wounds, the skeleton labelled by Wenham (1989: 123) as 'Victim II', a male aged 20–25 years, had thirty bone injuries catalogued, with seven cranial and eleven post-cranial blows, blows to the back of the head, blows to the back of the trunk, and blows to the arms. 'Victim III', a male aged over 35, had a single cranial injury, but also had a projectile wound to the third lumbar vertebra, with the iron projectile remaining in the spinal column (see Colour Plate 7). This arrowhead came to rest on the third lumbar vertebra. Manchester (1983a: 61) believes that its position indicated that the 'arrow was shot at the upright victim, probably from fairly close range to his right. The injury did no more damage than create great pain, some bleeding and, in this instance at least, an insignificant opening in the spinal canal. This was insignificant because the victim was felled shortly afterwards by a tremendous blow to the right side of the back of the head' (see Plate 11).

The linear wounds had fresh edges and showed no signs of healing. All had resulted in massive loss of blood and, in the case of Victim III, could have resulted in instantaneous death with the presumed sword blade having passed right through the brain. Wenham believed that all the blade wounds would have been caused by a sword (*seax*). Victims I, V, and VI had single injuries to the left side of the skull – classic patterning for a front-on attack by a right-handed adversary. Victims II, III and IV had multiple wounds as seen above – perhaps these were the result of more frenzied attacks. Victim II had wounds to the arms, which are indicative of unsuccessful self-defence (Wenham, 1989: 138). After being felled by blows to the back of the head, he suffered wounds to his back. Given that this was a cemetery site, it was impossible to tell through stratigraphy whether these burials were from a single engagement or whether they had been buried over a longer time period. Further to this assemblage it should be noted that a seventh skeleton, now lost, might have been female (*ibid.*: 123).

Table 3.2. *Wound summary of Eccles victims*

Victim number	Age (years)	Height (cm)	Head wound	Other wound
I	25–35	163	16cm-long cranial wound	
II	20–25	170	Seven cranial wounds	Eleven post-cranial wounds: to shoulders, arms, spine and pelvis
III	35+	176	Single wound	Projectile wound to spine
IV	25–35	179	Three cranial wounds	
V	25–35	172	Single 13cm-linear cranial wound	
VI	20–25	165	Single 12cm-linear cranial wound	

Source: Wenham (1989: 124–7).

UNKNOWN WARRIOR 6

Burial G, an Anglo-Saxon combat victim from Eccles in Kent

Victim number III from Eccles was a 176cm-tall man of over 35 years of age when he died. He had been hit from the side by an arrowhead, which had lodged in his spine causing great pain if not death or paralysis. The man was then dispatched by a blade that passed right through the back of his head, severing the brain.

FOUR

Chivalry's Price:
Footsoldiers of the Middle Ages

O God of battles! Steel my soldiers' hearts.
(Shakespeare, *Henry V*, IV. i. 342)

For the purpose of this work, the period defined as 'Medieval' covers the time from the Norman conquest of Britain in 1066 to the sixteenth century – a period in which the use of gunpowder became more widespread and the arrow, rather than the cannon's projectile, was the main missile weapon. Although drawing some comparative information from the crusades, we will concentrate on Britain and northern Europe.

The relatively new discipline of battlefield archaeology has much to commend it in evaluating the flow of battles, troop movements and formation positions. It can also illustrate the weaponry used and elements of the lives of the soldiers in those violent hours of combat (Pollard and Oliver, 2002, 2003), providing information often not available to the historian. Much of our information derives from two mass graves, one at Towton, North Yorkshire, and the other at Visby (formerly Wisby), on the Baltic island of Gotland. Mass graves are the more likely resting place for the common soldier with gentry being afforded, even in death, greater respect (Strickland and Hardy, 2005: 280).

At Towton, a mass burial of footsoldiers killed on 29 March 1461 in a most bloody Wars of the Roses encounter has been particularly illuminating in terms of giving us an understanding of the many elements of the soldiers involved. Some of these men were young (16–25 years old), others were up to *c.* 50 years of age, with an average of around 30 years (Boylston, Holst and Coughlan, 2000: 52) – compare this with the average age of 19 for the American infantryman in the Vietnam War in the twentieth century.

At Visby, in the summer of 1361, a large Danish force of King Waldemar fought and defeated the town's forces. Old and young, able-bodied and disabled were killed in the heat of a July day and the town fell to the Danes. Although the local troops were wearing armour, these were outmoded pieces and failed to prevent their defeat. As the bodies rotted in the sun, the armour probably became irretrievable and was cast with the bodies into a series of mass graves, graves which were discovered by archaeologists in the twentieth century.

Some traces of the infantryman on major battlefields of the period have yet to be found archaeologically. Will it ever be possible to locate the stake holes of the timber spikes driven into the ground by English infantry at Agincourt (1415) to ward off the French cavalry? Or to find the ditch dug at Crécy (1346), again by the English, who, according to the chronicler Geoffrey le Baker, 'dug many holes in the earth in front of our first line, one foot deep and one foot wide, so that if it happened that the French cavalry were able to attack them, the horses might stagger because of the holes' (de Vries, 1998: 164)?

This chapter puts forward some of the evidence we have for material from the sites of conflict, material showing the very real aspects of fighting rather than the showy aspects of display demonstrated in the 'age of chivalry'.

WEAPONRY

Weaponry and armour from the Medieval period can be seen in many museums, castles and stately homes throughout the world; what we are particularly concerned with for the purpose of this study are those items that have left a trace in the archaeological record; of weapons and armour found on battle sites, and of clearly discernible weapon damage to equipment or the victims of conflict.

As in the earlier chapters, there are problems finding material from ancient battlefields when small items suffer the corrosive effects of time and are subject to unreported chance finds. Given the ferocity of the engagement at Agincourt, for example, one might have expected to find more than the one possible bodkin arrowhead revealed in a recent survey (Wason, 2003: 60). Perhaps the majority of armour was stripped from the dead and the arrows retrieved, or maybe material has been taken over the years. It is possible that the site is located slightly further from the area traditionally denoted, or perhaps the site simply needs more work. The archaeologist Tim Sutherland has undertaken a geophysical survey that might suggest more finds in the future on this battlefield – with a tantalisingly large anomaly being found on his geophysical survey close to the nineteenth-century crucifix commemorating the dead of the battle and supposedly marking the site of the French burial pit (*ibid.*: 65).

Tom Richardson of the Royal Armouries, Leeds, believed that the concentration of head wounds to the Towton skeletons, and relative lack of body wounds, might indicate a lack of head protection; perhaps the simple discarding of armoured headgear such as a *sallet* to enable a quicker flight from the battle. The wounds at Towton illustrate the variety of weapons in use against the infantry. Of these wounds, many seem to have been inflicted from the front by right-handed assailants. On twenty-seven of the twenty-eight crania there was evidence for perimortem trauma – 32 per cent of wounds on occipital, 32 per cent on frontal, and 31 per cent on left parietal bones (Novak, 2000a: 95). The types of wounds ranged from blade to crush to puncture. It was difficult to distinguish the type of weapon responsible for cut wounds – these could have been caused by poleaxe blade, sword or dagger. Perhaps the same can be said for crush wounds – war hammer, mace, sword-pommel – and for puncture wounds – longbow arrows, crossbow bolts. However, as the latter category of wounds 'were so distinct in shape and size, cross matching with weapons from the battle was attempted' (*ibid.*: 97). This was accomplished using weapons held in the collections of the Royal Armouries.

Table 4.1. *Towton puncture wounds classification*

Burial	Location	Force	Weapon
9	R. parietal/temporal	Blunt	Beak of a Medieval war hammer
16	L. parietal	Blunt	Top spike of a poleaxe
17a	R. parietal	Blunt/projectile	Beak of a Medieval war hammer/crossbow bolt
17b	L. parietal	Blunt/projectile	Beak of a Medieval war hammer/crossbow bolt
18a	Occipital	Sharp	Blade stab
18b	Occipital	Sharp	Blade stab
21	Occipital	Projectile	Flesh-piercing arrowhead
30	L. temporal	Sharp	Stab from Castillon sword
40	Frontal	Projectile	Armour-piercing war arrowhead
41a	L. parietal	Blunt	Top spike of a poleaxe
41b	R. parietal	Blunt	Top spike of a poleaxe
41c	R. parietal	Blunt	Top spike of a poleaxe

Source: Novak (2000a: 98).

Although these wounds are those suffered by rather than inflicted by Medieval infantrymen, it nonetheless helps to reveal the range of weapons that our study set was up against. From the puncture wounds alone they seem to have faced cavalry as well as infantry. The study was enough for Novak to state that 'what we are seeing is merely the result of hand-to-hand combat in a brutal battle using very efficient weapons of war' (ibid.: 100–1). Surveys of this battlefield have also yielded weapons, including sword scabbard chapes and, through a measured ferrous metal survey, several bodkin arrowheads (Sutherland, 2000b: 160–2).

Arrowheads have been found on several excavations of Medieval sites. One example is at Urquhart Castle on Loch Ness, Scotland. Work here uncovered bodkin heads of varying lengths, three heads with broader cutting edges and a possible crossbow bolt head. In addition, a corroded mass proved to be a group of arrowheads that were once probably stored in a canvas or fabric bag, but which are now rusted together (Strickland and Hardy, 2005: 176). Arrowheads of the Medieval period have been found at Portchester Castle, on the south coast of England, and were probably for use by the garrison. These included some from the thirteenth century, varying in form from heavy arrows with barbs and socket to those with flat blades. Several crossbow bolts were also excavated (Hinton, 1977: 198–9).

As expected, archaeology often confirms what is known historically. For example, work at Gorey (Mont Orgueil) Castle in Jersey has uncovered a number of crossbow bolt heads dating from around 1460. Documentary evidence for this site suggested that this castle was provided with a garrison of up to forty-four crossbowmen (Watts and Mahrer, 2004: 55).

It is a commonly held belief that the presence of yew trees in English churchyards was for provision of wood vital for the construction of the longbows that were the mainstay of the Medieval infantryman. Contrary to this belief, King Henry V expressly forbade timber being taken from ecclesiastical land for this purpose (Strickland and Hardy, 2005: 16).

In terms of offensive weapons found at Visby, several iron arrowheads were recovered, along with iron knives and a possible pike head (Thordeman, 2001: 134–5). Furthermore, several skulls, transfixed with crossbow bolts fired by Danish troops, seem to indicate that both horizontal fire at close quarters and enfilade fire (resulting in wounds on both sides of the skull) were used. From the evidence, it seems as though crossbows were more in evidence on the field of Visby than at Towton. As with all battlefields, much of the equipment was recoverable by the victors and thus the archaeological record is unlikely to retain large quantities of valuable equipment unless, of course, its damage had rendered it useless or it was embedded in a corpse. The skeletons themselves indicate a number of types of weapons used, from sword and axe blades to the circular craters left on skulls by clubs (Ingelmark, 2001: 190–1).

Towton and Visby mass burials illustrate the vast range of Medieval weapon types through the form of the damage they inflicted. Manchester has found an example of the use of another weapon that could cause huge crush injuries. One of the most malicious hand weapons of all time was the medieval 'morning star' or 'holy water sprinkler'. This flailing implement featured protruding metal spikes. 'A flail such as this in the hands of country peasants, who were accustomed to using it, must have been a terrifying weapon which could bash the finest helmets of the crusaders to smithereens.' An example of a depressed skull fracture caused by such a weapon has been described from the Sedlec Ossuary, Czechoslovakia [sic] and dated to the Hussite Wars of the fifteenth century' (Manchester, 1983a: 60; see also Courville, 1965).

Pollard and Oliver (2002: 54) have located several items relating to the infantryman's panoply of arms in their examination of a series of British battlefields. At the site of the Battle of Shrewsbury (1403), several arrowheads were found – including a probable 'bodkin' arrowhead – which were long, narrow and designed to punch through armour. These arrowheads had proved their worth for the English against mounted knights at the battles of Crécy and Poitiers (1356), as part of the Hundred Years War, and the bowmen would again show their might in 1415, at Agincourt.

The use of swords, pole arms and bows and arrows forms only part of the picture, representing finds that have been made through archaeology. As we have seen in previous chapters, environmental conditions will have affected our assemblage and, in particular, the survival of materials such as wood and leather; clubs and staves may well have been available to the common soldier, but are now no longer visible.

ARMOUR

'The men-at-arms, however, formed only a small proportion of the troops on a Wars of the Roses battlefield, and the equipment of the ordinary infantry, who formed the vast majority of these armies, is much more poorly understood and has received relatively little attention' (Richardson, 2000: 143). If this is so, our understanding of the armour worn by the common soldier in Medieval times is helped by the finds from mass graves, the wounds suffered by the deceased (indicative, perhaps, of areas of the body which were poorly protected) and of finds of armour itself.

Perhaps the head wounds inflicted on those whose bodies lay in the burial pit at Towton would indicate that there were failings in the efficacy of the head armour, unless, as has been said, the helmets were discarded as the troops fled. A small quantity of copper-alloy mail was found on the field of Towton (Sutherland 2000b: 160), but we must turn to Visby for clearer evidence of armour used in combat in the fourteenth century.

Possibly as a result of the putrefaction of the deceased, not all the armour was stripped from the bodies of the defeated peasant army at Visby. Men were cast into the grave pits wearing their mail shirts and coifs, with plate armour and gauntlets and even iron shoes still in place. This armour was almost certainly out of date by the standards of 1361, and had probably been handed down through families.

From the work at Visby it is possible to discern a series of types of protection worn by the combatants (for examples of these armour types, see Thordeman, 2001). The best-known pieces are the mail 'coifs', a type of hood worn to protect the head, constructed from bronze and from iron rings. Some of these hoods still encased the skulls of those who were wearing them when they died (see Colour Plate 10) and one was worn by an elderly man, indicating the irregular nature of the force defending the town (Thordeman, 2001: 168). Although the excavators also found several lumps of rusted mail that might once have served as gauntlets, shirts or breeches, they felt confident to state that approximately 185 coifs were recovered from the graves (*ibid.*: 99). These took a similar form, being 'provided with a collar drooping down over the shoulders, and with the opening for the face straight at the top and rounded at the bottom, this opening being so small that the forehead, chin and greater part of the cheeks were protected' (*ibid.*: 104).

When discovered on a body that was also clad in armour, the coif was tucked inside the reinforced coat (*ibid.*: 106). No helmets were found in the grave pits and it is likely that this mail formed the only head protection – that is unless the putrefaction that despoiled the corpses, and thus the mail, had less effect on the overlying helmets and they were retrieved. If this was the case, one might expect the other types of armour to have been taken.

In addition to the mail coifs, two mail shirts were found – each covering the body of the man who died in it. The first shirt (Regn. no. Vxx 6) was quite short, with only a *c.* 31cm length surviving, with the sleeves ending in a mail gauntlet – one of two found at Visby. The second example (Regn. no. Vss 13) was in better condition and found on a man who lay on his back in the grave. This shirt was around 1.45m wide at the base and probably around 50–54cm long (*ibid.*: 106–11).

Mail was an effective form of protection: 'Experiments undertaken by the Royal Armouries have shown that when chain armour is outfitted on a free-flowing dummy, effectively mimicking the human body in motion, as it would be in a military engagement, it is almost impossible to penetrate using any conventional weapon. Sword slashes are deflected, with spear, sword, and arrow thrusts effectively stopped by the ring defences. Even bodkin arrows are unable to penetrate the chain armour in these experiments. When layers of leather, felt, or even cloth undergarments are added to chain armour, the protection is even better' (de Vries, 2003: 25).

Elements of mail have been found by Professor Barry Cunliffe's excavations at Portchester Castle. Here a strip of mail that is now corroded into a solid piece of iron oxide was retrieved. Hinton postulated that this was either a piece that had been used to form the collar of the padded body protection, known as a 'brigandine', or a cut from a mail shirt that had been altered to provide a better fit for its wearer (Russell Robinson, 1977: 195).

Among the plate armour excavated from the burial pits at Visby, the excavators believed that they could identify some six types of lamellar coats, with iron plates attached to the inside of a padded coat (see Plate 12). In the majority of these coats, the rectangular plates were attached vertically. Such coats were closed at the back or sides with buckles, many of which were also recovered. The men did not have arm protection, although some had a protective skirt to cover the upper thigh and groin (Thordeman, 2001: 210–20). Plate protection for the shoulders, hands, elbows, armpits and knees was also discovered, and two groups of iron strips with rivet heads were recovered from Grave 2. It seems probable that the latter grouping of overlapping plates would have constituted armoured foot protection (*ibid.*: 112–16).

All this armour was worn on the same day even though its form differed considerably; not one coat was the same. This could illustrate the ad hoc nature of the force defending the Gotland town, which used any armour available, including heirlooms. It was the excavators' opinion that the lamellar plate armour was worn by Gotlanders (*ibid.*: 227) as the armour, although of different construction periods, was quite similar and the islanders would have had the resources to have funded its manufacture. Despite being a town force of irregulars, the infantry of Gotland was far from a standard 'peasant' force. Brigandines – the padded woven coats into which iron plates were sewn – were also seemingly in use at Portchester Castle in southern England in the fifteenth century where several fragments have been excavated (*ibid.*, 1977: 194–6).

It should not be assumed that everybody at Visby was protected by armour – only 25 lamellar coats and two mail coats were found. Even allowing for the stripping of the dead, it is more than likely that some went into battle with very little protection, perhaps only leather or padded clothing. We have seen that the absence of head protection at Towton might explain the quantity of head wounds. The authors in the report on the skeletons found on the site of the 1385 Battle of Aljubarrota, Portugal, also concluded that the large numbers of cuts on the crania of the deceased indicated that these soldiers here had not been provided with strong head protection (Cunha and Silva, 1997: 598).

One further find illustrates a form of protection used by Medieval infantrymen, in this case by the archer. Many bowmen would have worn wristguards to prevent the bowstring damaging their arm. A leather bracer from the Wars of the Roses period has recently been recovered by excavation work. It bears the inscription *Armilla* and was found in the bilges of the Newport Ship, laid up on the banks of the Usk at Newport, south Wales, *c.* 1467 (Strickland and Hardy, 2005: 380).

By finding the protection itself, and through an examination of body wounds, the archaeologist can build up a picture of the armour used in battle – of the functional pieces rather than display items discarded in combat. This information is not obtainable from documents, such as military manuals, which proclaim the optimum kit, not what is available or practical to the soldier in action.

PRACTICE AND DISCIPLINE

Practice was vital for the Medieval archer if he was to be capable of delivering the lethal rain of arrows that would win battles such as Agincourt. The long-term effect of such practice could leave traces on the skeletons of those for whom archery was a way of life. The maxillary incisors of the individual known as 'Towton 8', from the Wars of the Roses battle burial pit, display grooves consistent with frequent bow stringing (Holst and Coughlan, 2000: 79). Dr Chris Knüsel's examination of the infantrymen from this site has also revealed interesting physical traits. In many cases, the constant archery practice has resulted in skeletal stress – the left arm (that is to say the bow arm of the right-handed archer) can display hypertrophy of the left elbow, while the right arm (the draw arm of the right-handed archer) can display hypertrophy of the shoulder.

THE LIFE OF THE SOLDIER

The life of the Medieval infantryman was far from easy. A vast number of those on campaign with the English army in 1415 contracted dysentery, greatly reducing the ranks that faced the French at Agincourt (Hibbert, 1998: 73).

The Wars of the Roses soldier also suffered a hard physical life if the pathology of the Towton burials is anything to go by. In addition to conditions such as minor spina bifida occulta, several of the warriors suffered spondylitis which might have led to back pain. Schmorl's nodes were also present on the bones, indicating a physical lifestyle (Coughlan and Holst, 2000).

Eating

Analysis of skeletal material also hints at some of the dietary traits of the Medieval soldier. Iron deficiencies were detected in bone samples from the infantrymen in the mass grave at Towton (Boylston et al., 2000: 62–3). Looking at their teeth, wear was not extensive and there was very little gradation in the younger individuals, which would 'suggest that the diet was neither fibrous nor adulterated by particulate matter such as sand or ash' (ibid.: 50).

There are a series of animal bones in the grave pits at Visby, which, although probably residual and not connected to the peasant army, might just hint at food provisions carried by troops on their way to battle, including the femur and humerus of a cow, and lower maxillae of a goat (Ingelmark, 2001: 197).

Excavations of the field of the Wars of the Roses Battle of Barnet (1471) revealed part of a 'tiny, flattened, copper-alloy band . . . possibly the reinforcement around the handle of an eating knife, the part that stops the blade shaft splitting the handle into which it has been inserted' (Pollard and Oliver, 2002: 113). This may have been a fragment of the standard kit of the Medieval infantryman, for eating on campaign.

Fragments of copper alloy cooking pots or cauldrons, which appeared to be of fifteenth-century date, and thus possibly connected to the battle, were found on the field of Towton. They could have been part of the logistical back-up of one of the two armies (Sutherland, 2000b: 160).

Within castles, excavations provide evidence for some of the food consumed, although it must be said that it is next to impossible to prove that this was eaten by the footsoldier rather than by anyone else inside the fortification. Cunliffe's work at Portchester Castle seems to indicate that, although cattle bones were present, these animals had greater use for traction than for consumption. The analysis of the bones also suggested that pigs were slaughtered for food within the second to third year of their lives (Cunliffe, 1977: 231).

Gaming

As with soldiers down the ages, the Medieval warrior would have gambled and played games in his free time while on campaign or while performing garrison duty. A bone gaming counter with ring-and-dot motif, for example, was recovered from twelfth- to thirteenth-century layers within Portchester Castle (*ibid.*: 83).

Accommodation

On campaign, the Medieval soldier would be lucky to sleep under cover – if he slept in a tent, as with the Roman period, the chances of archaeological evidence having survived are minimal; if he slept under the stars, the chances are nil.

Much work has been undertaken on the main place of static residence of troops of this period: the castle. These are found throughout the British Isles, in mainland Europe and, with European influences, as far away as Syria and Jordan where crusader castles were built. Their study has fascinated archaeologists and soldiers for centuries with some, such as T.E. Lawrence ('Lawrence of Arabia'), falling into both camps. A study of castles would be far too large for the scope of this book.

Religion

Within the context of the Medieval period, religion was of great importance to the soldiers who fought. It was the main motivation for many who took part in the crusades. It was, of course, possible for both sides in war to invoke God with the victors deeming their cause had been approved. Agincourt is a case in point (Hibbert, 1998: 95–6). This was the period of Joan of Arc – burned, lest we should forget, as a witch in 1431. Memorial effigies of knights in their battle armour are found in many European churches of the Medieval period, but the common soldier is rarely commemorated.

In terms of traces of religion on battlefields, crucifixes and suchlike would be the best evidence for personal devotion. Archaeological excavations on battlefields have revealed traces of churches. At Shrewsbury, Pollard and Oliver discovered the remains of the Medieval chapel that stood by the 1403 battlefield, 'Now represented by nothing more than a few stones, these walls must have echoed to more than a few prayers both before and after the battle' (Pollard and Oliver, 2002: 72).

In one further quasi-religious link, several stories emerged from 1915 about the miraculous halting of the German armies at Mons in Belgium. Despite being almost overrun, Allied forces had held up the German advances and with it ended the chances of the Schlieffen plan's success. These stories claimed that the ghosts of soldiers from Agincourt and Crécy had appeared in the sky, showering the German troops with arrows and thus saving the beleaguered British in an act of God. Although fictitious, the story of the so-called Angels of Mons has endured.

Medicine

It is a common belief that Medieval soldiers had no recourse to medical treatment and that if a wound was serious, the soldier would have had a low level of life expectancy. A series of excavated results point instead to extensive treatment for troops and that, on occasion, medical practitioners were successful. Excavations at Lewes, Sussex, for example, took place on the site of a cemetery for inmates of the hospital. A number of the burials displayed weapon injuries, while one had lost a hand in a previous incident, an injury that had healed before death (Brown, 2003: 57).

Several of the soldiers whose remains were found at Towton displayed successful wound healing, in some cases of severe injuries. Nine individuals had well-healed head wounds – probably from previous engagements – with sixteen separate wounds; seven of sharp force, and nine blunt force wounds. 'Towton 16' had suffered a major blade wound to his jaw, which had sliced out an element of bone, fractured the jaw and which would have left the individual severely scarred. Yet there was no evidence for infection and he lived (Novak, 2000a: 95). As we shall see below, 'Towton 41' was another veteran with well-healed wounds. These are some early indicators that medical treatment of the age might not have been as inept as traditionally portrayed.

As with Towton, some of the men at Visby had survived previous attacks – perhaps helped by medical treatment; one cranium had a healed cut injury to the frontal bone of the skull (Ingelmark, 2001: 196). The site of the 1385 Battle of Aljubarrota, Portugal, also featured the remains of soldiers who had survived earlier wounds with well-healed lesions of various kinds (Cunha and Silva, 1997: 598).

At the Fishergate cemetery, York, a number of the burials appear to relate to the Battle of Fulford in 1066. Seventeen burials connected to the twelfth to fourteenth centuries also displayed weapon injuries – and these to individual events. In addition to the possibility that this was the final resting place of men killed during 'trial by combat' (see page 96), there is the possibility that Fishergate, as at Gilbertine Priory, may have acted as a specialist hospital with people who had suffered severe weapon trauma being brought here for treatment. That there were a number of men who had died from these wounds in the cemetery may suggest that cases with very little hope were also attended. 'Evidence was discovered of an experimental technique undertaken at the priory, for skeleton number 10266 had two copper-alloy plates attached to an injured knee' (Daniell, 2001: 225).

Archaeological work at the site of another hospital connected to a religious house, the twelfth- to seventeenth-century Augustinian Soutra hospital, near Edinburgh, also appears to have yielded results that point to extensive use of medicinal plants to ease the wounds of Medieval soldiers (Moffat, 1992). Dr Brian Moffat's examinations of the hospital drains for medical waste from operations produced bone evidence for amputations, such as an amputated heel (Moffat, 1995: fig. 5a), and soil with a high concentration of ancient blood trace, thankfully mixed with quicklime to act as a deodorant. The archaeobotanical evidence recovered seems to indicate that 'battle-scarred soldiers facing amputation were anesthetised with a cocktail of black henbane, opium and hemlock – several hundred years before the age of anesthetics [sic] is understood to have begun with the discovery of ether and chloroform in the 1830s' (Laurance, 1997). This site was one at which Edward I stayed in 1303 (Moffat, 1988a: 85).

In addition to the discovery of the medicinal plants that would have been used for anaesthetics, remains of fruit fragments of box and several fragments of burnt boxwood were excavated. This plant, probably not native, was not only decorative – in the Medieval period its medicinal usage included the treatment of leprosy and venereal diseases (Moffat, 1992: 3–4). It could have been used for the treatment of the local populace at large, but it may give further hints of illnesses suffered by soldiers passing through.

The surgeons – presumably members of the monastic orders – used various implements in their medical work, including 'blood-letting knives'. An example of such a tool was recovered from the base of the medical waste by work at Soutra: a double-bladed knife with a short tang used, according to Moffat, to make 'incisions of veins in routine blood-letting, without doubt the commonest type of surgical operation' (ibid.: 18).

At another Augustinian site, Waltham Abbey in Essex, excavations also revealed 486 seeds, including 448 of black henbane and 31 of hemlock, again to provide a stupefying drink 'so that one man may sleep while other men may carve him' (Moffat, 1988a: 81). Almost certainly, the experience of monastic houses would have been essential in providing succour to the wounded Medieval soldier, and for tending to their spiritual needs should treatment not be enough to keep them alive.

Further skeletal evidence for humans being able to survive major wounds is present in the form of a skull from Pontefract, Yorkshire. The cranium of an adult male dating from the Medieval period had severe wounds to the frontal and parietal bones, which would have exposed the interior of the skull and rendered the victim unconscious. The edges of these cuts were smooth, indicating a degree of healing, and it is possible that some form of medical care had been administered to enable the individual to live longer than might have been expected (Manchester, 1983a: 60–1 and Plate 32).

Although not the specific remit of this study, evidence for medical practices has been found on sites connected with the crusades, including pharmacy jars which were discovered in excavations of thirteenth-century levels of the Frankish city of Acre (Mitchell, 2004: 13).

THE PRISONER

This is said to have been the 'Age of Chivalry', of strict codes of conduct and of knightly behaviour, and a halcyon age for the treatment of prisoners. Scratch even a small amount below the surface and this myth is soon dispelled. During the Hundred Years War (1337–1453) it was notionally possible to obtain ransom for noble captives taken in battle, but this did not stop Henry V's army from slaughtering many of these same noblemen captured at Agincourt when they felt in fear of a French rally and counter-attack. Shakespeare was in no doubt why this act of brutality was carried out – the killing of those that were present with the baggage train:

> GOWER. Tis certain there's not a boy left alive, and the cowardly rascals that ran from the battle ha' done this slaughter: besides, they have burned and carried away all that was in the king's tent; wherefore the king most worthily hath caused every soldier to cut his prisoner's throat. O, 'tis a gallant king! (Shakespeare, *Henry V*, IV. vii. 3)

Even if Shakespeare's history was, unwisely, to be taken as gospel, it is clear that those of common origin would have been afforded little mercy when captured. Such niceties were even more uncommon during the often savage Wars of the Roses. Indeed, Pollard and Oliver (2002: 93) go as far as to state that,

> By the time of the Wars of the Roses, there was no room for half measures. If chivalry had been a Geneva Convention of its time, then the desperate demands of battles like Barnet [1471] left no room for such courtesy. Indeed, by the time of Barnet it was the noblemen who were the targets for the worst excesses. Throughout the Wars of the Roses, the turning-point in a battle was traditionally met with a cry from the winning leaders of "Spare the commons! Kill the lords!" The ordinary folk were supposedly allowed to return to their humble lives while the opposing

nobility, conspicuous in their expensive finery, were hunted down and slaughtered. Whether that is true is clearly hard to say. It is hard to imagine that in the slaughter at Barnet the common man fared any better than his social betters.

Perhaps a couple of the individuals from the Towton burial pit display this. Not only were all those thrown into the pit not afforded the usual burial traditions with an east–west alignment in sacred ground (and ideally as close to the high altar of the local church as possible), there may even be marks to suggest deliberate disfigurement of the corpses or torture of soon-to-die prisoners. The individual known as 'Towton 32' has a number of small injuries around the left ear, while 'Towton 12' has cuts to the nose region, suggesting that both of these men had body parts cut off. If one interprets the site as representing that of a rout and, perhaps, of the dispatching of prisoners – albeit wounded ones – then there would seem to be a possible element of what we would now call torture beforehand, or else a deliberate attempt to prevent the deceased achieving resurrection (Knüsel and Boylston, 2000: 186).

Strickland and Hardy (2005: 280) believe that the 'high incidence of head wounds points rather to the massacre of men deliberately stripped of their defensive armour before being repeatedly hacked at, probably while on the ground'. Of course, as has been mentioned, there are other interpretations of these wounds – perhaps being savage, but standard combat wounds for those fleeing a battle and having discarded head protection.

Visby seems also to illustrate the indiscriminate slaughter of all who fought, presumably including any battlefield prisoners initially taken: 'Four individuals from Visby had their noses removed by sharp weapons' (Knüsel and Boylston, 2000: 180). This would, most likely, have been done to men incapacitated, captive, or deceased, although it is possible that this was from above and thus by a mounted opponent (Thordeman, 2001: 185). Whatever the case, it seems that there was probably little opportunity for the vanquished of Visby to surrender and that, when felled, their bodies were subject to many blows. Prisoners were also slaughtered in the crusades by the armies of Richard I in 1191.

Documentary evidence linked to the interesting results of work at Soutra hospital, where ingredients for an anaesthetic to be administered prior to surgery involving amputation were recorded, hints at the harsh treatment of prisoners in the Medieval period. Some seven weeks after their rout at the

Battle of Bannockburn (1314), the 'Calendar of Close Records' gives unusual orders from the defeated king, Edward II, for the care of three lowly English soldiers. These orders were sent to the 'Masters and Brethren' of the hospitals of St John, Oxford; St Mary, Ospringe, Kent; and St John and St James, Brackley, Northamptonshire. The men, William, son of Thomas le Charetter of Grove, Henry le Lounge of Fletewyk, and John de Sheperton were to be provided with 'maintenance for life' as a result of 'the Scotch rebels having inhumanly cut off his hand while engaged in the King's Service' (Moffat, 1992: 65a–65b). If, as the document suggests, these men suffered amputation after the battle, were they archers whose mutilation rendered their future service impossible? If so, there could be an element of truth in the tale of origin behind the 'V-sign' gesture of the English. There are some suggestions that this most insulting of British gestures was originally aimed at the French, to indicate that the two fingers essential for drawing the bowstring were still intact; that the man hadn't been mutilated after capture and that he was still a potent threat to the French forces. After all, a French chronicle of the mid-fifteenth century quotes a speech by Henry V wherein he warns his bowmen that this is the fate that will await them on capture (Wason, 2003: 65). Whether or not this is an urban myth we cannot know; archaeologically we can simply trace the materials required for anaesthetics prior to such amputations.

MEMORIALS AND BURIALS

Although there are many effigies of armoured knights in the churches of Europe, the commemoration of the common dead of the infantry has often been undertaken by later societies. Two of the main sites we have examined, Towton and Visby, both have a later stone cross on the battlefield. The sites of other major engagements, such as Flodden, Bosworth Field and Agincourt, also have memorials either on the field or to mark places of supposed burial sites. It is interesting to note that there are often flowers or tokens of memorial placed on these monuments to this day (see an example at Towton (Fiorato, 2000: fig. 1.16)).

Burial for those killed in Medieval combat was not always immediate, particularly if the deceased was either on the defeated side or not of noble birth. The dead at Visby in 1361 were left decomposing for several days under the heat of the July sun before being thrown into a pit. The slain of

Aljubarrota were afforded even less dignity; their bodies lay open to the elements for several years before the disarticulated remains were collected and deposited, making the later tasks of archaeologists that much more difficult (Cunha and Silva, 1997: 596).

In addition to the burial pits that have been found, several from major battles have yet to be traced archaeologically though many were known to have been killed in the engagement. We have already mentioned the example of Agincourt, and the site of the 1403 Battle of Shrewsbury was also examined by Tony Pollard and Neil Oliver (2002: 58–63) using both geophysical survey and excavation with little success in locating the graves. Crécy, too, has yet to yield its dead, although chroniclers noted that 'the dead of both sides were then buried in pits near where they had fallen' (de Vries, 1998: 173).

THE FALLEN

Most of our evidence for combat victims of the Medieval period comes from a series of mass graves, as we shall see. There are some individual bodies that display weapon wounds, including skulls found at Safed, Israel (a Frankish town and castle of the crusades). One of these skulls had an unhealed diamond-shaped lesion on its top indicating an arrow wound (Mitchell, 2004: 113). Others included the skeleton of a 30–40-year-old man from Grenå Sygehus in Denmark, which dated from *c.* 1050–1536. This man had suffered a slash wound to his right femur, about 9cm from his knee and about 1.6cm in depth. A similar wound was in place on the other leg. Although these would have resulted in much loss of blood, the individual would not have died as a result of them. What had proved fatal was a vertical blow to the skull (Bennike, 1985: 105–6). Bennike (*ibid.*: 106) was unsure whether this was definite proof of battle wounds and thus the mass graves seem to provide clearer proof of the effects of Medieval combat.

Several mass graves connected to major battles in the Medieval period have been discovered, including those from Aljubarrota in Portugal, Visby in Gotland, and Towton in England. The quality of information recovered from these sites varies, but enables us to derive information on the battles, which is not included in the written histories. The bodies are almost exclusively of men, although it was thought, initially, that female remains were present among the slain at Visby and that there were bones of children in the burials at Aljubarrota (Cunha and Silva, 1997: 597). These graves illustrate the types of weapons used in combat, the presence of men who have experienced combat on more than one occasion, and the nature of the combat encountered. These are not the graves of nobles, for whom burial could be grand and commemorated with reclining effigies. These remains are of the footsoldiers, those in the defeated army.

Archaeological work at the Templar fortification of Jacob's Ford in Galilee, a site stormed by the armies of Saladin in 1179, are starting to yield skeletal elements to point at the levels of violence suffered by combatants and the tactics and weaponry used by the Islamic armies of the crusades. Arrowheads have been found among the bodies of the deceased indicating early wounds, as the same men had suffered blade injuries to the shoulder, face, skull or jaw. One skeleton clearly illustrated that a member of the Frankish garrison had had his arm amputated by a blade injury through the elbow (Mitchell, 2004: 119–20).

Excavations at Lewes hospital revealed the presence of a number of skeletons displaying weapon injuries. 'The evidence of trauma seen in this sample ranges in severity from unhealed cuts, which are likely to have been the cause of death, to minor well-healed injuries' (Lucy Sibun, pers. comm.). The archaeologists detected unhealed cut-marks to the bones of four males. A fragmentary skull of a middle-aged man (Skeleton 180) showed a total of five blade cuts, ranging in length from 38 to 72mm. Three of the blows had removed a segment of bone, which would have resulted in the death of the individual. The first blow, inflicted to the base of the individual's skull from behind, would have proved fatal, with the other wounds to the top of the head, superfluous and perhaps simply hacks at a prone body (Brown, 2003: 59).

Wounds to other individuals included a skull fragment with two deep cuts and the jaw of another individual (Skeleton 143) which had been sliced in half (Lucy Sibun and Martin Brown, pers. comm.). From the dates of these burials and the fact that they had probable sword wounds it is tempting to postulate that these men were victims of the Battle of Lewes fought from 12 to 14 May 1264 between the Earl of Leicester, Simon de Montfort, and the army of King Henry III. In this engagement de Montfort's forces defeated those of the King and captured the King's son, Prince Edward. As a result, de Montfort gained overall power in England. However, as Sibun has pondered, if these individuals were battle victims, why were they interred at the hospital rather than in mass graves such as those discovered during work on the nearby turnpike road? The severity of some of the trauma wounds indicates they were dead on arrival and so there is no reason for them to have been taken to the hospital for care (Lucy Sibun, pers. comm.). Why, too, were the graves so spatially dispersed in the hospital graveyard? It could mean that these people were not killed in battle and therein lies a problem. Unless bodies are found on known martial sites, or with military equipment, the presence of trauma on the skeleton – even when in the vicinity of a known battle – need not equate with them being war victims. These men could have been killed in domestic disputes or murdered, resulting in them having been buried at different times, in separate areas of the graveyard.

Chris Daniell has put forward another interesting possibility for the presence of weapon injuries – trial by combat. Between 1985 and 1986, York Archaeological Trust excavated the site of St Andrew's Church, Fishergate, York, and uncovered 402 articulated skeletons of which 29, all male, showed evidence of weapon trauma. Some of these skeletons, as we have seen, may relate to the Battle of Fulford in 1066 – double burials in graves, with weapon injuries, and with the strong likelihood of a single violent event. Others cannot be explained away by one large single episode of combat and, as they occurred over a period of time from the twelfth to fourteenth centuries, must have a different cause. As trial by combat was known for the Medieval period this would certainly be a plausible explanation (Daniell, 2001).

These caveats notwithstanding, some of the human remains that have been excavated belonged, indisputably, to those who fell in combat, most notably those found in the mass graves from Towton and Visby.

UNKNOWN WARRIOR 7

. . . there was a great conflict, which began with the rising of the sun, and lasted until the tenth hour of the night, so great was the boldness of the men who never heeded the possibility of a miserable death. Of the enemy who fled, great numbers were drowned in the river near the town of Tadcaster, eight miles from York, because they themselves had broken the bridge to cut our passage that way so that none could pass, and a great part of the rest who got away who gathered in the said town and city were slain, and so many dead bodies were seen to cover an area six miles long by three broad and about four furlongs.

(George Neville, Bishop of Exeter, in Boardman, 2000: 15)

On 29 March 1461 one of the bloodiest battles of the dynastic Wars of the Roses took place in the small village of Towton in North Yorkshire. Fought in a blizzard, the Yorkists eventually broke the Lancastrian armies and put the fleeing to the sword. Chroniclers refer to some 28,000 casualties numbered by the heralds (*ibid.*: 15). It was a most bloody engagement and one which was to prove decisive in this phase of the wars; Edward, Duke of York, was crowned King Edward IV later that year.

Some 535 years later, ground preparation for a new garage at Towton Hall was to provoke a macabre discovery. Human bones were unearthed and, as a result, an archaeological investigation of the vicinity took place. What followed was one of the most interesting archaeological discoveries of battlefield remains (Fiorato, 2000: 2). A rectangular mass burial pit was uncovered with tightly packed bodies generally orientated in an east–west/west–east axis in prone or supine positions (Sutherland, 2000a: 41) (see Plate 13). These bodies were then covered in a mound of soil. Analysis has shown that the bodies were of rugged males – and the skeletal remains represented thirty-seven or thirty-eight individuals (Boylston *et al.*, 2000: 45).

On closer examination the true horror of the wounds suffered by these men became clear. Thirteen men (33 per cent) had post-cranial wounds; there were thirty-seven sharp injury wounds and six blunt weapon wounds, mostly to the hands and arms. This wound pattern is consistent with 'parrying a blow from an assailant' (Novak, 2000a: 91). The majority of these were also to the right arm or hand, indicating the right-handed attributes of the sufferer. As these wounds seem absent from the torso of the deceased, perhaps they were afforded good body protection – padded armour or brigadine (*ibid.*: 93–4).

Shannon Novak's analysis (2000a) is important in drawing a fuller picture of the men. For example, nine of the soldiers had well-healed cranial trauma wounds from previous battles or conflicts. This set of sixteen separate wounds ranged from minor superficial nicks to deeper flesh wounds.

'Towton 16' had suffered a truly dreadful facial injury with a section of bone sliced from the lower jaw with subsequent fracture. This, though scarring, had successfully healed – perhaps revealing a better quality of medical care than we often attribute to this period. The man was thus a true veteran – some 46–50 years of age. Would he have inspired confidence in his younger brothers-in-arms, who perhaps faced such brutal conflict for the first time? His luck finally ran out as he sustained eight blade, blunt and puncture wounds in his death at Towton (Novak, 2000a: 95; Novak, 2000b: 246–7). The wounds found here were caused by arrows, swords, war-hammers and pole arms. Arrow wounds might be expected for those killed in the mass flight of arrows in early stages of battle, but they were relatively rare and the evidence seems to point towards the killing of these men in a violent episode towards the end of the battle, perhaps the rout of the fleeing Lancastrian forces. Other trauma also illustrates the most basic of human emotions – fear. There is enough evidence of damage to teeth to suggest that clenching of teeth in a situation of extreme stress occurred (Knüsel and Boylston, 2000: 178).

The infantryman catalogued as 'Towton 41' was another individual who had had prior experience of warfare (see Colour Plates 8 and 9). In addition to the wounds that caused his death at Towton, he had a series of scars that had been inflicted beforehand, some of which had healed. On his skull was a small depression fracture of the frontal bone, an old fracture by the left eye, along with a v-shaped 39mm-long blade injury that had cut the top of the man's head to a depth of 4mm, and a well-healed adjacent depression. An examination of his skeleton by Knüsel (2000: 109–11) revealed the traits of development that suggested he was experienced at using the bow – like 'Towton 16', the man was a veteran.

During the battle, Towton 41 suffered dramatic and fatal injuries. Shallow blade wounds were present on the front of the man's face, on the left-hand side. He also had a blade wound to the left frontal bone of the skull and a small depression fracture close by. These wounds were inflicted from the front, presumably in face-to-face combat. In addition to these blade wounds some other severe injuries were noted that had been inflicted from behind. The man's right hand, arm and leg were cut deeply and there was a further blade wound to his spine. A 46mm segment of bone was removed by a blade to the upper left part of the skull just above the mastoid process (for an analysis of this individual, see Novak 2000b: 262–4; see figs 35 and 36).

Three small square perforations were located on the top rear (posterior parietals) of the skull ranging from 7 to 8mm in size, encircled by a bevelled margin. Again these wounds were inflicted from behind and above, and seem to correspond with the top spike of a poleaxe (ibid.: 263). All in all, Towton 41 had thirteen cranial wounds and nine other wounds – both those inflicted in the encounter that led to his death and others from earlier engagements.

> ## UNKNOWN WARRIOR 7
>
> ### Towton 41: an infantryman from the mass burial at Towton, 29 March 1461, probably an archer of the defeated Lancastrian army
>
> This is the body of a man aged between 26 and 35 years. The body, orientated north-west/south-east was of an individual 172.5 ± 2.99cm in height (Holst *et al.*, 2000: 208) who, in similar fashion to many who had ended up in the burial pit at Towton, had lived a rugged lifestyle as indicated by the presence of Schmorl's nodes (*ibid.*: 208).
>
> This man was not new to combat, displaying both old wounds and physiological traits consistent with him practising archery over many years. He had wounds both to the front and inflicted from behind, perhaps indicating a degree of frenzy in dispatching a wounded man. His location in the mass burial pit, far from the supposed centre of the battlefield, and the types and specific location of his wounds, may all point to him having been killed in the rout of the Lancastrian forces.

UNKNOWN WARRIOR 8

ANNO DOMINI MCCCLXI FERIA III POST JACOBI ANTE PORTAS VISBY IN MANIBUS DANORUM CECIDERUNT GUTENSES HIC SEPULTI. PRO EIS

The battle was fought outside the gates of Visby, between Danes and Gotlanders, in the year 1361, on 27 July, and the victory went to the attacking foreign army.

(Thordeman, 2001: 1–2)

As recorded on the later battlefield cross, in 1361 an army of Danish regulars fighting for King Waldemar Atterdag appeared before the gates of Visby on the island of Gotland. The forces arrayed against the Danes were no match – the old and the young, the sick and disabled, all were pressed into service of the town and none had the training of their opponents. According to contemporary Swedish chronicles, some 2,000 townspeople were killed (*ibid.*: 23). Waldemar entered the town in triumph while the bodies of the slain lay around putrefying for days in the heat before being cast into great burial pits. Visby fell to the Danes.

On 22 May 1905, during the excavations of an arbour, several human skulls covered by mail were discovered. By early July, the whole of a mass grave was exposed and the first of the victims from the Battle of Visby some

544 years before was found. In 1912, as part of the preparations for a road, further remains were found over a wide area, and more excavations took place in the 1920s and in 1930 (*ibid.*: 56–60).

Several stories were connected with these archaeological excavations. Supposedly, 'though the flesh had disappeared from the bones and grinning skulls of these warriors during the six centuries since they fell for their country, the moist earth had become so saturated with the decay that only men with abnormally tough nerves could endure the overpowering odour that rose from the excavation'. Indeed the archaeologist, Dr Wennersten, 'could not work in the pit without fainting' (*ibid.*: 87). While the 1912 excavations took place an illustrious visitor arrived: Kaiser Wilhelm II of Germany. Prophetically, Dr Wennersten was alleged to have greeted the Kaiser: 'Here you see, Your Majesty, how frightful are the consequences of war. I hope you will remember!' (*ibid.*: 88). As we shall see in Chapter 7, the results of the Kaiser's battles were also to create their own archaeological record.

What had been found, and excavated in a grid system, were five mass graves (three main graves) with Common Grave 1 being some 5.5m wide and 7m long, and 1.5–2m deep (skeletal material being 0.5–1m thick). Common Grave 2 was 12m long, 6m wide and 2m deep with 0.5m thickness of bone. Although the archaeological technique of the time meant that remains were excavated by grid rather than by individual skeleton (the technique successfully adopted at Towton), the excavators felt confident enough to make several observations about the men found. They believed that Grave 1 held between 258 and 268 individuals, Grave 2 some 710–98, and Grave 3 had 119 people. Graves 4 and 5 had a large enough quantity of victims to realise a total of up to 1,572 deceased. Perhaps it is safe to suggest that those in the mass graves represented the town's defeated peasant army rather than Waldemar's dead for whom greater respect would have been shown, as the victors and holders of the field.

The filling of the graves was subject to some sort of deliberate spatial patterning, with large discrepancies between the number of young individuals and those of military age. Dominant wound types varied, with more cuts to the extremities of the bodies present in Common Grave 3.

Ingelmark (2001: 152) was unable to reassemble the skeletons recovered from the excavations. Initial examinations indicated that there might be nine female pelvises within the mass graves, but this was something that the

Table 4.2. *Comparison of skeleton details within the graves*

Skeletons	Common Grave 1	Common Grave 2	Common Grave 3
% of young individuals	37	16	8
% of 'military age'	80	45	53
Average heights of individuals	*c.* 168.92 ± 0.27cm	*c.* 168.81 ± 0.19cm	*c.* 167 ± 0.30cm

Source: after Thordeman (2001: 80).

author was uncertain of on later analysis. It is hoped that current work under the aegis of Professor During (pers. comm.) might be able to provide more information.

What is beyond doubt is the range of wounds to the men in the mass graves. The results of attack by sword, axe, crossbow, morning star, mace, lance and even – as with Towton – war hammer, can be witnessed (Ingelmark, 2001: 160). Cutting weapons, such as swords and axes, had caused some 456 wounds, while arrow wounds were present in 126 cases, 60 of which also had cuts. One tibia even retained the arrowhead as the body was thrown into the pit (Thordeman, 2001: fig. 167); skulls retained crossbow bolts that perhaps preceded the main assault (*ibid.*: figs 179–81). A further astonishing example of leg wounds is that of a man whose lower legs were cut off 'probably by a single blow' (Ingelmark, 2001: 164–5).

Several of the wounds might indicate that, alongside infantry, there were a number of mounted troops – damage to the unprotected lower legs of the men being a vital clue. One such body had had the right foot severed from the lower leg by a cut through both tibia and fibula. Indeed, a large quantity of wounds seems to have been 'aimed vertico-horizontally from below' (*ibid.*: 177). These wounds may also reflect damage inflicted upon a wounded, prone foe – as per those in the grave pit of Towton.

Although much of the armour used by the town's forces might have been outmoded by the standards of 1361, mail coifs were still capable of preventing some wounds – only 40 per cent of wounds were to the skull. Nonetheless, some skulls do still show injuries – in Grave 1, 42.3 per cent of the bodies had cuts on the cranium. Grave 2 had a total of 52.3 per cent of skulls with wounds, though in Grave 3, only 5.4 per cent of the skulls were damaged – perhaps as a result of better head protection worn by those thrown here.

Ingelmark's study illustrates some facets of the battle through the palaeopathology of its victims: '80 per cent of the blows struck vertically from above belong to the group "not more than one cut", it indicates that these blows were difficult to strike. The cuts belonging to the group "two or more cuts" have probably been struck at warriors who had fallen, were retreating or were attacked from behind; whereas the injuries in the group "not more than one cut" were received in hand-to-hand fight' (*ibid.*: 184). It seems likely that those not killed in combat were dispatched with little mercy. The army of the inhabitants of Visby, the old, the young, the lame and disabled, were slain before their town's gates in the July heat.

UNKNOWN WARRIOR 8

One of the defenders of Visby, killed in July 1361 and thrown with the bodies of his comrades into a mass grave (see Colour Plate 10)

This man was protected by a mail coif – its presence in the grave may indicate that it was too unpleasant a task to remove it from the body. He was found in Common Grave 2, excavated in 1928 (Regn no. VII:10, Cat. no. 18872 (see Thordeman, 2001: 104, 464–5)). Although killed at the Battle of Visby in 1361, his exact cause of death remains unknown (Annica Ewing, Statens Historiska Museum, pers. comm.).

FIVE

The Flash of Powder:
War in the Tudor and Stuart Period

Our enemies, consisting of about 800 horse and 300 foot, with ordnance, led by the Earl of Northampton . . . intended to set upon us before we could gather our companies together, but being ready all night, early in the morning we went to meet them with a few troops of horse and six field pieces, and being on fire to be at them we marched through the corn and got the hill of them, whereupon they played upon us with their ordnances but they came short. Our gunner took their own bullet, sent it to them again, and killed a horse and a man. After we gave them eight shot more, whereupon all their foot companies fled and offered their arms in the towns adjacent for 12 pence a piece.

(Neremiah Wharton, August 1642, in Ede-Borrell, 1983: 10)

The period from the sixteenth century to the mid-seventeenth century encompasses a dramatic change in the lot of the soldier – it sees the last days of the use of archery by the infantry and the emergence of the large-scale use of gunpowder. Although cannon were present in the years spanned by the previous chapter, and it was not until 1595 that Queen Elizabeth I's Privy Council ordered the general replacement of the bow with a firearm – the 'arquebus' (Strickland and Hardy, 2005: 390) – the sixteenth and seventeenth centuries saw an enormous growth in the use of firearms in European war. Ships were provided with firepower, such as the vessels that served Henry VIII, including the *Mary Rose*, and those that fought the Spanish Armada in 1588.

By the time of the English Civil War, 1642–51, musketeers using firearms known as matchlocks formed one of the two branches of the infantry, the other being armed with pikes and still protected by elements of armour. Although pikemen would continue to use such protection, the use of gunpowder meant that armour would become almost redundant in this period and that sieges were frequently brought to quicker conclusions. Until the emergence of the bayonet, musketeers would still benefit from the protection of pikemen against cavalry attacks, when their own swords or the stocks of the musket would have been insufficient.

Infantry in this period was used to man ships and provide the soldiery on board during naval engagements, they were present as forces on set-piece battles on land, and also played a vital role in sieges, manning both defensive and offensive works, which they and engineers constructed. Their role was varied, and it often left its trace in the archaeological record. Although impressive, we shall not be examining the great castles or ships of the period. This chapter will look at the evidence left of the footsoldier's life and often their death. It also sees the emergence of a well-trained standing army, the revolutionary (in more than one sense) New Model Army, from the earlier tradition of the trained band.

WEAPONRY

The Tudor warship *Mary Rose*, which sank on 19 July 1545, is an exceptional resource of information pertaining to the later years of archery. In addition to sailors, there were many men on board who were effectively infantrymen – soldiers with the county militia. Longbows were found across the site of the wreck of the *Mary Rose*, scattered as the great warship slid to her final resting place in the Solent. Some were complete, some broken, and a number were recovered from storage chests on the weather deck. One chest contained forty-eight bows, the other thirty-six. The yew bows in these chests were 1.82–2.13m in length (Strickland and Hardy, 2005: 6–7). On the upper deck of the warship another chest was found. This held 1,248 arrow shafts. Fifty-two sheaves tied in bundles of twenty-four, with up to 6,000 arrows eventually being found (*ibid.*: 7–9). Eighteen leather spacers, pierced to take either twenty-four or thirty-six arrows, and armguards (bracers), mostly of leather and nearly all stamped with various marks, were retrieved (Stirland, 2000: 122). Twenty-four of the latter have survived along with one example made from horn, which had survived thanks to the preservative action of tar from one of the ship's ropes (Strickland and Hardy, 2005: 10).

Dr Matthew Strickland discusses another aspect of infantry war in our period – the possibility of the use of poisoned arrows, something that the French alleged as a result of the high level of combat fatalities among men sustaining arrow wounds: 'recent evidence from the *Mary Rose* arrows shows that there was some substance in the French complaint . . . a copper-based compound was used to protect the fletchings and to help firm the glue used to fix them on the arrow shaft. It is possible that the copper sulphate may (albeit unintentionally) have served to exacerbate a wound inflicted by the arrow head itself' (Strickland and Hardy, 2005: 286).

Although the early sixteenth century continued to see the presence of the longbow and of pole-arms that would have been familiar to the soldiers who fought and died at Towton, Agincourt and Crécy (see Chapter 4), the firearm was increasing in importance. Tony Pollard and Neil Oliver's important work on the 1513 battlefield of Flodden bears this out. At this battle, the Scots suffered a grievous defeat at the hands of the English, a defeat that included the death of their king, supposedly 'struck down . . . by an English bowman's arrow, fired into his mouth as he battled to within a spear's length of the Earl of Surrey' (Pollard and Oliver, 2002: 121). This defeat still has resonance today leading, as it did, to the bagpipe lament 'The Flowers of the Forest'. The archaeological work not only retrieved a lead cannonball, probably fired at the Scots by English artillery pieces, but also discovered a lead ball that would probably have been fired at the English using an 'arquebus' or 'hackbut' (*ibid.*: 159).

In 1588 the Spanish put together a huge force with the intention of landing in and defeating England – the famous 'Armada'. The ships were not just a large naval force, they also carried a strong infantry element. The defeat of the Armada was absolute and saw the sinking of many of the major Spanish vessels around the coast of the British Isles, vessels that are now yielding some of their secrets to maritime archaeologists. One such ship was the mighty *La Trinidad Valencera*, which, at 1,100 tons, was the fourth largest of the Armada. She had received damage in engagements off the Flemish banks and eventually ran aground and broke up on a reef off the north Donegal coast after her crew had escaped (Martin, 2001: 73).

Spanish footsoldiers would still have been armed with the pike – a long wooden pole, which was tipped with a metal blade and had strips of metal along the top to prevent the head of the weapon being lopped off by a sword. Pikemen acted in units, rather like the Ancient Greek phalanx, with pikes extending to the front and using force of weight to drive through units – the 'pike-push'. Pikemen were also vital to protect musketeers, who could seek shelter within the square. The excavation of this Spanish vessel included retrieval of several pike staves – a bundle of the lower ends was recovered, the greatest length being some 3m. Two metal pike heads were also found and the excavators calculated that the original pike would have been composed of a 5.5m ash stave, some 3.5cm thick, tapering to a 2.4cm diameter end. The head was a small pointed iron 'shoe' and, with the side strips, the whole weapon weighed around 5kg (*ibid.*: 82).

The contents of this vessel are most useful in illustrating the increasing importance of firepower to the infantry. Seven wooden matchlock gunstocks were retrieved, all of which were plain and undecorated and thus probably the basic infantry weapon. There appeared to be no standardisation of weapon type – clearly there was no regular weapon issue. Thousands of lead bullets were also discovered, in two main sizes: 13mm/14g for arquebuses and 19mm/40g for muskets (*ibid.*: 82). Such weapons worked by pouring black powder down the barrel of the gun, followed by the lead shot and any wadding, which was rammed down. More powder was added to a primer pan, which led to the main charge. The priming powder was ignited by the touch of a burning cord, which set off the main charge, expelling the round from the gun. As barrels were not rifled, weapons were not accurate to any great distance. There was the added danger of leaving the ramrod in the barrel when the weapon was fired, as this would also be projected from the weapon, something of which modern re-enactors are acutely aware.

La Trinidad Valencera yielded several of the main powder flasks and examples of smaller powder flasks, presumably used to charge the pan (*ibid.*: 82–3). Another wreck site from the Armada – that of the *Girona* – was investigated by maritime archaeologists. This vessel was a galleass of the Naples Squadron, which sank off Lacada Point, County Antrim, on 26 October 1588 (Flanagan, 1987: 8). A wooden arquebus stock and ramrod were retrieved from the vessel. The stock still retained the round of shot that had been put into the barrel (*ibid.*: 6).

Since lead, as well as stone, was the raw material for musket balls, infantrymen did not have to look far to replenish their supplies. Excavation work within the Friary buildings at Jedburgh Abbey revealed traces of lead waste, which was interpreted as being the waste product from window repairs or cut fragments from the casting edges (Dixon *et al.*, 2000: 50–1). But, as several traces were found in quite late deposits both inside and outside the building, and displayed heat damage, Ian Barnes, who examined the magnetic susceptibility and viscocity of the site (*ibid.*: 80), believes there might be another explanation. He suggests that the traces of lead are the result of the stripping of window lead and its reforming into musket balls by the soldiers who sacked the Friary (Barnes, pers. comm.). This might be corroborated by the discovery of a lead shot within the finds assemblage, a piece of ordnance that would have been fired by an artillery piece of the fifteenth to seventeenth century. Historic documents indicate that the Friary was burned first by Lord Eure, and then the Earl of Hertford, 1544–5 (*ibid.*: 87).

Lead musket balls have been found all over English Civil War sites, including those which were uncovered in the ditch surrounding Basing House, Hampshire, ranging from 9mm to 18mm in diameter (Allen and Anderson, 1999: 85). Earlier excavation work on this site had recovered parts of the muskets themselves, with two of the priming pans that held the powder that would ignite to fire the full charge, two musket locks, and the iron nozzle of a powder flask with its lid 'actuated by a see-saw lever' all recovered (Moorhouse, 1971: 52–3). Ammunition that had been fired has also been excavated from this siege site: a 'fired lead shot was found above or embedded in the gatehouse cobbles' (Allen and Anderson, 1999: 81). The same is true for the lead musket balls from Sandal Castle in Yorkshire. Some 15 per cent of the eighty pieces of lead shot found appeared to have been flattened from impacts (Credland, 1983: 261). In terms of matchlock pieces, three trigger locks were found at Sandal, as were priming pans and pan-covers alongside several lead covers from powder holders; 105 lead balls were found during excavations at another Yorkshire castle, Pontefract (Eaves, 2002: 345).

Part of a matchlock was recovered from Nottingham Castle (Harrington, 1992: 23). When under siege, there would have been difficulties in obtaining new projectiles for the muskets and thus it should not have been a surprise to find moulds for manufacturing new lead balls – rather like the discoveries of impromptu moulds at the Roman siege site at Velsen (see Chapter 2). At Scarborough in Yorkshire, excavators found sprues from two-piece lead shot moulds (*ibid.*: 56), a hearth at Dudley had a bowl cut into it in which lead was found – probably evidence for a similar practice (*ibid.*: 55), and another example was discovered at Beeston Castle in Cheshire (Ellis, 1993: 122). A further mould for two bullets was perhaps found at Pontefract Castle in Yorkshire though the excavators remained somewhat uncertain of its use (Roberts, 2002). All of these would have used lead stripped from roofs and windows, as at Jedburgh, and the excavators of Pontefract believed that the kitchen might have served as a small-scale munitions factory with evidence of recycled copper alloy and lead (*ibid.*: 431).

At its best, careful study can show the distribution of artefacts and thus the concentrations of activity. Foard (2001) has produced a distribution plot for the presence of shot on the small Northamptonshire site of Grafton Regis, besieged by a force of 5,000 over three days in 1643 – a force to which the 200-strong garrison succumbed.

Battlefield sites have as much evidence of shot for the presence of infantry as siege sites in terms of the location of musket balls. Marston Moor, close to York in the north of England – the site of a decisive battle in 1644 – has been examined and through fieldwalking thousands of these objects have been retrieved. 'Some of the bullets had been flattened or hammered before being fired, possibly to create a more lethal projectile; other bullets bore the marks of human teeth, probably from "biting the bullet", while in a few instances, bullets were fused together, suggesting that the soldier had rammed two bullets into his weapon' (Harrington, 2004: 84).

Further research on the Marston Moor site has yielded lead priming nozzles and caps and powder bottles from bandoliers – a similar situation to studies of the 1645 battlefield of Naseby (*ibid.*: 84; for a plot of musket ball finds, see Battlefields Trust, 2004). Musket balls are frequently found by metal detectorists and their finds need proper recording to facilitate accurate distribution plots of troop movements. Foard (2001: 97) has also produced a distribution plot of musket balls on the important 1645 battlefield, which saw the decisive defeat of the king's armies by those of the New Model Army of the Parliament. Pollard and Oliver have found many musket balls on the 1642 battlefield of Edgehill, Warwickshire, some of which are flattened indicating that they have, perhaps, struck a target – these too have enabled a distribution plot (Pollard and Oliver, 2003: 112–13). Caps from powder boxes and powder flask tops have been found at Beeston and Sandal Castles – with experimental work suggesting that these were lost most frequently in hand-to-hand fighting (Foard, 2001: 94).

The excavation of a V-shaped ditch with flat bottom, forming part of the English Civil War defences of the castle of Newcastle-upon-Tyne, discovered much by way of the accoutrements of the infantry within the fill of the ditch. Artefacts included musket balls, the rest for a musket and powder flasks that would have held the charge for the musketeer's firearm. These flasks were worn in a leather belt slung over the musketeer's shoulder and were known as the 'twelve apostles'. More unusual was the pottery grenade discovered (Harrington, 1992: 22–3). Although there is no full context for the ceramic grenades found at Leicester in 1854, Courtney and Courtney (1992: 70) concluded that the weight of probability lay in these being 'left by one of the royalist or parliamentarian garrisons of the conflict [English Civil War]'. The ceramic grenades were all unglazed and predominantly of oxidised red earthenware. They show that gunpowder was of huge importance in combat.

The pikeman's panoply of weapons may also be represented at Newcastle-upon-Tyne with the finding of an iron pole-arm blade (Harrington, 1992: 22–3). The long thin blade of a pike head, with flattened diamond section, and a further example with a lozenge-shaped blade, hollow shaft socket and two extending prongs, which would have run along the length of the pike staff to prevent it being lopped off by a sword, were found by excavations at Basing House (Moorhouse, 1971: 53). Swords were carried both by cavalry and infantry, although lower ranking infantry would have had far less ornate pieces. Some blade weapons do survive – the English basket-hilted sword fragment, dating to around 1645, found in the siege trench at Sandal Castle, Yorkshire (Credland, 1983: 265), and the sword blade and hilt from Pontefract (Eaves, 2002: 327) are examples.

Although the finds of armour and weaponry may not be especially common, Foard (2001: 94) makes an important point that the presence of pikemen and their location on the battlefield can be discerned with other methods: 'In each regiment during the Civil War they [the musketeers] were typically deployed in two bodies, one on either side of the pike, which comprised the remaining third. Hence although archaeologically the bodies of pike will be largely invisible on the field, their location can be inferred from the evidence for the musketeers.'

ARMOUR

Pollard and Oliver discovered a small metal button with a simple design on its face 'and typical of the garb of a medieval Scottish soldier' from the site of the 1513 Battle of Flodden. Furthermore, an armour square that would have fitted within padded armour of similar style to the sets we have seen at Visby (see Chapter 4, pages 84–5), and a fastening for a leather belt or piece of armour were found (Pollard and Oliver, 2002: 159, 160). Although the firearms of the period were often inaccurate, cumbersome and of little impact on the battle, a direct hit would have rendered armour relatively useless. It was the ending of an era.

Armour was also in use by the infantry of the Armada. The work on *La Trinidad Valencera* has found a number of interesting pieces, including several *morion*-type helmets. These have peaked ends to the fore and back and flat sides to deflect blows. The *morions* on board the ship appear to have been highly decorated with etched designs and brass rosettes, and provided with plume holders. This decoration seems to have been important enough to have required covering to prevent damage as concretion on one example seems to indicate the presence of a fabric cover. Another helmet still had its internal padding present – vital if it was to be of any use to the infantryman. This padding was composed of a coarse cloth stuffed with pine needles and led the excavators to state that 'this would have effectively absorbed impact transmitted via the surface of the helmet, and is very similar in concept to the well-designed German infantry helmet of WW1 [the first issue of which was the M1916 – RO]. Sixteenth-century Spanish *morions* were clearly designed with the hazards of combat engineering and trench warfare in mind' (Martin, 2001: 84).

Breastplates of a type which would have been used by pikemen were also recovered from *La Trinidad Valencera*. Such breastplates were supposed to be proof against firearms from some distance – witness the later Civil War examples with impressions of musket balls as a type of 'quality seal'. Although this may have been the case, by the end of the English Civil War, the back- and breastplate with tassets was generally abandoned by pikemen, who opted instead for the leather 'buff' coat, as it was durable, relatively efficient against blade weapons and, above all, light.

Although losing its efficacy, armour has been recovered from secure archaeological contexts of the English Civil War period. The top of a metal collar or 'gorget', over which a helmet would have fitted, was found at Basing House (Moorhouse, 1971: 54), and another at Pontefract Castle (Eaves, 2002: 330–1). It is this latter site which provides us with the best archaeological source for armour used by the infantry in the English Civil War. From Civil War layers, such as the fill of the garderobe, and from within a countermine came several fragments representing some of the protective equipment used by the defenders. The surprising fact is that many of the pieces were quite old.

Helmets featured among the assemblage. The right cheek-piece of a 'burgonet' helmet and two *morions* (see Plate 15) were found in the

In Memory of
THOMAS THETCHER
a Grenadier in the North Reg.
of Hants Militia, who died of a
violent Fever contracted by drinking
Small Beer when hot the 12th of May
1764. Aged 26 Years.
In grateful remembrance of whofe univerfal
good will towards his Comrades, this Stone
is placed here at their expence, as a fmall
teftimony of their regard and concern.
Here fleeps in peace a Hampfhire Grenadier,
Who caught his death by drinking cold fmall Beer,
Soldiers be wise from his untimely fall
And when ye're hot drink Strong or none at all.

This memorial being decay'd was reftor'd
by the Officers of the Garrifon A.D. 1781.
An honeft Soldier never is forgot
Whether he die by Mufket or by Pot.

The Stone was replaced by the North Hants
Militia when difembodied at Winchester
on 26th April 1802 in confequence of
the original Stone being deftroyed.

And again replaced by
The Royal Hampshire Regiment.

1. The cautionary tale of an infantryman's death, Winchester Cathedral. *(Photo courtesy of Phil Abramson)*

2. A Late Bronze Age shield from Long Wittenham, Oxfordshire. This Nipperwiese-class shield was used in combat; note the lozenge-shaped weapon perforation to the second shield rib. *(Ashmolean Museum, Oxford)*

3. A flint projectile embedded in a rib of Unknown Warrior 1, Stonehenge, Wiltshire. *(Photo by courtesy of the late Professor John Evans)*

4. A section through the Middle to Late Bronze Age linear ditch at Tormarton, South Gloucestershire. This was the final resting place of Unknown Warrior 2 and up to four other young men. *(Author's collection)*

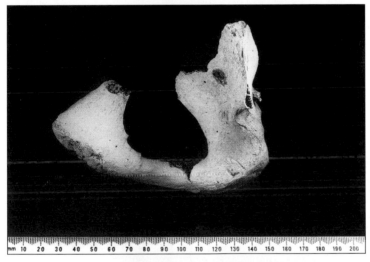

5. A Bronze Age spear embedded in the pelvis of Unknown Warrior 2, Tormarton, South Gloucestershire. *(Photo by Ian Cartwright)*

6. The perforated skull of Unknown Warrior 2, Tormarton, South Gloucestershire. The *coup de grâce* is thought to have been inflicted by the ferrule of a spear shaft. *(Photo by Ian Cartwright)*

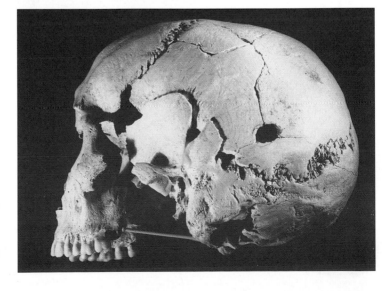

7. Remains of the Roman barrack block at Caerleon in Wales. *(Author's collection)*

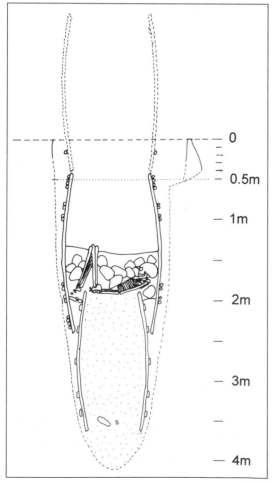

8. A section through the well at Velsen, in the Netherlands, showing the position of Unknown Warrior 4. *(After Morel and Bosman, 1989: 169)*

9. The Lewis Chessmen, probably made in Norway around AD 1150–1200; found on the Isle of Lewis, Outer Hebrides, Scotland. Note the 'Beserker' footsoldier on the right of the group. *(Copyright British Museum)*

10. Viking runes carved inside the Neolithic tomb of Maes Howe in Orkney. *(Copyright Homer Sykes/CORBIS)*

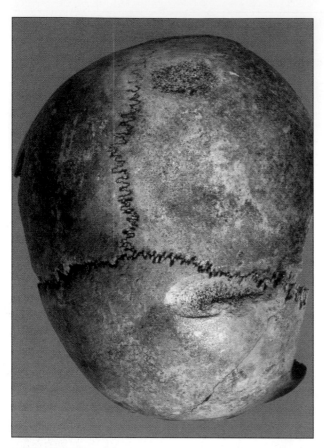

11. The skull of Unknown
Warrior 6, Eccles, Kent,
showing weapon trauma.
(Copyright Bradford University)

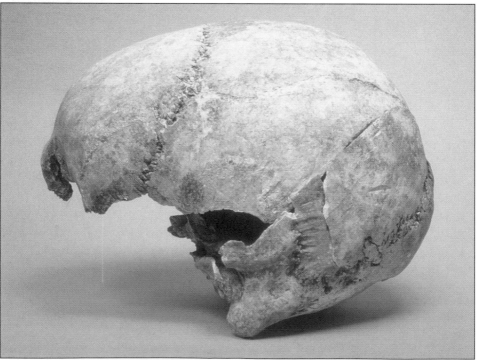

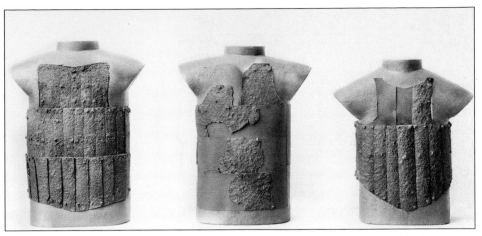

12. Lamellar armour excavated from the burial pits at Visby, Gotland. *(Copyright Nationalmuseet, Copenhagen)*

13. The mass grave at Towton, North Yorkshire, illustrating the position of Unknown Warrior 7. *(Copyright Bradford University)*

14. Objects retrieved from the *Mary Rose*, reflecting the pastimes of those on board. *(Copyright Adam Woolfitt/CORBIS)*

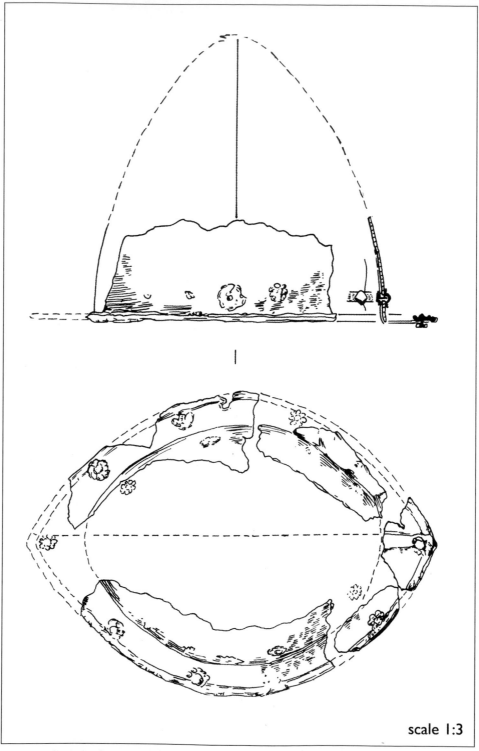

scale 1:3

15. Pontefract Castle armour: Morion helmet number 9. *(After Roberts 2002: 328, fig. 134)*

countermine shafts in the bakehouse and the Elizabethan Chapel (Eaves, 2002: 325–9). Body armour was also found: a backplate, with evidence for replacement of one of its shoulder straps, and another heavy backplate that was unlikely to have been made post-1630 (*ibid.*: 327). Fragments of the armoured 'skirt' extending from the body armour of the pikeman to protect his upper thighs during pike-push and tassets were found (*ibid.*: 338).

Armour of a type used at Visby and Flodden was also in evidence during the English Civil War period, with examples of the iron plates sewn into fabric jackets being found at Pontefract (*ibid.*: 341) and Beeston (Ellis, 1993: 160–2). Two pieces of iron plate for such a coat were also discovered in Keep Area F at Sandal Castle (Credland, 1983: 266). This was supposedly obsolete even by the fifteenth century, let alone the mid-seventeenth century, but still it was pressed into infantry use.

In terms of clothing, work on *La Trinidad Valencera* revealed elements of the costume of those on board, presumably both of the infantry and the seamen. Woollen garments dominated, including heraldic surcoats, and several pairs of durable rope-soled shoes (*alpargatos*) were found.

On land, the excavations of Pollard and Oliver on the site of the Civil War Battle of Edgehill located a number of buttons. Some of these were silver-plated and with ornate designs, perhaps belonging to officers, and others were plain and 'fastened the more modest attire of the rank and file' (Pollard and Oliver, 2003: 112). Elements of footwear, so vital for infantrymen, have been excavated from English Civil War sites. Finds at Basing House included a boot heel with iron shoe and nails, and a leather sole and upper dating to the second quarter of the seventeenth century, which probably represented soldiers' boots from the siege of the house and were sturdy enough to have survived over 350 years (Moorhouse, 1971: 62).

PRACTICE AND DISCIPLINE

Skeletal evidence may be as good as many sources in pointing to extensive military practice in the sixteenth century. Continued use of the longbow had resulted in pathological changes to the skeletons of those found on board the *Mary Rose*, in much the same fashion as those men found at Towton (see Chapter 4). Also, fourteen of the skulls found on the vessel displayed wounds that were not fractures and might have been inflicted on experienced fighting men. One of these skulls seemed to have suffered a penetrating arrow wound with the angle of wound indicating a blow from above, a blow from which the man recovered. 'He was probably wearing a helmet, and small fragments of helmets were found during the excavation of the wreck. The bone around the wound was healing, so the attack was a fairly recent one. Alternatively, it has been suggested that a practice arrow at the butts, rather than during battle, could have caused this wound. In the former case, the bodkin arrowhead would have been wrapped, so that it did not cause permanent injury or death, although it may have penetrated his helmet. During battle, however, the arrow would have been naked and would easily have penetrated any helmet, probably fatally' (Stirland, 2000: 104–6).

Several treatises were written by the time of the English Civil War, including Thomas Jenner's *The Military Discipline Wherein is Martially Showne The Order for Drilling the Musket and the Pike* (1642). Although many combatants of the officer class had learned their martial trade through fighting in the Thirty Years War (1618–48) in central Europe, trained militias, such as the London Trained Bands, provided the backbone for the armies of the Parliament at the start of the English Civil War. Despite some successes, their results were not to the level hoped for by Parliament, and so the New Model Army was created, with an emphasis on the importance of discipline and practice. This army provided a radical military rethink, culminating with stunning victories such as Naseby in 1645. As the first genuine standing army in England, the New Model effectively held power for some ten years after the execution of Charles I. Training would certainly have been required to use a musket effectively or to play a role in the pike square. Without training, the results could be dreadful – historical references exist for musketeers blowing themselves up at Pontefract Castle by overcharging their weapons, and also for shooting their comrades by mistake (Roberts, 2002: 431).

Part of this practice and discipline would undoubtedly have involved essential maintenance by the footsoldier of his weapon to ensure that it was kept clean, lessening the chances of it fouling or misfiring in battle. Such fatigues are still an important part of the infantryman's duties. A barrel scourer pertaining to this work was found in excavations at Beeston Castle. This object was 'screwed into the end of a ramrod and then used to clean scale from gun barrels' (Ellis, 1993: 157). So, although historical sources may still be the best evidence for training and discipline, the archaeological record also provides fascinating insights into essential work.

THE LIFE OF THE SOLDIER

The finding of a Jew's harp in excavations of English Civil War layers at Gloucester indicates one of the pastimes of the soldier when not in action. A further element that shows that the life of the soldier was far from monastic was the find of ten animal-membrane condoms from the garderobe (latrine) of Dudley Castle, which was slighted, and thus sealed, in 1647. The deposit was composed of 'both the domestic and organic remains of the occupying Royalist force which had defended the castle under siege conditions between 1643 and 1646' (Gaimster, *et al.*, 1996: 129). Five of the condoms were in very fragmentary condition, but the other five were more complete with surviving lengths of 47, 47.1, 20.5, 51.5 and 56.2mm (diameter 30.5, 34.3, 31.0, 30.3 and 38.0mm). These may have related to officers' activities, but it is an important indicator that life went on despite conditions of privation for many within besieged sites.

Drinking

The skeletons of the crew of the *Mary Rose* perhaps reveal the use of flavourings within their drinks in the decay of their teeth. 'Apparently, the crew of the *Mary Rose* is the earliest known group to show a modern pattern of decay . . . Although there was no widespread consumption of sugar in the first half of the sixteenth century, it had been suggested that the crew probably used honey "and other cariogenic foods and drinks"' (Stirland, 2000: 84).

In addition to evidence written on the bones of the crew, artefactual evidence points to the consumption of alcohol on board, particularly beer. Oak-staved containers with willow hooping were found on the wreck alongside seventeen spiles. This latter item, most frequently of poplar wood, was a tapering wooden object which would have been hammered into the container in place of the bung to allow the beer to flow freely. Drinking vessels were also located on the ship, with wooden tankards lined with pitch being present, and leather flasks, again with an internal pitch coating, being recovered (see *Mary Rose*, 2005).

Survival conditions are key to the archaeological dataset in terms of any bias that might otherwise creep into our understanding. It is an archaeological cliché that 'absence of evidence is not evidence of absence', and this is something that Margaret Rule (1989: 19) highlights when she considers the drinking equipment on the ship: 'the almost complete absence of objects made from horn within the ship does not mean that the men drank only from wooden or pewter tankards; we have to recognise that horn is food material for micro-organisms and that most of the horn objects were "eaten" by bacteria.'

The soldiers on board *La Trinidad Valencera* were also provided with drinking vessels – leather goatskins for wine and for water were found by the excavators. These skins were lined with pitch in similar fashion to the flasks on the *Mary Rose* and plugged with wooden stopper funnels in their necks (Martin, 2001: 84).

Around the gatehouse and ringwork terminals of the besieged Basing House, bottle glass was found in relative abundance, though in poor condition. Most of these fragments were green and probably from wine bottles (Allen and Anderson, 1999: 76). Pottery assemblages, which included drinking vessels such as flagons, have been found on several sites of the English Civil War period – particularly siege sites. Pontefract and Beeston castles (Noake, 1993: 203) had such collections. Dudley Castle contained a communal drinking vessel known as a 'tyr' (Harrington, 2004: 115), which may have been used by the military garrison in more carousing moments. Excavations from Newcastle-upon-Tyne uncovered a stone-lined pit with detritus dating from 1645 to 1675. Clay pipe fragments, glass and pottery, along with coinage – predominantly Scottish – hinted both at the domestic nature of the fill and, perhaps, of the nationality of some of the troops. The earliest levels held material of pre-Civil War vintage which might have been in use in the siege and there were many tin-glazed wares and vessels known as 'Bellamine' jars (Ellison *et al.*, 1979: 159).

Eating

We are fortunate to have evidence for the food of the soldier from sites where provisions were collected – from ships and castles. The former reflects victuals provided to crewmen on active service, while the latter reflects a particular set of circumstances – food available to the besieged. This category also shows the increasing privations suffered by those cut off from regular supplies.

Although some of the skeletal material on the *Mary Rose* provided evidence for malnutrition in early life, including rickets and prolonged deficiency of vitamin C (Stirland, 2000: 87–8), the excavations of the ship produced evidence for the quality of some of the victuals provided to troops of the Tudor era. Admittedly, these foodstuffs were for sailors and archers alike in situations not encountered by the infantry per se, but the infantrymen on board would have had access to these rations. Stirland discusses this material and her work is worth quoting at some length:

> The meat consisted of beef and pork and one fallow deer haunch, probably for the officers. The beef had been butchered according to the King's regulations and consisted entirely of flat bones, devoid of marrow. It was all of a high quality from immature animals. There was one cask of pork, which included some marrow-containing long bones, as well as vertebrae and ribs. A large deposit of pork and ham, which had been butchered in quarters, was also found loose in the hull. All the meat had been salted. The fish was stockfish and largely consisted of headless cod . . . As well as plum stones and grape pips, there were the remains of grape skins in a barrel, although these could have been left from wine. (Stirland, 2000: 148–9)

Large quantities of animal bones were found during the excavations of the gatehouse, ditch and kitchen of Basing House, some of which were burnt or butchered. From the layers of the 1645 English Civil War siege, the animals represented included cattle and sheep (these two being the largest set), pig, horse, roe deer, red/fallow deer, domestic bird, fish and rabbit, although the latter may have been intrusive, as is the case on many archaeological sites (Allen and Anderson, 1999: 87). It seems reasonable to suggest that the food was available to infantry among the besieged, as well as its commanders. The animal bone assemblage at Beeston Castle, demolished under the orders of the Parliament in 1646, included sheep, cattle and pigs (Harrington, 2004: 51).

Siege conditions were also apparent at Dudley Castle, where the Royalist commander, Colonel Leveson, and his force held out against Parliamentarian opposition, before eventually surrendering to Sir William Brereton. As the castle was slighted, the sealing of the garderobe provides a secure Civil War date for deposits. Studies concluded that there was much evidence of food within these layers, including coriander, figs, grapes, pumpkins and strawberries, and of animal, bird and fish bones (Gaimster et al., 1996).

The butchered mammal bones from Civil War layers at Pontefract Castle included cattle, sheep and pig, but much of this comprised skull and foot bones, perhaps illustrating that cuts of meat not normally consumed were eaten when supplies became shorter during the siege. The excavators believed the assemblage included a greater dependence on former 'inedibles' – these included three butchered horse bones and a dog and a cat bone in context 116 (first–second siege) and a horse bone from the third siege deposits (Richardson, 2002: 378–9). A large collection of fish bones was also present at Pontefract, associated with the first to second siege. These were almost all large and very large cod (*c.* 1m in length), though halibut, conger eel and plaice were also included. 'The range of the excavated skeletal elements would suggest that these fish had been brought to the site as stockfish (salted and dried to keep for many months), rather than being beheaded at the castle' (Nicholson, 2002: 393).

Smoking

This era sees the emergence of a new pastime of the infantryman – smoking. It is a habit that endures right through to the present day and is still traceable in the archaeological record of the First World War. Tobacco was first seen in Europe and used as a narcotic in the sixteenth century. Most of the excavations of the English Civil War period sites of the seventeenth century have a great deal of clay pipe evidence.

At Southgate Street in Gloucester, excavations of a 5.5m wide and 2.3m deep V-shaped ditch of the English Civil War defences of the town yielded over 500 clay pipe fragments (Harrington, 1992: 33). Some of these pipe bowls were found pressed into the floor levels of buildings on the city's outskirts which had been deliberately destroyed by fire on 10 August 1643. They were of an identifiable type – such as the example with 'RR' stamped on its base (Atkin, 1989: 7).

Clay pipes were excavated from the fill of a Civil War defensive ditch dug by Royalist troops at Sandal Castle in Yorkshire (Harrington, 1992: 21) as they were at Newcastle-upon-Tyne within a new defensive system around the old castle (*ibid.*: 22).

Basing House retained a number of clay pipe fragments from the citadel – including London-style pipes (*c.* 1640–60). Some of these pipe fragments showed signs of external burning, which the excavators took as probably being inflicted at the time the building was razed (Allen and Anderson, 1999: 78). Pontefract Castle in Yorkshire had a collapsed countermine which contained fragments of clay pipe (Roberts, 2002) and Beeston Castle in

Cheshire also had many of the ubiquitous pipes. Here there were some seventy-three clay pipes of the English Civil War period – with stamps on them including 'NE', 'OP', 'SE' and 'AL' – all of which are common in Chester (Ellis, 1993: 172).

Toilet

Curiously, human toilet activity is important for our study of the sixteenth- to seventeenth-century infantryman, for the very end product of the act as much as for its indication of the diet of troops.

Urine was a vital ingredient in the production of saltpetre. Cord, when soaked in saltpetre, could ignite and smoulder and thus apply the requisite flame to the charge of matchlock and cannon. 'The process involved, though somewhat dangerous, was not unduly complicated; it involved the extraction and refinement of saltpetre from the "earth", found in decomposing organic matter in cattle-sheds and dovecotes; the saltpetre was then blended with charcoal and brimstone, and the mixture finely milled' (RCHME, 1964: 53). Human urine was also used, and people were employed to collect it on siege sites of the English Civil War.

Gaming

Although it was not to be, after the catastrophe that befell them, the soldiers on board the *Mary Rose* might have expected long periods of boredom when not in action. As their martial predecessors had done on many occasions, the troops took gaming equipment onto the ship with them. The excavations recovered part of this important assemblage. Finds included bone dice in wooden chests, many gaming counters, and even a backgammon set in the carpenter's cabin (Rule, 1989: 22). A leather pouch was discovered that may have served as the shaker for dice in a game (see Plate 14).

Their seventeenth-century counterparts also played games – one of the finds of Pollard and Oliver's work at Edgehill with the most human poignancy was a piece of lead caseshot that had been 'converted into a gaming piece by having a series of lines incised into one end' (Pollard and Oliver, 2003: 115).

All of these pleasures had, in theory, to be paid for, although many were those who complained of privations caused by having troops billeted upon them, and much was taken in the aftermath of siege or when an army moved through a village, town or city. Although standard coinage of the 1640s has been found in besieged towns and cities, other sites issued specific 'Siege Money'. A case in point is Newark. Here there were two denominations of coins produced in 1645 and with the legend 'Newarke': 1s, and 1s 9d. Those coins marked 'Newark' were of 2s 6d, 1s, 9d and 6d from 1645; and 2s 6d, 1s, 9d and 6d from 1646. They are all lozenge shaped with a crown between the letters C and R and the value on one face, and OBS (*obsessum*, 'besieged'), the place name and date on the other. Many such tokens have been found around Newark. It is probable that the origin for the manufacture of these tokens was a scarcity of regular coinage in the isolated town (RCHME, 1964: 73). Siege coinage has also been located in Pontefract Castle where it was produced by the garrison (Wright, 2002).

Writings

The English Civil War was the first war in Britain to have war correspondents, with accounts of battles, atrocities and heroism appearing in newspapers and pamphlets published by both sides. Propaganda was spread among the troops, as were radical theories of religion, the rights of men and of suffrage among the forces of Parliament. A degree of literacy would have been required even if only by a small number of men to read this material to others in a regiment.

We are also fortunate to have the writings of some of the common footsoldiers of the age, such as Neremiah Wharton who wrote of his service in the Parliamentary armies of the early years of the war before his probable death at the Battle of Edgehill in 1642 or soon after (Ede-Borrett, 1983).

Graffiti provides us with further evidence of literacy among the serving soldiers of the seventeenth century. At Pontefract Castle we see pieces of wall plaster and the walls themselves with names and dates carved into them. Graffiti in the Constable Tower relating to the Royalist garrison of the first and second sieges of 1644–5 include the names 'William' and 'John'. Those on the walls of the cellar, mostly in capitals, were from the time of the Parliamentarian garrison 1648–9; the names in this graffiti may also relate to the imprisoned. As such they are a fascinating record – their testimony includes '16 Geo 48 BeALe' (George Beale 1648), 'ROBERT BRIER 1648', 'IOHN 1648 SMITH' (John Smith 1648) and 'IAMES 1648 BROVSTON' (James Brouston 1648) (Bostwick and Roberts, 2002: 296–8). We even have a record of two of the men whose names appear: Robert Greathed (recorded as captured in

October 1648), and John Grant, a gunner (*ibid.*: 296–8) (see Plate 16). Most infantrymen on board the *Mary Rose* appear to have marked their possessions with simple graffiti marks (see *Mary Rose*, 2005), although writing material such as leather parchment made from sheepskin was found on the ship.

Several churches lay claim to have been 'defaced' by soldiers during this turbulent time, with buildings used as billets, prisons and stables, and with soldiers carving their names into monuments. One such church is Bromham in Wiltshire, which claims to have graffiti carved all over the reclining alabaster monument of Sir Roger Tocotes, a veteran of the Wars of the Roses. This was said to have been carved by Parliamentarian troops after the nearby Battle of Roundway Down in 1643. Although some of the names may indeed have been carved by these men, it is impossible to blame them for starting such sacrilegious actions as there is at least one pre-existing date on Sir Roger: 1641. It is a common claim that such iconoclasts as the Puritanical elements of Cromwell's armies were responsible for such damage. Often it is not true, but simply a good story. On occasions, however, the evidence seems more clear, the inscription in Burford Church, Oxfordshire, which we shall examine below in the section on The Prisoner (see page 126) being a case in point. Another church that retains graffiti from this period is that of Old Basing, next to Basing House, Hampshire.

Accommodation

Tents were clearly used for accommodation by armies on the move – even those troops being transported by the great ships of the Armada brought such items along with them for the intended campaign on land against England (Flanagan, 1987: 10).

The work at Flodden seems to have located the possible site of the Scottish pre-battle camp on Branxton Hill. On stripping the site, excavators discovered an arc of stones set into a shallow slot across one of the excavation trenches. 'Just possibly this is the sort of trace a tent or temporary shelter may have left behind, the stones perhaps supporting thin stakes, which would prop up a hide or oil-cloth roof, pretty much like the "benders" that modern travellers live in. There were also a couple of post-holes elsewhere in the trenches, and these stone-line holes may have once supported the central posts of other tents' (Pollard and Oliver, 2002: 156). Although this evidence might seem a little thin for such a claim, further along the hill an earthen bank running behind a gun emplacement they had located, may support this hypothesis, as it may have been part of a defensive bank thrown up around the camp to protect it from attack. If this is the case, then historical accounts of the battle seem to be accurate in this respect (*ibid.*: 156–7).

Camp sites leave elements relating to the time when soldiers were stationed there. The siege of Newark, Nottinghamshire, between 1642 and 1646 is a case in point. Parliamentary forces dug a bank and ditch around the town to cut it off, gun batteries and forts were soon constructed with Scottish forces building an encampment known as 'Edinburgh' to the west of the works. Archaeological fieldwork has recovered numerous artefacts from the site of this encampment: iron slag – the by-product of the smelting process activities of the armourer – the lid of a large powder flask, hinges from a wooden box, musket balls (including one with sprues) and lead sheeting for the making of musket balls (*ibid.*: 234). In addition to these finds, the presence of bricks in these fields intrigued the authors as it might indicate that 'the camp [included] not just tents but also more substantial buildings. If so, this would tie in with the portrayal of what looks like houses among the tents on Clampe's contemporary map of the siege of Newark' (*ibid.*: 239).

Sieges of this period present their own problems, as one of the methods of protecting the town or city concerned would be the deliberate destruction of the suburbs by defenders. This would deny cover for any offensive actions undertaken, creating an effective killing ground; it would also deny accommodation to the enemy. Burned layers for such destruction can be found at Gloucester, the only Parliamentary garrison between Bristol and Lancashire. Here, the suburbs of 214 houses and a church were burnt down on 10 August 1643. The clay floor of one of the destroyed houses, in Southgate Street, was seen through archaeology to have been sealed 'by piles of debris from a fire and building rubble, including stone roof tiles, and the cesspit was left open and derelict. This event could be dated archaeologically (by the clay pipes and pottery) to a time bracket 1640–60, with the most likely historical context being that afternoon of 10 August 1643' (Atkin, 1989: 9).

Within the context of siege warfare, soldiers must have spent at least some of the time in trench systems cut either to protect or to encircle the town or city concerned. At Gloucester, much material, as we have seen, has been recovered from the great defensive ditch cut around the city. Other excavation work has uncovered the remains of a possible Royalist attack trench or 'sap'. This work would have been cut on a perpendicular from the encircling Royalist trenches to get closer to the defenders' positions (*ibid.*: 9). Some of the fiercest actions in this siege supposedly took place in these trenches with accounts describing 'our muskettiers sending plenty of shot into their trenches, and cast divers granadoes provided ready' (*ibid.*: 10). Were one to describe the image of a trench raid with firearm and grenade, and with several of the troops involved smoking nearby, one would be forgiven if this conjured up images of Vimy Ridge, Messines or Verdun in the First World War – this was, however, 1643.

Study of the distribution of metal artefacts has also possibly led to the location of the 1651 camp site of the Parliamentary armies at Worcester (Foard, 2001: 92).

Religion

In Europe, the fifteenth and sixteenth centuries were an age of enormous religious turmoil with the emergence and rise of Protestantism on the mainland, the Reformation in Britain, and the Thirty Years War.

Although Henry VIII was responsible for the Reformation in England, closing the monasteries and generally crushing the Catholic Church as a result of his failure to gain papal approval for the dissolution of his marriage to Catherine of Aragon, Protestantism was not always his chosen path. Earlier in his reign, Henry had written a treatise condemning the heresy of Martin Luther for which he had been awarded the title 'Defender of the Faith' by the Pope. This title has been retained by British monarchs despite the break from Rome and can be seen on British coinage to this day – with the abbreviation *Fid.Def.* The *Mary Rose* sank in the post-Reformation period of Henry's reign and thus it is perhaps surprising to find wooden and bone rosary beads and their containers on the wreck. A wooden box for these was found on the orlop deck, amidships, and a fruitwood container from the stern of the main deck (for these items see Rule, 1989: 22; *Mary Rose*, 2005). Catholics were subject to severe persecution and thus, unusually in our study, it is likely that these men would have tried to keep their religious beliefs secret.

Religious houses did not escape the ravages of military actions in this period – the Friary at Jedburgh (see pages 106–7) was razed by Lord Eure and the Earl of Hertford (1544–5). Excavations on this site pointed to this military destruction: 'Extensive burnt deposits in the north and south range indicate that the Friary was destroyed by fire. Building debris, roof slate and glass, in particular, indicate that the Friary may have become a roofless, windowless ruin in the wake of this episode.' Or, as a contemporary author wrote, 'The people thus fled, and the town given to the Englishmen by the chance of war, the gunners burned the Abbey, the Greyfriars and divers bastells and fortified houses' (Dixon *et al.*, 2000: 87).

The footsoldiers on board the ships of the Spanish Armada who were to undertake the invasion of England in 1588 would in many cases have had strong religious beliefs. They were, after all, the army that was to crush Elizabeth I's heretical nation. Finds retrieved from several of the sunken vessels investigated include elements of Catholicism, though it is more likely that these relate to the nobility – the officers on board. Among the assemblage was a gold *Agnus Dei* reliquary from the *Girona* that contained wax pellets made from paschal candles and blessed by the Pope (Flanagan, 1987: 6).

Religion was also an important element of the English Civil War, although it is not possible to divide allegiances down purely religious lines; it would be too simple to state that all Parliamentary supporters were of Puritanical leaning, for example. At the foot of Edgehill, there was once a church by which the Royalist armies must have passed en route to the battle. Geophysical survey and excavation by Pollard and Oliver (2003: 107–9) have located this building, which is likely to have been the site of prayers by those going into battle, both those for whom this was a new experience and those already hardened by participation in the Thirty Years War in central Europe.

Medicine

The survival conditions on the *Mary Rose* have enabled us to obtain some of the best evidence for the tools of the surgeon's trade for a specific engagement in any of the eras covered by this book. In the cabin of the barber surgeon, a walnut chest was discovered. In it were the preparations required for the immediate treatment of sailors and infantry in the forthcoming battle. Rows of lidded, turned wooden containers and still-corked medicine jars, probably from Raeren in Germany, contained ointments; one still retained the fingermarks of the last user.

On examination, it seems that the range of medicines on board the *Mary Rose* offered treatments

mainly for wounds, burns, and other skin complaints. However, most were probably fairly effective, as they contained active ingredients used in medicine until the start of the 20th century – and in one case, to the present day. One preparation for burns consisted of zinc mixed in animal fat – similar to modern calamine lotion whose active ingredient is zinc oxide. Another consisted of copper salt in animal fat, an antibiotic ointment used until recently to treat necrotic skin ulcers.

The chest also contained large quantities of pine resin, an antibiotic dressing for wounds which prevents fluid loss and dehydration. Scraps of bandages were found in the chest, and perhaps most surprisingly, a jar of peppercorns, which textbooks recommended both as a dressing for rheumatic aches and, for internal use, to treat gastric spasms. According to Brendan Derham, a doctoral student at Bradford University who conducted the research, the chest contained almost no medicines for internal consumption because barber-surgeons (including ship's surgeons) were prevented at the time from prescribing them. This remained the prerogative of physicians, an elite group who rarely went to sea. (British Archaeology News, 1999)

In addition to field dressings, impregnated with herbal infusions, and wooden spatulas for applying ointments, there was a heavy mortar for pounding the drugs, a bone earscoop, a brazier, a pewter bleeding bowl and a chafing dish. Perhaps the cherry wood feeding bottle in this assemblage was there to enable the very weak or those with severe facial injuries to eat (for this collection, see *Mary Rose*, 2005). Other pewter items from the cabin of the barber-surgeon included drug flasks and an item which seems more akin to an implement of torture, a urethral syringe (Rule, 1989: 23). Although being treated for injuries sustained during this period must have been, on occasion, a truly hellish experience, it was certainly not for lack of care or thought.

At Sandal Castle in Yorkshire, four small, unglazed white ware jars were found in the kitchen. These were not local wares, they had been imported from abroad or elsewhere in the country. Along with the presence of several glass bottles and the nearby English Civil War period cemetery of nine skeletons, the excavators believed that this might suggest that the kitchen had been converted into either an impromptu field hospital or a medical dispensary during the siege (Mayes and Butler, 1983: 213).

Excavation work also reveals that some of the other sufferings of troops of the sixteenth and seventeenth centuries included lice. Hair lice have been retrieved from the fine teeth of the combs on the *Mary Rose*, and such parasites seem to have afflicted soldiers from all eras (Strickland and Hardy, 2005: 7).

THE PRISONER

The excavation of the bodies of at least sixty men from the Battle of Good Friday in Uppsala (1520) revealed that the majority seem to have been killed while they were fleeing; with wounds to the back and to both sides of the skulls (Kjellström, 2005). One of the men (Skeleton A4:00) had been decapitated – his sole wound being from a very sharp blade from behind that had severed his head. His body had been placed on its back in a grave pit, with the skull to the right of his waist suggesting that his head was perhaps not severed during the battle. The osteologist examining the burials postulated that 'the direction of the blow and orientation of the cut together with the burial context points towards the man being executed' (*ibid.*: 36, 44). If this is indeed the case, then the archaeological record has another example of a probable prisoner of war executed following his capture.

The English Civil War, as with all civil wars, brought out bitterness and rancour that, on occasions, could manifest itself in appalling treatment of wounded or captives. For example, 'On Christmas Day 1643 Lord Byron accepted the surrender of some 20 Parliamentarians at Barthomley, Cheshire. "I put them all to the sword," the Royalist commander boasted, "which I find the best way to proceed with these kind of people"' (Carlton, 1991: 19). This being said, not all those captured were killed – many were treated with kindness and respect, especially the nobility. Footsoldiers could actually be 'encouraged' to change sides to fight for their captors.

Some information derived from Beeston Castle might just relate to the last desperate moments of infantrymen before being captured. Excavations discovered a number of matchlock priming pans which seemed to indicate that the guns had been deliberately destroyed – perhaps akin to an artilleryman's 'spiking' of the guns – to prevent them falling into enemy hands (Harrington, 2004: 115). Archaeologically our main traces of the imprisoned relate to inscriptions left by the incarcerated, and through cemetery evidence.

Excavations at Abingdon, Oxfordshire, have yielded possible information about the fate of prisoners from the English Civil War. Being some 6 miles from the King's capital of Oxford, Abingdon was a Royalist centre until May 1644 when it was taken by a group supporting the Parliament. Within the context of the grounds of the abbey church, 50m from the contemporary town gaol, a mass grave was found. The remains of one of these men had a musket ball in his ribcage. Were these men those included in the burial register for 1644–5 with the entry 'for the burial of nine prisoners from the town gaol' (T. Allen, 1990: 27)? If so, perhaps we are either seeing the execution of one or more of these captives, or the fatal results of a failed escape attempt. Given the ledger entry, were these men Royalist prisoners of war?

Some of the strongest buildings of the Civil War period were churches and this made them suitable not simply for religious use, but also for use as fortified centres and prisons. St Mary's Church at Painswick, Gloucestershire, is a case in point. The Parliamentarian governor of Gloucester, Colonel Massey, established an outpost in this town, but, in March 1644, his troops were all forced into the church after attack. The doors of the church were fired on and grenades were thrown resulting in many casualties and the capture of those within. The church then changed roles from place of shelter to place of imprisonment for the Parliamentarians. One of those imprisoned, Richard Foot, left his name carved in the church in association with a quote from Spenser's *Faerie Queene*, 'Be bold, be bold, but not too bold' (Wroughton, 1999: 212). Huge numbers of people were taken prisoner during the Civil War – Carlton (1991: 18) has calculated the numbers as being 34,393 Parliamentarians and 83,041 Royalist captives, a total of 117,434 – a figure greater than his estimate of 84,378 fatalities.

An inscription carved by a prisoner of the English Civil War is present in the dungeon of Pontefract Castle (see page 119), where the legend 'John Grant 1648' is carved onto the walls. His name appears three times scratched into the sandstone during a five-month incarceration – this being the same man who, from letters written between the two sides, appears to have requested a visitor's pass for his wife (Bostwick and Roberts, 2002: 296).

It wasn't only the opponent's forces that were locked away when captured; for discipline to be maintained, it was necessary to clamp down harshly on any dissent within. The formation of the New Model Army revolutionised the fortunes of Parliament in the Civil War. There was a large tranche of radicalism in the ranks – with political and religious pamphlets to the fore, reinforced by the orations of preachers. One such radical sect, the Levellers, called for political reform, for greatly increased enfranchisement to permeate Britain as a result of Parliament's victory. This was more than the leaders of the army, including Cromwell, were willing to tolerate and the Levellers were suppressed. Not only were several members of the sect shot at Gloucester Green in Oxford, but, at nearby Burford, Cromwell captured some 340 members and imprisoned them in the church. One prisoner, Anthony Sedley, carved his name on the font: 'Anthony Sedley Prisner 1649'. Sedley's fate is not known, but three leaders of the insurrection were shot against the wall of the church.

MEMORIALS AND BURIALS

Soldiers from this period were afforded memorials in churches, too. For example, the stained-glass windows at Middleton Church, near Manchester, depict sixteen archers who fought alongside Sir Ralph Assheton at the Battle of Flodden (C. Bartlett, 2002: 62–3). English Civil War soldiers are also depicted in the church window at Farndon, Cheshire – a Royalist memorial. Unknown pikemen and musketeers are both depicted.

Memorials were also placed on the sites of conflict to commemorate the unknown soldiers who had died. The 1642 battlefield of Edgehill – the first major battle of the Civil War – was a case in point (it is now Ministry of Defence land).

As with the victims of Visby (see Chapter 4), burial was not prompt in every case. Some of the bodies from the mass grave of the 1520 Battle of Uppsala, Sweden, were left exposed for some time before burial. Although the skeletal material showed relatively few teeth marks of scavengers, the bones were largely disarticulated. Perhaps this corroborates a note from the Swedish Archbishop Trolle of Uppsala, allied to the Danish king, to the effect that the bodies of fallen men were 'left to dogs and ravens in bogs' (Kjellström, 2005: 45).

There are records for burials in the seventeenth century being given to those killed in battle by later societies, long after the actual event. Claverton Church, near Bath, records the burial within its grounds of victims of the

1643 Battle of Lansdown. These were individual soldiers who were discovered, supposedly in their armour, in the nineteenth century and reburied with Christian dignity. Other early excavations found mass burials, which supposedly related to Civil War actions, but left little by way of record and thus we cannot conclude much from the results of the work – an example being the possible soldiers' bodies from the siege of Leicester (for discussion of earlier finds, see Courtney and Courtney, 1992: 69).

The work at Abingdon revealed the presence of an English Civil War period cemetery, which contained around 500 burials, 250 of which were excavated. Of particular interest was the alignment of these graves: north–south. This seems to have been a deliberate attempt to avoid the more Catholic east–west alignment and would thus sit well with the mid-seventeenth century, with its more Puritan outlook. Finds from the graves included a silver penny of Charles I, Scottish silver shillings of Charles I or James VI, and a coffin plate of 1650–75 (T. Allen, 1990: 27). What was especially intriguing about this cemetery was the presence of the mass grave of possible Civil War prisoners (see page 125). Perhaps a 'dignified' burial was not deemed the right of a captured opponent.

THE FALLEN

Many of the crew, mariners and archers alike, perished with the rapid sinking of Henry VIII's flagship the *Mary Rose* on 19 July 1545. Following the excavation and recovery of the ship, Anne Stirland examined the human bones that formed an element of the archaeological deposit. She found that a total of ninety-two relatively complete skeletons were present and that the skeletal assemblage represented a minimum number of 179 individuals, all male (Stirland, 2000: 74–5). The heights of these men ranged from 159 to 180cm with an average of 171cm, the majority being between 18 and 30 years of age (*ibid.*: 79–80).

Stirland attempted to discern differences in skeletal traits that might reveal whether particular skeletons belonged, in fact, to the infantrymen on board – the archers. The shoulder blades were particularly important in this research. Ten of the fifty-two complete pairs of shoulder blades displayed a condition called 'os acromiale' – a non-fused epiphysis of this bone. Stirland believed that the most likely cause of this trait was the continuous use in practice and in combat of the longbow; after all: 'Every boy aged from 7 to 17 had to be provided with a bow and two arrows by his father and, after 17, had to provide a bow and four arrows for himself. Practice butts were also supplied in every town' (*ibid.*: 122). Such long-term use of a weapon that puts considerable strain on the body seems to have affected the shoulders of certain men. Also, many of these skeletons had more developed thigh and buttock muscles, something one would also expect for bowmen (*ibid.*: 134). One of these men was finally buried as an 'Unknown Mariner' in Portsmouth Cathedral, 1984.

In 2001, archaeological work on the slopes of Uppsala Castle in Sweden unearthed a mass grave. The bones were radiocarbon dated to 1440–1650, at the 95 per cent probability level, and this, along with their context and evident trauma, resulted in them being related to the Battle of Good Friday in 1520. On a cold and snowy 6 April 1520, Swedish troops attacked Danish forces stationed in Uppsala. As at Towton (see Chapter 4), the weather had made the use of early models of firearms problematic. Swedish forces were composed of groups of organised peasants, who found themselves up against paid mercenaries from Germany, France and Scotland (Kjellström, 2005: 24). Fortunes changed throughout the day, but early successes for the Swedish troops soon ended and the Danish forces prevailed. Overall losses for the battle were said to be over 4,000.

The grave found in 2001 contained the bodies of at least sixty comparatively tall men, aged between 25 and 34 years, one of whom had been decapitated. Trauma patterns on the skulls – the location of most of the wounds – seem to indicate that these men were trying to flee when they were cut down; there were few defensive wounds to their front or hands, while wounds to their posteriors, and to both sides of the head, were common (*ibid.*: 46).

As with so many of the combatants featured in this book, the rank and file of defeated armies of the Civil War period were probably buried in mass graves, or, in some cases, were buried where they fell. Despite this, burial rites were seemingly well observed, if the writings of the period are to be believed (Harrington, 2004: 109). Although multiple burials of this period have been found at places such as Leicester, Tantallon Castle in East Lothian, and Taunton, it is not fully possible to link them directly with the Civil War, although this explanation remains a distinct possibility (*ibid.*: 108–9). There are records of the discovery of Civil War burials throughout England, such as that of a number of Royalist skeletons, some of which retained traces of clothing, on the Warwickshire Sites and Monuments Record (SMR).

Castles also have information relating to those who fought in the wars of the seventeenth century. Pontefract Castle in Yorkshire held the remains of men probably killed in the siege. Six graves from this period have been found – possibly part of the Royalist garrison – with one skeleton, Grave 043, displaying a clean unhealed blade-weapon wound to the frontal bone (Roberts, 2002). Sandal Castle, also in Yorkshire, yielded the remains of nine men from the Civil War levels, all of whom had been deliberately buried – one had been in a coffin (perhaps Major Ward) and the green stains on some of the bones of the other men indicated the presence of a now-corroded shroud pin. These men ranged from 16 to 40 years of age and had an average height of 169cm. Two men were between 16 and 18 years old, and seven between 20 and 40 years. One of the younger men had suffered a severe soft tissue injury to his right hip. This tear had resulted in ossification of the wound (Manchester, 1983a: 55, plate 18).

UNKNOWN WARRIOR 9

Five of the men buried at Sandal Castle displayed signs of trauma; Graves 535, 536 and 541 had small irregular pieces of ferrous metal on the floor of the grave. In Grave 536 this was near the left loin of the skeleton, in 541 the metal was present below the right innominate/right loin, and in 535 below the left innominate. 'It is probable that this metal is from one or more of the mortars which exploded within the castle during the siege . . . [this] metal may have been responsible for death, either immediately due to haemorrhage from soft tissue injury to spleen, liver or kidneys; or subsequently due to consequential wound sepsis' (Manchester, 1983b: 337).

Burial 535 had serious congenital abnormalities that Manchester believed might have precluded him from active combat duties due to the flattening of the femur heads as a result of bilateral congenital acetabular dysplasia. This would have caused No. 535 to have had the unusual gait which is associated with this degenerative joint disease and he would have been in some pain. Manchester postulated that this illness would have meant it was more likely that the man performed domestic duties within the castle, or, perhaps, might have been the blacksmith as he was tall and powerfully built (ibid.: 337). That he had a healed forearm or 'parry' fracture might be indicative of the kick of a horse.

On the other hand, a further wound suffered by this man in conjunction with his death in the siege, possibly as a result of mortar fire, and his

UNKNOWN WARRIOR 9
Burial 535 at Sandal Castle, Yorkshire
This powerfully built adult man was killed in the siege of Sandal Castle in the English Civil War. He had suffered a blow to the arm some time before his death and a cut to the head just before his demise. The danger of this latter wound had probably been offset by the wearing of some form of helmet. Burial No. 535 seems perhaps to have been killed by mortar fire brought against the castle by its besiegers (see Plate 17).

powerful stature might indicate that he performed some martial role, thus warranting his inclusion as one of our 'unknown warriors'. He had suffered a 30mm-long linear injury to the calvarium of the left frontal bone, perhaps the result of ante-mortem aggression. With this man, his frontal bone was abnormally thin and a straight blow would probably have caused more damage: 'the superficial nature of the injury may in fact indicate a cutting wound, or possibly a blow the force of which was impeded by head protection of some kind' (Manchester, 1983b). The man may also have been wearing some form of helmet.

UNKNOWN WARRIOR 10

A postern gate was located on the eastern side of the citadel at Basing House in Hampshire. As we have seen, this building, held by the Royalists, was besieged and taken by overwhelmingly superior Parliamentary forces in 1645 – a decisive year of the Civil War. Archaeological work to a gully inside this gate in 1991 produced a fascinating discovery within the gully's fills: a human skull and two cervical vertebrae and fragments of a third were recovered (see Colour Plate 11). Although some of the right side of the head was missing, the majority was intact and enabled investigators to make several observations. The head was almost certainly male and probably of someone 18–25 years of age (judging from the attrition of the teeth). The man suffered from quite severe dental pain, and the wear on the teeth suggested that this led to him favouring the use of the left side of his mouth to avoid having to use his right teeth. Allen and Anderson (1999: 99–100) suggested that the high levels of dental caries in a young individual might indicate the increased carbohydrate consumption of post-medieval populations. The skull also indicated that the young man suffered from iron deficiency anaemia.

The skull itself had a severe wound to its top – a 40mm-long lesion caused by a blade weapon. Although there is no evidence for this wound healing, it would not have been enough to have caused death, although blood loss could have been severe. The authors believed that the most likely scenario was that the man may have been rendered unconscious by this blow, and was then decapitated – hence the presence of only three vertebrae (*ibid.*: 100).

What set this man's skeleton apart from those of other individuals is that it both displays weapon injuries and comes from a securely dateable context, to a most violent single event in the English Civil War. Unfortunately, apart from the skull, there were no other elements of the skeleton that would enable further statements about the individual, though the material recovered revealed much.

UNKNOWN WARRIOR 10

One of the victims of the 1645 siege of Basing House, Hampshire

The remains of a man found in the destruction layers of Basing House, stormed and razed in 1645 during the English Civil War. The man was probably killed in hand-to-hand fighting by decapitation following a blow to the head. There is no evidence to suggest whether this is the head of one of the defeated Royalist defenders or of a Parliamentary attacker – the latter also lost many men in the fight for the house (Harrington, 2004: 10).

SIX

The Revolution of Industry:
Soldiers of the Nineteenth Century

Then it's Tommy this, an' Tommy that, an' 'Tommy, 'ow's yer soul?'
But it's 'Thin red line of 'eroes' when the drums begin to roll, –
The drums begin to roll, my boys, the drums begin to roll,
O it's 'Thin red line of 'eroes' when the drums begin to roll.

(Rudyard Kipling, 'Tommy')

The nineteenth century must surely have been one of the periods in which the lot of the infantryman changed most. Industrialisation ensured that the potential for them to kill or be killed increased exponentially – in greater numbers and at greater distance than before. Where 'industrialised' forces met those of more 'traditional' societies, slaughter could be huge; though not always of the latter. Training of troops was more commonplace, and, by the close of the period, the wounded private could at least expect a reasonable chance of good medical treatment for wounds afflicted or maladies suffered on campaign.

As literacy of the common man increased, so do our opportunities to study their written thoughts of campaigns, army life and privations. Further to this, we are also able to read accounts of their opponents. The infantryman's life and death are also covered in greater immediacy than ever before – in paintings and poetry, and by the new medium of photography. For the first time, images of the dead were available for mass consumption on the home front, and the role of the press would change forever.

It should also be remembered that not all those who served in nineteenth-century armies were male. The muster-out rolls of the Union armies in America, referred to by William Fox in 1889, included the following individuals:

Forty-sixth Pennsylvania, Company D: Charles D. Fuller; detected as being a female; discharged, date unknown.

One Hundred and Twenty-sixth Pennsylvania, Company F: Sergeant Frank Mayne: deserted Aug. 24, 1862; subsequently killed in battle in another regiment, and discovered to be a woman; real name, Frances Day.

Second Michigan, Company F: Franklin Thompson; deserted. (Charge of desertion removed by the House Committee on Military Affairs, Washington, Feb. 1887, the soldier having had a good record and had fought well in several battles, but proved to be a woman; real name was Miss Seelye.)

(Fox, 1889)

Since the nineteenth century is, in archaeological terms, very close to our era, we have much evidence, including upstanding fortifications, parade grounds, spreads of battlefield detritus and the remains of the combatants. In this chapter we shall examine some of these strands to evaluate the nature of the evidence for the life of the infantryman.

WEAPONRY

The soldier could now kill at a greater range and with greater speed. The nineteenth century saw a change from the standard use of musket to rifled breech-loading and, ultimately, bolt-action weaponry. Industrialisation enabled vast quantities of munitions to be used, which are still traceable on the battlefields of the era. Musket balls, bullets, and cartridge cases have been recovered from Waterloo to Khambula, Antietam to Spion Kop. Thus the fairly new discipline of battlefield archaeology is enriched. For example, although fundamentally a cavalry action and not in the remit of this book, movements of individual soldiers of the Seventh Cavalry are traceable through studies of the ballistics evidence retrieved from the site of the Little Bighorn battlefield (Custer's Last Stand, 25 June 1876) in the United States (Scott *et al.*, 1989).

The study of the infantry through scatters of munitions is not without its problems. Recent examinations of the Crimean War battlefield at Balaclava (25 October 1854) have found not only spent munitions of this period, but also ammunition from the Second World War rendering metal-detecting spatial analysis surveys difficult to say the least (P. Freeman, pers. comm.).

Before we left Lisbon we had served to us, seven day biscuit, five day meat, and two day wine. Each man's kit consisted of one blanket, one watchcoat, two shirts, two pairs stockings and two pair boots, one pair of soles and heels, besides all other little etceteras, necessary to make up the soldiers kit. Sixty rounds of ball cartridges in the pouch . . . (Wheeler, 1999: 51)

As the account of his kit, written by Private Wheeler, light infantryman in the 51st Regiment in the Napoleonic period (from 1809), shows, the early nineteenth-century soldier had large quantities of musket balls available to him. Vast amounts of these were expended in the campaigns of the Peninsular War (1808–14) and also at celebrated set-piece battles such as Waterloo (18 June 1815). To date, relatively little systematic study of battlefields such as Waterloo has occurred, though much by way of spent musket balls has been retrieved, British musket balls being of .75 calibre while the French were of .69 (Pericoli, 1973: 73).

Large monuments, like the 'Butte du Lion', have irrevocably altered the landscape and made specific cluster studies more problematic. In many cases, the presence of an action is visible, in terms of buildings or trees pockmarked with musket-ball holes or stray munitions, but little else can be inferred from the artefacts. On other sites spent munitions indicate the areas of the line that came under pressure through attack.

Although rifles, including the Baker Rifle, were used by some Light Infantry regiments, such as the 95th Regiment, the standard weapon for the British Napoleonic infantryman, both in regiments of the line and in garrisons, was the 'Brown Bess' musket. It was muzzle loaded, the charge and ball being forced down by a ramrod, but its accuracy was poor, and, although the rate of fire was higher than a rifle to a ratio of around 3:1 or 4:1, the main tactic with their utilisation was to provide an overwhelming volley at point-blank range. There would be no need to aim – simply to produce a maelstrom of lead through which opposing cavalry and infantry could not pass unscathed. Excavations of a Victorian cottage close to the Berry Head Forts in Devon yielded artefacts associated with the late eighteenth- and early nineteenth-century activity locally, including a hammer from a Brown Bess musket (Armitage, 2004: 6).

The Crimean War (1853–6) was not just fought at well-known sites like Balaclava; many actions took place further afield. The massive Russian fortress of Bomarsund, on the Ålund Islands between Sweden and Finland, was bombarded by British warships and assaulted by *c.* 12,000 French troops.

In 1982, at the Notvik tower, rubble was cleared away and archaeological research carried out. Several finds relating to the infantry garrison were recovered, revealing information as to the weaponry used. Musket and rifle bullets (mostly spherical lead balls of diameter 16.5–17.5mm and up to 21mm) were uncovered, as was evidence for use of Belgian-made Lüttich smoothbores. Perhaps most interesting were the finds of two broken musket butts and at the bottom of a cistern, cartridges with paper wrappings and gunpowder (Löndahl *et al.*, 2001: 217). So archaeology can reveal a change in type of firearm with cartridges now being seen to replace the powder flasks of preceding generations.

Recent archaeological work has given us further clues as to the nature of combat and the myths surrounding a number of engagements. Artefacts relating to weaponry are included in this. At the crossover of musket to rifle use there are an increasing number of academically rigorous studies of fields of conflict by archaeologists such as Tony Pollard, on the Anglo-Zulu War (1879), and several individuals on the American Civil War (1861–5).

Excavations of American Civil War sites show the vast range of firearms available to both Confederate and Union infantrymen. More than 370 different types of guns and at least 65 different calibres, ranging from .220 to .858, were used throughout the war, and it was a taxing logistical challenge to keep all the weapons supplied with the proper ammunition (M. Espinola, pers. comm.).

At Brawner Farm (Second Manassas) on 28 August 1862, intense fighting around Brawner's House left many traces of the battle. About forty artefacts have been excavated from their original historic context here. The study by Potter *et al.* (2003: 14–16) revealed the presence of the following: fired and unfired percussion caps, both impacted and unfired .69 calibre musket balls, impacted .58 calibre three-ring bullets, impacted .54 calibre three-ring bullet, impacted .54 Gardner bullet, knapsack hook, Austrian Lorenze rifle-musket gun-tool and even a bullet carved as a chess piece. As we know from written accounts that their right flank was located around these outbuildings, it is inferred that the 4th Virginia Regiment was using all these weapon forms. The rings on the bullets mentioned above would have facilitated spinning of the projectile, enabling greater range and accuracy.

At the battle site of Ox Hill (Chantilly), fought on 1 September 1862 during a thunderstorm, numerous artefacts associated with Pender's North Carolina and Field's Virginia Regiments also serve to illustrate the plethora of available arms and multitude of suppliers. Italian Carcano bullets (frequently associated with North Carolina militia units), a Prussian .69 calibre bullet, a Belgian .69 calibre bullet and even an English .75 calibre (Tower Musket) ball were recovered (M. Espinola, pers. comm. – see also Nash, 2004, for this site). The problems encountered with these firearms are revealed by the findings of tools designed to correct faults. If powder was wet, as would have been the case in the storm at Ox Hill, then the gun would not function and powder and lead projectile would have to be cleared (wet powder could lead to battles being abandoned (see Holmes, 2001: 196)). One .69 calibre all-in-one gun-tool found here included a screwdriver, nipple wrench, and a vent pick to remove powder from the fouled touch-hole of the weapon. If this failed and the wet powder rendered the weapon useless as a firearm, there was no choice but to use the bayonet, or the butt of the gun as a club – a situation that occurred at Ox Hill.

A tool known as an Enfield 'worm', which acted as a type of corkscrew to remove blocked projectiles, was also found. This could be fitted to the end of a soldier's ramrod and used to extract the bullet. In this case, a .58 calibre 'minié' bullet was attached to the end of the worm and there were other bullets that seem to show that they have been pulled twice by a worm, having misfired both times (M. Espinola, pers. comm.).

During the salvage survey of the Ox Hill battlefield, unfired lead bullets were recovered that were discarded when the paper cartridges had become wet during the violent storm. The discarded wet paper cartridges, of which only the lead bullet remained, clearly outlined where the combatants had stood in their regimental line of battle. Even during the storm some of the weapons would still fire but after being gradually exposed to the rain, most of the ammunition in the soldier's cartridge box had become wet and unserviceable. Impact zones represented by groupings of fired bullets were also able to provide information on what parts of the battleline had come under fire and were under the heaviest attack. These groupings of fired bullets and the 'bread trail' of discarded bullets were critical in determining where the combatants had been positioned. This was especially helpful in determining where the second Confederate battleline was established to stop the Union breakthrough on the Confederate centre and for identifying the previously unknown location of the battleline on the east side of the battlefield. (M. Espinola, pers. comm.)

Cornelison Jr has examined the archaeological potential of the battlefield of Chickamauga (18 September 1863), using metal-detecting surveys to evaluate the nature of retreat of Union units. Artefacts from this site included unfired minié balls, caltrops (iron spikes for use against cavalry), percussion caps, bullets of various calibres, an Enfield-type ramrod, iron rifle-band spring clips, a bayonet scabbard tip, 14 buckles (two of which came from a knapsack), and an army belt buckle (Cornelison, 2003: 298–300). The author concluded that the scatter of artefacts showed that, in retreat, some units were 'stable' as they passed through the area, though other 'individuals or units passed through the area in tactically unstable conditions with little to no semblance of military order' (ibid.: 304), their munitions and equipment being freely discarded with no clear evidence for a fighting retreat.

Sterling (2003: 324) also notes the wide range of firearms used by the American infantryman in the Civil War and the effectiveness of the new rifled weapons: 'Minié's bullet design led to an increased effective range for the musket from a smoothbore's 100 yards to 400 yards for a rifled musket.' This could also have had its downside, as such development of firepower did not always go hand in hand with an updated style of battle plan; as Sterling (ibid.: 325) noted 'the new rifle musket made Napoleonic tactics both obsolete and more deadly. The average Civil War infantryman suffered from the combination of technological improvements and the resistance of many field commanders to adopt tactics suited to the improved fire power and accuracy.'

The British Empire came into conflict with indigenous peoples across the globe as part of its nineteenth-century expansionism, wars against local forces in Africa being a case in point. In 1879, Imperial troops faced the Zulu warriors of King Cetshwayo in the Anglo-Zulu War and by the turn of the century were again engaged in South Africa – this time against the Boers (1899–1902).

The 1879 campaign is frequently depicted as one of the greatest clashes of military styles – of highly disciplined, well-armed, well-drilled, well-supplied troops up against a 'savage' spear-wielding opponent. This is as erroneous as it would be to depict the defeat of Custer at the Little Bighorn as being by 'savages' armed with bows and arrows. Indeed, from Doug Owsley's studies it appears that Custer's foes were, in fact, armed with more modern, efficient weapons than were the Seventh Cavalry (Scott et al., 1989).

For years, collectors were able to retrieve artefacts from the battlefields of the Zulu War with the majority being taken from Isandlwana and Rorke's Drift, the two best-known engagements of the campaign. This highlights one of the problems for archaeologists intent on discerning much about individual engagements through artefact studies. The rebuilding of the mission station at Rorke's Drift in 1882 and the use of a bulldozer in 1979 to organise the site for the centenary celebrations have severely altered the potential for spatial analysis – in much the same manner as the Waterloo monument.

Those who were not killed at this place formed again in a solid square in the neck of Isandhlwana. They were completely surrounded on all sides, and stood back to back, and surrounding some men who were in the centre. Their ammunition was now done, except that they had revolvers which they fired at us at close quarters. We were quite unable to break their square until we had killed a great many of them, by throwing our assegais at short distances. We eventually overcame them in this way. (Uguku of the UmCijo ibutho [regiment], in Emery, 1977: 87)

One of the great legends of the disastrous (for the British) battle of Isandlwana on 22 January 1879 was that the British position was taken by the Zulus as a result of the infantry running out of ammunition for their Martini–Henry rifles, because the men found it extremely difficult to open the ammunition boxes in the battle. Studies by Tony Pollard, Neil Oliver, Ian Knight and Len Van Schalkwyk on this battlefield are perhaps changing this hypothesis.

According to historian Ian Knight, the survey team on the battlefield found spent cartridges – some further forward than the British front line had been thought to be – strapping from ammunition boxes and camp debris (Knight, pers. comm.). Other finds of foil handles and possible foil from the tops of the ammunition boxes right up at the front line were made, as were the nails and hinges of an ammunition box (Andrew Greaves, 2000). Supplying the front line with ammunition was not the problem – it was much more likely that the British were simply outnumbered, out-generalled and outfought on the day. Some evidence for last, desperate and futile stands made by British infantrymen is also inferred from distinct clusters of Martini–Henry cases. One such grouping, in this case of five cartridges behind a large rock, was thought perhaps to be a last shelter for a British soldier, who used the boulder as cover for sniping at the Zulus until he, too, was probably killed (*ibid.*: 5).

Further items pertaining to weaponry have been recovered from excavations on combat sites of the Anglo-Zulu War. It was already known that the Zulu army was not simply armed with stabbing spear (assegai) and club (knobkerry); a large number also had firearms, admittedly generally obsolete, with weapons such as the muzzle-loading Tower Musket and percussion Enfield. As is confirmed by Laband (1987: 23), writing on the aftermath of the Battle of Khambula on 29 March 1879 and the capture of weaponry, 'of the 325 taken, only 15 were breach-loaders. One of these was a Snider Carbine marked as belonging to the Royal Artillery, and the other 14 had belonged either to the 24th or 80th Regiments, showing that they had been captured wither at Isandlwana or Ntombe Drift on the 12 March'.

Excavations took place during 1983–93 at Rorke's Drift, where a handful of British troops held off a series of attacks by Zulus who were largely the reserve of the force that had overwhelmed the camp at Isandlwana. Though much artefact collection has gone on here – from 1879 onwards – there is still enough material to offer clues to what the fighting was like, particularly for the infantryman.

One major reason for the British success in holding the mission station was the fact that the Zulus were unable to get the better of the British infantry in the firearms stand-off. Although the Zulus were generally armed with inferior weaponry, it is the topic of current debate as to whether several Martini–Henry rifles from those fleeing the carnage of Isandlwana were picked up by the Zulus and used against the British here (Adrian Greaves, 2002: 414–15). The Zulus were firing from caves on the slopes above the mission station, known as the Oskarsberg (Shiyane). Greaves (*ibid.*: 341) wrote: 'At least three slugs of a .577 calibre were recovered from a cave overlooking the battlefield. Furthermore, during construction of a car park in front of the battlefield, similar wax-moulded, fired slugs were recovered. These discoveries suggested that the team were recovering bullets that had been used during the battle of 1879. The fact that many of these slugs were recovered from the car park area (to the north of the battlefield) confirms reports that the Zulus were overshooting their targets.'

Although the rifle butt could also be used in an offensive role for hand-to-hand engagements, at close quarters 'cold steel' would still be the weapon of choice. The bayonet would have been a feared weapon and, in close square formation, would have been enough to deter or defeat cavalry actions superseding the role of the pike. Scabbard tips for bayonets have been recovered from places such as the battlefield of Antietam in the American Civil War, 17 September 1862 (Potter and Owsley, 2003). The bayonet had to be used to force home an action when powder became wet, as at the Battle of Ox Hill. However, this most visceral of combat forms probably resulted in relatively few casualties when compared with the destructive capabilities of artillery and massed firearm use. Indeed, Martin Howard, when writing on the subject of Wellington's doctors from the early nineteenth century, stated: 'The cold steel of the bayonet may have had a psychological effect, but actual bayonet wounds were rare. In a French study of the casualties of a hand-to-hand mêlée between French and Austrian troops, the musket ball wounds outnumbered the bayonet wounds by more than twenty to one' (Howard, 2002: 127).

Archaeological discoveries of weapon parts (especially munitions) can therefore help to determine the presence (or otherwise) of the infantryman in certain locations, and sometimes even of individual units. They can help to dispel myths put forward to explain particularly damaging defeats and can illustrate exactly what types of weapon were available to the soldier in particular battles. Clearly, the nineteenth century was one of huge change for the footsoldier as the efficacy of his firearms increased considerably.

ARMOUR AND COSTUME

The place is completely strewed with broken shells, breastplates, pouches, scabbards and caps, both of French and English.
(On the aftermath of battle in the Napoleonic period;
Wheeler, 1999: 80)

By the seventeenth century armour was going out of favour with the infantry and by the nineteenth century it had all but disappeared. Breastplates were still being used by the cavalry during the Napoleonic period, though even this branch of the armed forces had no real use for such protection as the twentieth century dawned, firearms having rendered it useless. Armoured covering would only again be widely seen with the advent of the tank in the First World War, with the exception of snipers who would sometimes make use of armoured protection.

After major engagements in the nineteenth century, the battlefield was often littered with artefacts associated with infantry costume. Buttons, hats, boots and other such items would be scattered across the area of conflict either still attached to the dead, or torn off as a result of explosion, looting or the agonised death-throws of the vanquished. As archaeologists, we can benefit from these traces by being able to denote the presence of particular units or to see the types of costume worn into battle. Indeed, the nineteenth century was a period of great change; not only was armour abandoned, by the close the British had even swapped their famous red coats for a camouflage-friendly 'khaki'. 'Khaki (from the Persian for dust-coloured) made its appearance in the Mutiny [the Indian Mutiny, 1857], when white uniforms were dyed locally with materials that included coffee, curry powder and mulberry juice: the 32nd cooped up in Lucknow, even used the office ink' (Holmes, 2001: 191). British troops would still wear their famous red coats in the Zulu Wars of 1879, but the need for camouflage was evident during setbacks in the Boer War. This was a harsh lesson to be learned and something that the French 'Poilu' would get to understand in the First World War, as their red trousers were highly visible to the enemy. 'It had been the fate of many hundreds, when they had sat down because of weakness or necessity, that their clothing had been brutally torn from them and, where they could not defend themselves, they froze to death naked' (Walter, 1991: 90).

At the site of the burial pit of many of Napoleon's ill-fated forces of 1812 in Vilnius, much by way of costume has been found. An officer's hat and military boots are included in this inventory. The skeletons found were not simply of males; the army would have included many women – wives, cooks, tradeswomen, washerwomen or suchlike. The remains of at least twenty-seven women have been positively identified here, one of which was wearing a jacket of the 61st Line Infantry Regiment – perhaps taken in an unsuccessful attempt to defeat 'General Winter' (Jankauskas, pers. comm.). Jankauskas also attributes the cutting marks on the left shin of one individual as perhaps being the marks left when somebody tried to remove the shoes from a frozen body.

The fact that clothing was taken from the bodies of the dead by the barely living in the terrible struggle against the cold is born out by a German infantryman Jakob Walter, who wrote in some detail on the subject of the 1812 retreat: 'It was not possible to recognise one another except by voice. Everyone was disguised in furs, rags, and pieces of cloth; they wore round hats and peasant caps on their heads, and many had priests' robes from the churches. It was like a world turned upside down' (Walter, 1991: 71).

Walter was one of many non-French troops serving among the ranks of the Grand Armée – the Lithuanian excavations have shown this in great detail. Certainly the 123rd Infantry Regiment was at Vilnius – a fact revealed by the presence of buttons from this unit in the death pit. In addition, buttons of the 21st and 29th Infantry Regiments have been recovered.

Excavations at castle, barrack and prison sites also indicate that the presence of particular units and buttons, as we have seen, is an excellent indicator. Archaeological fieldwork at Portchester Castle, Hampshire, has yielded evidence for both prisoner and guard regiments. The French buttons from this site, dating to the French Revolutionary and Napoleonic Wars, included the 4th, 14th and 16th Infantry and also the 65th, 66th and 82nd Regiments. In addition, other buttons were of the Garde de Paris First and Second Battalions. Going on the button evidence, the British regiments used to guard the prisoners included the Shropshire Militia and the 12th (East Suffolk) Regiment of Foot (Cunliffe and Garratt, 1994: 108). Shoe buckles were also recovered from the gravel surface of the airing yard, and, as this surface was not laid until 1810, this shows that shoe buckles were still used in the early nineteenth century (*ibid.*: 89).

Brixham Heritage Museum has been excavating a series of Napoleonic forts guarding the approaches to Torbay in Devon, and the work has revealed much information relating to British soldiers of the period. The buttons from this site included examples of the 3rd (East Kent), 62nd (Wiltshire) and 51st (2nd Yorkshire) Regiments of Foot stationed here from 1808 to 1810, while one from the 28th (North Gloucestershire) Regiment was found, once having belonged to a soldier who was here on recruiting duties and stationed in the fort between 1811 and 1813 (see Berry Head Archaeology, 2000; Armitage and Rouse, 2003). Intriguingly, a button of the 37th Line Regiment (France) was also found (Armitage and Rouse, 2003: 31).

Buttons had other uses for unscrupulous members of the infantry, as Rifleman Harris of the 95th Regiment recounted when referring to a stern speech on the subject by Marshall Beresford: 'I can tell you, it was a discourse which our men (some of them) much needed; for they had been in the habit of tearing off the buttons from their coats, and after hammering them flat, passing them as English coin, in exchange for the good wines of Spain' (Hibbert, 2000: 68).

Work on sites of the Zulu Wars adds colour to our picture of the action. At both Rorke's Drift and Isandlwana it is well known that the 24th (Warwickshire) Regiment of Foot provided the major portion of the British forces involved in both engagements. Excavations at Rorke's Drift yielded one of the distinctive sphinx badges of the 24th Regiment (Adrian Greaves, 2002: 340).

Perhaps more interesting were the finds associated with the defeated British forces at Isandlwana including a 1st Battalion 24th Regiment belt buckle on land known as Black's Koppie – possibly representing retreating British troops (Andrew Greaves, 2000: 4) – from a site designated as Area 3 of the battlefield by recent fieldwork. Here seven 1st Battalion 24th Regiment buttons were found in a row, around 8cm apart. This was presumed by the author to represent a British tunic that had been looted by the victorious Zulu army from one of the bodies of the British infantrymen and subsequently discarded on the eastern slopes of Isandlwana (*ibid.*: 3).

Buttons and elements of costume have been recovered from many of the fields of conflict of the American Civil War, and, as we shall see later, some of these are in direct association with the remains of those who paid the ultimate price of service as an infantryman in a combat force. The buttons from the archaeological investigations at Kenmore (close to the action of Fredericksburg in December 1862) were found in the formal gardens and outbuildings by a house. These reveal information on the contrasting sides of the war. The Confederates fighting here were largely composed of the Virginia militia and the buttons had the state motto *Sic Semper Tyrannis* under and image of Victus standing over defeated tyranny, and thirteen stars representing the states in the Confederacy with an initial eleven and possibly Missouri and Kentucky. The Union troops, on the other hand, had some rubber buttons as it was hoped that these would be non-reflective (George Washington's Fredericksburg Foundation, 2005).

The finds made during Espinola's salvage survey of the Ox Hill (Chantilly) battlefield over the years show that 'uniform' is something of a misnomer in many Civil War instances. On both sides, much of the fighting was undertaken by state militia (with their own particular costume), while Confederate forces were dressed in a more eclectic fashion than their Union counterparts – certainly this was the case post 1863. Prior to 1854, US Army general service buttons had an eagle with the letter 'I', 'C', 'A', 'R' or 'D' on them (depending on whether the serviceman was in the 'Infantry', 'Cavalry', 'Artillery', 'Rifles' or 'Dragoons'. Of the six burials where the main field hospital had been located at the Centreville fortifications, two had buttons stamped 'I', while others were of later non-unit-specific issue. A nondescript gilded flat button was also found on the Ox Hill battlefield, where a homesick Confederate soldier had crudely scratched his home and the initials F.E. as a form of a personal dog tag. Although one could purchase a patriotic identification tag from a sutler, many soldiers would instead write their name on a scrap of paper and put it in their pocket before going into battle. As was the case with 'Private F.E.', some soldiers found other creative ways of identifying who they were so that their families might know what became of them (M. Espinola, pers. comm.). The truly terrible effect of artillery on infantry ranks ensured that identification of the infantryman killed in combat was becoming increasingly problematical.

PRACTICE AND DISCIPLINE

At length the court martial was handed to the Colonel, he pointed to a deserter, saying, try him now, or he will escape tonight. The court martial was read, the sergeant and corporal was to be reduced and receive 300 lashes each, and the private 500.

(Wheeler, 1999: 70–1)

In terms of training, the Napoleonic infantryman had to be able to fire his musket or rifle, but perhaps even more important than this, other than for riflemen, was the ability to move into formation to give and frequently to receive fire. To manoeuvre into square to receive cavalry was also essential if the infantryman was not to be cut down in the open – as such, drill was vital.

Although with written sources there are many treatises on the disposition of troops for various required formations and texts on the methodologies of drill and discipline, in terms of archaeological deposits we are less likely to witness such works. However, Professor Barry Cunliffe's excavations in the Barrack Field at Portchester are interesting. Here, layers of well-trampled chalk marl were found, separated by a lens of grey chalky soil and then sealed by a layer of beach shingle – the whole being drained by underlying gullies. The excavator believed this excavation trench revealed a parade ground, something annotated in the plan of 1815 (Cunliffe and Garratt, 1994: 51–2). As such, this area might have witnessed some of the everyday training of British troops of the Napoleonic era.

Riflemen were a different case from infantry of the line: their weapons were far more accurate and had greater range, and they did not act as a unit. Instead, they were able to seek cover, to act on initiative and to choose their own targets, aiming to deliver a deadly, individual blow. Practice in use of the weapon was, for them, vital. Throughout the nineteenth century, the emphasis on proficient gunnery increased so that by 1853 it was possible for Lord Hardinge to establish a School of Musketry at Hythe, Kent, and by the turn of the century several ranges had appeared. In Britain, the range at Bisley, Surrey, was also important – and still exists in a similar capacity today.

Britain's role in conflicts in South Africa in the nineteenth century highlighted the need for practice in use of the rifle. Zulu marksmanship was comparatively poor in the 1879 war, as we have seen, but the Boers were able to inflict casualties far out of proportion to the size of their force by using their Mauser rifles against the British – this with good marksmanship abilities. Ranges became more common in Britain from the late nineteenth century to the beginning of the twentieth century, as the need to improve and practise shooting skills became paramount. Ranges are often seen on the Ordnance Survey maps of this time – the 1901 map of Pipley Bottom, Bitton, shows one such range, with its users firing from a position in Gloucestershire at targets in Somerset.

Practice works from the Napoleonic period have been found in Crowthorne Wood in Berkshire, England (N. Smith, 1995). A number of these appear to have been the legacy of military manoeuvres on Easthampstead Plain in order to practise the latest training manual in the light of the French Revolution (*ibid.*: 424). A series of small redoubts was constructed (six being marked on the 1876 Ordnance Survey 6-inch map) – perhaps to practise artillery usage.

The need to practise building trenches for defence and also for methods of overcoming such defensive barriers was to become all too apparent in the years of the First World War, as we shall see in Chapter 7. Perhaps less well known are examples of training trenches connected to conflict in the wars of the closing years of the nineteenth century. We know that such trenches were present on the British Army training area on Salisbury Plain at least by 1902. Here 'three 4 foot deep S-shaped Boer trenches, filled with standing dummies, were fired at both by guns and howitzers with fair effect' (quoted in McOmish *et al.*, 2002: 139). Nineteenth-century practice trenches are also located in Crowthorne Wood, perhaps cut by cadets from the nearby Royal Military Academy at Sandhurst. These have stretches of communication trench – possible areas for flanking fire and for signalling or observation (N. Smith, 1995: 433).

THE LIFE OF THE SOLDIER

Alcohol has always played an important role in the life of the infantryman: something to forget one's predicament, to pass the time, to instil courage and, at times, to ensure enlistment. The latter was the view of the Duke of Wellington, who said of his common soldiers, 'the scum of the earth' (Holmes, 2001: 148), that 'people talk of their enlisting from their fine military feeling – all stuff – no such thing. Some of our men enlist from having got bastard children – some for minor offences – many more for drink' (Howard, 2002: 156).

Once they had taken the king's shilling, drink continued to fulfil a role. Archaeological sites dating from throughout this period reinforce this view, as do the writings of individual soldiers. Private Wheeler, of the 51st Light Infantry Regiment of Wellington's Army, wrote of his embarking to mainland Europe: 'Our situation here is not very pleasant, the weather is cold and we have not much room to exercise ourselves on deck; one comfort attending us is gin and tobacco is cheap, so we can enjoy ourselves over a pipe and a glass' (Wheeler, 1999: 39). Cheap gin was ubiquitous, and it was stated by an early nineteenth-century magistrate that gin was the 'principle sustenance' of more than 10,000 people in London (Howard, 2002: 156).

Excavations by Barry Cunliffe at Portchester Castle, Hampshire, have revealed large numbers of finds relating to drink. Indeed, on the subject of the early nineteenth-century ceramics, he went as far as to say that the interest of the assemblage 'lies solely in the fact that they reflect military supplies' (Cunliffe and Garratt, 1994: 70). Portchester was used as a prisoner-of-war camp in this period. Many of the inmates were French, though, later, British military deserters were also interred. From Pit 260 (dating to *c.* 1794–1815), a grey stoneware tankard was recovered. This was covered in a brown slip and stamped 'Crown Inn Portchester' – the delights of the tavern were not off-limit to the infantry militia guards. Additionally, 111 fragments of wine bottles were found. All were dark green; seventy-three were base sherds and the remainder were of necks and shoulders, all of late-eighteenth- to early nineteenth-century date (*ibid.*: 84).

In Southern Africa British forces took alcohol with them as part of their supplies. These materials were in the camp at Isandlwana, and the noxious liquids fell into the hands of the victorious Zulus in January 1879:

> all of the white men had been killed, and then we began to plunder the camp. We found *tywala* [drink] in the camp, and some of our men got very drunk. We were so hot and thirsty that we drank everything liquid that we found, without waiting to see what it was. Some of them found some black stuff in bottles [ink], it did not look good, so they did not drink it; but one or two men [who] drank some paraffin, thinking it was *tywala*, were poisoned. (Warrior of the uMbonambi at Isandlwana, in Emery, 1977: 84–5)

Gin was still an important spirit at the time of the Zulu Wars, and the excavations of the remains of the mission station at Rorke's Drift have yielded large numbers of glass fragments. Although many items had melted, perhaps as a result of the fire in the hospital building as part of the action, much was identifiable. Around the store buildings were a number of dark-green glass fragments, which 'probably derive from spirit bottles. Two square-based gin bottles were partially recovered' (Adrian Greaves, 2002: 343). Holmes recounts a tale of the drive for alcohol in the Crimea: 'Few British soldiers could match the single-mindedness of a Zouave [French soldier] who sold his boots to buy drink and blacked his feet for the sake of appearances' (Holmes, 2001: 406).

British military forces did not only consume alcohol. Alongside eight nineteenth-century port bottles and nine or ten whisky bottles, a ginger beer bottle was also recovered from the rubbish dump of the Boer War period British Fort Schanskop, near Praetoria, South Africa (Pienaar, 2002).

If spirits were the poison of nineteenth-century European armies, troops in the American Civil War did not go without. Recent excavations of the large US Army Civil War depot in Jessamine County, Kentucky, have also revealed the popularity of beer. Among the glass and ceramics were many tavern wares – most common of which was the 6oz tumbler. There were also eight ale glasses. In terms of bottles, seven whisky, three gin, eleven wine and seventeen beer vessels were recovered (McBride, *et al.*, 2003: 99). The presence of a soda water bottle at this site also showed that non-alcoholic drinks were not ignored.

Smoking, too, continued to comfort the troops. In a letter written in the year of Waterloo (from Grammont in Belgium, 29 May 1815), Private Wheeler wrote: 'We are in excellent health and spirits and have the best of quarters. The people are remarkably kind to us. I with one man are quartered at a tobacconists, so we do not want for that article . . .' (Wheeler, 1999: 162).

Clay pipes have been found at several nineteenth-century military contexts including the Crimean War site of Brännklint (Löndahl *et al.*, 2001: 222) and at Portchester Castle, Hampshire. Finds at the latter included one known to have been made by a certain James Frost of Portchester, who was born in 1743 and died in 1827. In this assemblage there were 'Ten bowls. Seven had Prince of Wales plumes and arms on the bowl, all with the initials I.F. on the spur. One pipe commemorated the Battle of Trafalgar: it bore the word Trafalgar between figures of Nelson and Britannia' (Cunliffe and Garratt, 1994: 89). A further decorated pipe bowl was found during excavations at the American Civil War site of Fort C.F. Smith, where one of the garrisons had a pipe decorated with the likeness of a soldier in a kepi hat (Balicki, 2003: 143). So not only were these items used by the military; their bowls have martial statements on them.

Perhaps the most poignant evidence for the soldier's penchant for tobacco has been found at the recently discovered burial pit of the victims of Napoleon's retreat from Moscow at Vilnius. The director of these excavations, Professor Rimantas Jankauskas, a physical anthropologist at the University of Vilnius, has studied the skeletons that were excavated. Among the bodies was the skull of a young male (*c.* 20–25 years of age). This revealed extensive wear of the upper and lower left molars leaving a circular peroration to the upper and lower bite of the jaw. This was consistent with the frequent smoking of a clay pipe, which wears the teeth down over time (Jankauskas, pers. comm.).

I have had to endure sufferings and privations that are almost beyond belief . . . I have had to pass four nights out of five in the trenches under a constant fire from the Russian batteries. The ground was wet and sloppy . . . all our clothes are wet and in some cases this is what caused the death of so many of my fellow countrymen . . . I can say we have had plenty of biscuit and salt beef but were unable to eat it – no means of cooking. (I Death, 50th Company 1 Btn Coldstream Guards, Balaclava, Crimea; Suffolk Record Office, ref. 1970, Bury St Edmunds)

Famously, Napoleon believed that an army marches on its stomach (although this was perhaps not best illustrated by his planning for the 1812 campaign). Food remains should perhaps be expected on sites habituated by the nineteenth-century soldier. For this we are more reliant on camp and barrack sites, there being little time to eat and bury remains in a battle, although the defeated might leave traces of their preserved foodstuffs.

The remains of animal bones within rubbish pits can perhaps reveal the soldier's diet of choice. Excavations by the Brixham Heritage Museum of the Napoleonic period forts at Berry Head, guarding the approaches to Torbay, recovered several thousand animal bones, which had been thrown out by the garrison. If these are taken as being a representative sample, then it seems the soldiers subsisted on a diet of beef, mutton and fish (hake) with very little by way of pork or chicken (Berry Head Archaeology, 2000). Perhaps contemporaneous with these remains are the excavated mounds taken as being possible field kitchens at Crowthorne Wood, Berkshire. Here charcoal and sand, which had been scorched as a result of fire, were found in association with early nineteenth-century pottery in an area of military practice works (Manning, 1964; N. Smith, 1995: 424).

Despite the protestations of Private James Cook, D Company 24th Regiment of Foot that 'it is nothing but mountains here; all biscuits to eat' (Emery, 1977: 95), the British army in the Zulu wars was generally provided with meat. This is born out by finds of the remains of sheep, goat and cattle close to the front of Fort Bromhead at Rorke's Drift, where documents suggest they were slaughtered for food (Adrian Greaves, 2002: 342). Among the bottles recovered from this site, 'one bottle stopper bore the embossed letters of Lea and Perrins' (ibid.: 343), a well-known British sauce manufacturer.

Excavations at the British Boer War period rubbish dump at the site of Fort Schanskop, Praetoria, also yielded a Worcestershire sauce bottle alongside animal bones. In addition, one ceramic toothpaste container and two wooden toothbrushes were recovered – perhaps a necessity following this consumption (Pienaar, 2002).

Excavated sites relating to the American Civil War show not only the same presence of animal bones, but, in some cases, also the area of cooking. The discoveries by Potter, Sonderman *et al.* (2003: 23) at Brawner Farm are interesting: 'Excavation of the surrounding soil revealed a Confederate pewter copy of a US model 1858 canteen. Still in their original context were the iron roller buckles from the canteen sling and stains from the iron chain that had held the stopper to the canteen.' This was 'found alongside fire-cracked rocks, burned brick and mortar fragments and bones from cow, pig and horse with marks of crude butchery and burning' (*ibid.*: 24).

In the nineteenth century we benefit from the frequent press articles that were written during lengthy wars, discussing the conditions endured by soldiers on campaign. The American Civil War is a major case in point; an article in the *New York Times* of 1862 discusses the state of Confederate soldiers, their rations and the misleading belief that this indicated imminent defeat for the South:

DESTITUTION OF REBEL TROOPS

Correspondence from the vicinity of the rebel armies, and the reports of all those who visit their lines under flags of truce, concur in stating that 'extreme destitution' prevails among them. The men are found with rags tied around their feet instead of shoes; they are seen eating ears of green corn, cob and all; they search for, pick up and eat the bits of hard bread that our own troops throw away; while for clothing and tents a set of vagabond gipsies would excel them.

All of this sort of information is interesting, and it makes readable letters. We have had much that was similar heretofore, and it used to convey a certain degree of confidence to the country that the rebels were on their last legs, and might soon expect to succumb from sheer exhaustion of nature. But such delusive hopes no longer fill our breasts when we read these stories. They have augured nothing in our favour heretofore, and we do not trust them anymore. We have found that a shoeless army marches fifty miles in forty-eight hours, and surprises the best-shod army that any country has ever turned out . . .

The truth is, the rebel Generals strip their armies for a march, as a man strips to run a race. Their men are 'destitute' when they reach our lines, because they cannot cumber themselves with supplies. They come to fight

– not to eat. They march to a battlefield, not a dress parade. (*New York Times*, Monday 10 September 1862: 4, col. 4)

The size of armies engaged in this war entailed huge logistical organisation and, as part of this, large supply depots. At the US Army Civil War depot at Jessamine County, Kentucky, we have gained useful information as to the nature of food supplies for the troops. Tin cans, including of sardine, were recovered, as were 82 butchered bones (pig, cow, sheep, rabbit, fish – bass and pike – chicken and turkey. Additionally, Owen's House had 20g of eggshell. (McBride *et al.*, 2003: 99).

It was not only the British soldier who enjoyed preserves and pickles with his food, work at Fort C.F. Smith had finds of 'food bottles . . . for the garrison including bitters and medicine bottles also cathedral-style pickle jars and sauce bottles, ribbed mustard jars . . .' (Balicki, 2003: 143).

These days are passed as follows. After the morning parade every one is busy employed in cleaning appointments. This done the day is devoted to Athletic exercises, boxing, wrestling, running, picking up a hundred stones, some times on foot at others on horse back, cricket, football, running in sacks and any other amusement we might fancy. (Wheeler, 1999: 195)

Time spent in actual combat filled a relatively small proportion of a soldier's life. As a consequence, the infantryman suffered long periods of boredom punctuated by short, terrifying episodes of fighting. Archaeological work has uncovered elements of a soldier's life in terms of filling the duller moments of spare time, when they were left to their own devices.

Much of this may well have revolved around gaming of various sorts. The Napoleonic sites mentioned in this chapter yield traces of such activities; bone dominoes were recovered from the forts at the end of Berry Head (Berry Head Archaeology, 2000). Cunliffe's work at Portchester seemed to suggest a similar picture with three fragments of small boxes, made to hold gaming pieces, being found (Cunliffe and Garratt, 1994: 114). Indeed, several dice and six dominoes were also found on site – an apposite discovery, as the latter were a 'game introduced to Britain in late 18th Century by French prisoners' (*ibid.*: fig. 32). Finally, 'Two gaming fish were found in the outer bailey. They were used in connection with card games such as quadrille and are mentioned by Jane Austen in *Pride and Prejudice* published in 1813' (*ibid.*: 113).

Board games and dominoes were also popular in the American Civil War, the excavations at Brawner Farm producing a specially carved projectile. The author believed that 'judging by its shape, one bullet was probably a chess piece. During the Civil War, it was common for soldiers on both sides to carve bullets as a way of alleviating boredom' (Potter *et al.* 2003: 16–17). On the battlefield site of Chickamauga, lead gaming pieces were also recovered (Cornelison, 2003: 298–300), and dice and dominoes were recovered from Kenmore Farm. This latter site revealed a particularly poignant element pertaining to an individual infantry private. A stencil, belonging to Private Charles R. Powers, Company G, 19th Maine Regiment, was found in the garden of the site – this had been used to mark his belongings. 'Private Powers received a severe wound during actions at nearby Chancellorsville (May 1–3, 1863) and was taken to a Union hospital established at Kenmore. It was here that he died. His stencil, no longer of value to anyone, was discarded in Kenmore's gardens' (see George Washington's Fredericksburg Foundation, 2005).

Writings

The nineteenth century saw frequent war dispatches in the newspapers of countries involved in conflict, and there are great contemporary literary works of celebrated novelists such as Thackeray and Tolstoy. Increased literacy at this time has enabled the historian to examine a large number of letters written by the 'common man', by infantry privates rather than just the commanders. The soldiers also left their own personal scribblings on site. Prisoners (see page 162) often inscribed their name, initials or regimental number on the walls of their place of confinement. There is also the legacy left by soldiers in their campaign theatres – various monuments in Egypt were carved with the names of combatants in Napoleon's army.

The British, too, were keen to display regimental pride by carving their unit's crest. The best example of this is the crest of the 24th Regiment carved into the rocks of the Oskarsberg terraces overlooking the mission station at Rorke's Drift, South Africa, after the battle (Adrian Greaves, 2002: 348). This was perhaps accomplished not only to commemorate the remarkable action at the mission station itself, but also in memory of those other members of the regiment who had not been so fortunate at Isandlwana.

Regimental insignia are also carved and painted on to the rock faces at several places along the road close to the fort at Ali Masjid on the Khyber Pass on the northern frontier with modern-day Pakistan and Afghanistan – the Gordon Highlanders, South Wales Borderers, Royal Sussex, Cheshire and Dorset regiments are all represented. Some of these depictions are nineteenth century, others from the early twentieth century, including the 2/4th Battalion of the Border Regiment inscribed 1917–1918 (its Battle Honours list the Northern Frontier of India 1916 and 1917, and Afghanistan 1919).

Individual soldiers also carved names and regimental details as reminders of their presence. On analysis of a series of late-eighteenth- and early nineteenth-century inscriptions at the Brimstone Hill Fortress on St Kitts, West Indies, V.T.C. Smith (1995: 102) believed that such carvings can be separated into seven categories: 1. soldiers' names; 2. initials; 3. regimental references; 4. sayings; 5. dates; 6. drawings; 7. unknown. The graffiti could, of course, use combinations of all seven categories and thus we are able to distinguish individual soldiers and their regimental affiliations. 'George Swales' of the '3rd Buffs', for example (ibid.: 102), or 'J. Sutherland' '93 High . . .' '24 Oct 1829' – the 93rd Regiment, 2nd Argyle and Sutherland Highlanders (ibid.: 104). 'F' or 'T' 'Duffy' of the '28th' (28th Regiment – the 1st Gloucestershire Regiment) also left his mark (ibid.: 105). This shows that many soldiers were literate to a degree and desired to leave evidence for their existence.

The great rise in the interest in the common footsoldier in the poetry and paintings of the age is also interesting. Perhaps the most famous (and sardonic) of these poems is 'Tommy', by Rudyard Kipling – again, back to Private Thomas Atkins – the eponymous infantry private. The stanzas include the following:

Then it's Tommy this, an' Tommy that, an' 'Tommy, 'ow's yer soul?'
But it's 'Thin red line of 'eroes' when the drums begin to roll, –
The drums begin to roll, my boys, the drums begin to roll,
O it's 'Thin red line of 'eroes' when the drums begin to roll.

We aren't no thin red 'eroes, nor we aren't no blackguards too,
But single men in barricks, most remarkable like you;
An' if sometimes our conduck isn't all your fancy paints,
Why, single men in barricks don't grow into plaster saints;

The infantryman in the poem decries the public for its hypocritical attitude to the army at time of war and at the same time confesses that discipline could not possibly be maintained at all times. Kipling's own son, John, was killed while fighting in an infantry regiment, the Irish Guards, at the Battle of Loos, in September 1915 during the First World War.

Poetry does not simply examine the common soldier per se, but also deals with the 'heroic' figure of the Unknown Soldier killed in battle. It serves to emphasise the sacrifice of the soldier killed on campaign and demands remembrance, yet there is a strong streak of romanticism, lacking the bitter pathos of some of the poetry of the First World War. It should, however, be noted that many poems of the First World War, especially in the early years, could also verge on the sentimental – for example, Rupert Brooke's 'The Soldier', which contained the lines:

> If I should die, think only this of me;
> That there's some corner of a foreign field
> That is forever England.

(Silkin, 1979: 77)

In Britain, the Boer War was the subject of much attention from poets, leaving us with the celebrated 'Drummer Hodge', by Thomas Hardy:

> They throw in Drummer Hodge, to rest
> Uncoffined – just as found:
> His landmark is a kopje-crest
> That breaks the veldt around;
> And foreign constellations west
> Each night above his mound.

(Silkin, 1979: 75)

and also the 'March of the Dead', by Robert Service:

> They left us on the veldt-side, but we felt we couldn't stop
> On this, our England's crowning festal day;
> We're the men of Magersfontein, we're the men of Spion Kop,
> Colenso – we're the men who had to pay.
> We're the men who paid the blood-price. Shall the grave be all our gain?

You owe us. Long and heavy is the score.
Then cheer us for our glory now, and cheer us for our pain,
And cheer us as ye never cheered before.

The private in the American Civil War was also the subject of poetry – for example, the words of Margaret Junkin Preston in 'Only a Private':

Only a private – it matters not
That I did my duty well,
That all through a score of battles I fought,
And then, like a soldier, I fell.
The country I died for will never heed
My unrequited claim;
And History cannot record the deed,
For she never has heard my name.

Accommodation

In one corner of the room I have collected a quantity of dry fern, this forms my bed, it being necessary to strip to keep free from vermin. Every night the contents of my haversack is transferred to my knapsack. This forms my pillow, at the same time secures my kit and provisions from midnight marauders. The haversack is then converted into a night cap. Being stripped, my legs are thrust into the sleeves of an old watch coat, carefully tied at the cuffs to keep out the cold. The other part of the coat wrapped around my body served for under blanket and sheet.

(Wheeler, 1999: 74)

A soldier's accommodation would depend on whether or not he was on campaign. If he was, then his lot would vary from tent to billet or, particularly close to or during actual periods of combat, out in the field with little to no cover, as highlighted by Wheeler (above). Sleeping in the open was often unpleasant and a frequent gripe of the private, occurring throughout the nineteenth century. One shouldn't assume that those who served in Africa were spared the cold – Private Henry Moses wrote a mournful letter home during the Zulu War: 'We may never meet again. I repent the day that I took the shilling [enlisted]. I have not seen a bed since I left England. We have only one blanket and are out every night in the rain – no shelter' (Emery, 1977: 95).

For the archaeologist we are presented with the problem that sleeping in the open air under a blanket or similar will generally, bar the odd fire pit or slit trench, leave little or no trace in the archaeological record. We are thus reliant on excavations of barracks sites or of castles and forts at which the soldier was stationed, such as those of the Napoleonic and Crimean. Examples include the wooden prefabricated barrack huts that were provided for the troops at Berry Head in 1803 (Armitage and Rouse, 2003: 2).

Excavation evidence shows that soldiers who served as the guard for prisoners of war at Portchester Castle (1794–1810) gained accommodation in a place of much former grandeur. They were billeted in the southern sector of the inner bailey at Portchester Castle – in the old hall range of Richard II. This dwelling included a brick-built cesspit and well and also a fireplace, and was drained by a brick-built fire sewer flushed with water from the castle moat (Cunliffe and Garratt, 1994: 49).

Barracks of the American Civil War could have been temporary, flimsy constructions.

Architectural drawings show that building superstructures rested on either brick footers or wood posts. Excavations at Fort Ward in Alexandria, Virginia, uncovered brick piers associated with that fort's barracks. Considering that buildings were temporary, it is likely that little effort went into their construction. Evidence supporting the inferior construction was the destruction of a barracks by a summer storm in 1865. (Balicki, 2003: 132)

Now the whole camp was studded with several hundred bell tents as white as snow and as regularly placed as if it had been the work of much labour and time. (Wheeler, 1999: 111)

Within fortifications or entrenched positions there was always the possibility of tents providing shelter for the soldier. Pollard's (2001: 234) archaeological examinations of the fort at Eshowe, Zululand, showed that such cover was included in the British supplies; finds included 'tent hooks and brass eyelets, from tents or wagon tarpaulins: heavy iron wagon fittings, and an artillery shell . . .'.

Religion

In terms of artefactual evidence from archaeological sites, religion might be in the form of surviving religious texts, of inscribed devotional comments or the presence of the dead in cemeteries of a particular religious denomination, or with headstones to the same effect.

The religious affiliation of regiments is sometimes traceable through regimental chapels and the survival of nineteenth-century infantry colours in a particular cathedral or resting place. For example, the Queen's colour of the 24th Regiment of Foot, which was present at Isandlwana, is now in the Regimental Chapel of Brecon Cathedral. This standard was as important to British troops as was an Eagle standard to their nineteenth-century French counterparts or to Roman legions before them.

The presence of religious elements within the graves of the deceased is, perhaps, to be expected. On excavations at the bloody battle site of Antietam in the American Civil War (17 September 1862), which resulted in 23,000 soldiers being killed or wounded, Potter and Owsley examined one particular burial that had strong evidence for the Catholicism of the interred. The body was of a male aged 40–49 years with some arthritic changes. From his uniform and belongings it was inferred that the man was an infantryman of the Irish brigade that perished attacking Confederate positions at Antietam.

Three 'Miraculous Medals' and a crucifix with five wooden rosary beads were found in a civil war grave from Antietam (found in 1983 in a field on a sunken road or bloody lane). The rosary beads and crucifix were in Grave 4, which had the following inventory:

> 11 30 cal. buckshot (unfired)
> 3 .64/.65 cal. round balls (unfired)
> 13 percussion caps (unfired)
> 4 plain-shield eagle coat buttons
> 1 New York State cuff button
> 10 tinned metal, 4 hole buttons
> 1 white porcelain, 4 hole button
> 1 small iron roller buckle
> 1 knapsack hook
> 1 brass, cap box finial
> 1 brass, bayonet scabbard tip
> 1 clasp knife

1 miraculous medal
1 crucifix with 5 wooden rosary beads
1 .58 cal. CSA Gardner bullet (fired)
2 .577 cal. Enfield bullets (fired)

(Potter and Owsley, 2003: 62, table 4.1)

A knapsack tool and a roller buckle indicate this soldier was carrying his knapsack . . . A brass finial from the cap box and a brass bayonet scabbard tip suggest he was wearing his waist belt when he was buried . . . All of the soft-lead bullets – one .58 calibre Gardner and two .577 calibre Enfields struck bone, causing marked deformation in two of the slugs. It is very likely that these bullets caused the man's death. (*ibid.*: 63, 65)

Medicine

At six o'clock I took the knife in my hand, and continued incessantly at work till seven in the evening; and so the second and third day. All the decencies of performing surgical operations were soon neglected; while I amputated one man's thigh there lay at one time thirteen . . . It was a strange thing to feel my clothes stiff with blood.

(Charles Bell, surgeon, anatomist, on the subject of his work during the
Battle of Waterloo, 1815; Howard, 2002: 126)

The nineteenth century saw a gradual change in the lot of wounded soldiers. Armies often had respected surgeons (though these frequently prioritised treatments for officers (see Howard, 2002: 44)), and the understanding of the nature of treatment of wounds and the requirements for more sanitary conditions for patients grew. Celebrated campaigners for the treatment of soldiers emerged, such as Florence Nightingale in the Crimean War and Clara Barton in the American Civil War. Although hospital conditions at Scutari in the Crimea left a huge amount to be desired, the lot of patients was beginning to be highlighted and thus improved.

Traces of an American Civil War period field hospital at Winchester, Virginia, have survived long enough to be excavated. This tent hospital had been ordered by Surgeon James T. Ghiselin on 22 September 1864 (Whitehorne *et al.*, 2003: 158), and fieldwork revealed 'forty-one rectangular and two nearly square depressions [which] were identified as sub-floor features, constructed to serve as platforms for tent structures' (*ibid.*: 160). Limestone and handmade bricks on the site might also suggest the presence of hearths and chimneys.

The infantryman was still often subject to virulent spreads of diseases, and much of an army's strength was often incapacitated through illness. The wounded were not deemed as important as fit troops, who could still influence the outcome of a battle, and their transportation to places of treatment was often archaic – in rickety carts and whatever else was available.

Essential stores in the panniers included 'lint, surgeon's tow, sponges, linen, both loose and in rollers, silk and wax for ligatures, pins, tape, thread, needles, adhesive plaster ready spread, and also in rolls, opium, both solid and in tincture, submuriate of mercury, antimonials, sulphate of magnesia, volatile alkali, oil of turpentine, etc. etc.'. (M. Howard, 2002: 33)

The surgeons who worked close to or even on the battlefields of the nineteenth century had much to take with them in order to perform their allotted task. Some of this material has made its way into the archaeological record, but, as much is perishable, it is usually the containers that are recovered. Brixham Heritage Museum's excavations of the forts guarding the approaches to Torbay at the end of Berry Head have yielded medicine vials (see Berry Head Archaeology, 2000), while at another Napoleonic period site, Portchester Castle, parts of nine syringes (to deliver an enema) were found. These were common from *c.* 1800, although they all predate the gravelling of the airing yard in 1810 (Cunliffe and Garratt, 1994: 117, fig. 33). This technique was one certainly known to be used by the nineteenth-century doctor: 'Where all oral medications were seen to fail, and this was often the case, the army doctor might try other approaches, such as a variety of enemas, or the application of irritant substances to the skin to raise blisters' (Howard, 2002: 165).

Battlefield treatment was not always possible; recovering one's wounded comrades when under fire is still, today, a difficult action, and there were times when the wounded were simply left on the field to suffer often excruciating pain from ghastly wounds. Biting soft lead bullets was sometimes the only means available to ease their pain.

Mario Espinola's survey at Ox Hill recovered a .550 calibre Enfield bullet with a boxwood plug – a unique version of the Enfield pattern designed to provide a more snug fit with the barrel. Massachusetts units at the Battle of Ox Hill were armed with Enfield rifles imported from England, and it seems that a wounded soldier had bitten this bullet to alleviate some of the pain of his wound.

Casualties

> I could not without pity and some degree of horror look at the desolating scene around me . . . the dead and dying lying about covered with blood, sweat, and dust looks frightful, the wounded some in their last agony begging for water, others writhing under pain calling on some one to shoot them.
>
> (Wheeler, 1999: 32)

Casualty rates could be quite horrifying in nineteenth-century battles, though disease was generally a bigger killer than combat. For example, in the Crimean War, the British Army lost some 4,600 men in battle, while a further 13,000 were wounded and 17,500 died of disease. The casualties were just as bad in the Boer War, during which 45,000 Empire troops were reputed to have been killed. Single battles also had startling losses: 'On the second day at Talavera the 24th Regiment had 343 casualties out of a starting strength of 787. At Waterloo the 28th Regiment had 253 casualties from 557 men' (Howard, 2002: 34).

Given the perception of the infantry as being 'cannon fodder' in this period, the study of Howard into the medical profession of Wellington's Army is illuminating. He noted that, at least at the start of the nineteenth century, 'Officers also had a greater likelihood than the private soldier of dying in battle. In the last three and a half years of the Peninsular War, when the British Army had a field strength of just over 60,000, the total annual mortality from battle, including fatalities on the field and later deaths from wounds, was 6.6% for officers and 4.2% for the ranks' (*ibid.*: 33).

Many of those men wounded in battle would have gone on to die in hospital, which is probably what happened to Unknown Warrior 12 (see pages 170–1), and many of the victims of Napoleon's retreat from Moscow: 'At no point was there time to take care of the wounded. The most able-bodies had to advance as best they could; the rest found themselves in a hospital – and died there. This is what happened at Vilnius' (Bahn, 2002: 76).

With all the dreadful injuries inflicted by musket, rifle, cannon or sword, the stoicism displayed by the individual infantryman was often astonishing. Even taking into account a possible degree of exaggeration, there are many stories relating to private soldiers, such as this: 'A private in the 92nd Regiment had his arm removed close to the shoulder by a cannon ball, but was still able to walk off the field and casually remark to Morris's Regiment, "Go on, 73rd, give them pepper! I've got my Chelsea Commission!"' (Howard, 2002: 37). 'Chelsea' was a reference to the Royal Military Hospital in that part of London.

THE PRISONER

After a battle, the defeated soldier would face a couple of options if still alive; either he could attempt flight or otherwise he would be made a prisoner of war. This is, of course, assuming that his foe was willing to offer quarter. This was certainly not always the case in the wars of the nineteenth century. Private Wheeler wrote a chilling line on the actions of some of his Napoleonic War comrades: 'If you knew but the hundredth part of the atrocities committed by men calling themselves British soldiers it would chill your blood' (Wheeler, 1999: 196).

The Zulu War also saw the killing of wounded and defeated by both sides, something attested to by both Zulu and British combatants. Private John Snook stated: 'On March 30th, about eight miles from camp, we found about 500 wounded, most of them mortally, and begging us for mercy's sake not to kill them; but they got no chance after what they had done to out comrades at Isandlwana' (Emery, 1977: 173).

On the other side, a Zulu warrior, Muziwento, wrote of the British at Isandlwana: 'Some covered their faces with their hands, not wishing to see death. Some ran away. Some entered into the tents. Others were indignant; although badly wounded they stood at their post' (Laband, 1985: 17).

According to historian John Laband, after the Zulu defeat at Khambula, the British pursuit of the fugitives was dreadful, resulting in many Zulu deaths. 'It is well known that most of the dying Zulu expected no quarter (they usually gave none themselves), for they received none. Their pursuers were out to avenge Isandlwana and Hlobane only the day before, and as Major D'Arcy of the Frontier Light Horse exhorted his men: "No quarter, boys and remember yesterday"' (Laband, 1987: 28).

Those soldiers who were captured and incarcerated might have considered themselves to be, in some ways, fortunate. Archaeologically, we are able to denote the presence of prisoners on several sites. This can be registered through epigraphy, through the excavation of the prison camps, and through artefacts made by the prisoners themselves.

French prisoners of war from the Napoleonic period were held in several sites in England – at Norman Cross near Peterborough, Portchester Castle in Hampshire, and even in prison hulks (ships) in Portsmouth, reminiscent of Dickensian Britain.

Portchester Castle

Prisoners began to arrive at Portchester in March 1810 in the first instance decanted from the prison hulks in the harbour . . . the main influx took place between June and October, many of the men brought from the Mediterranean and from Portugal.

(Cunliffe and Garratt, 1994: 56)

The prisoners wasted little time leaving their mark on Portchester Castle. They inscribed their names, generally initials in the case of the nineteenth-century detainees, and dates on the walls; for example, along the outer face of the north side of the corner bastion. All recognisable names were French and dates recorded were '1796 (2), 1797 (9), 1799 (1), 1800 (2), 1805 (1), 1808 (2), 1810 (2), 1811 (3)' (ibid.: 69). There were a few possible American names (John Yarold, F. John Gill, Thomas Collins, and John Rigby) from 1796 to 1798 (ibid.: 69).

The phase that Cunliffe refers to as 'Period 3' (1794–1810) saw the castle's preparation for its role as a prison, resulting in several changes to the Medieval building, 'Nine prison huts provided accommodation for 4,500 prisoners. The keep and north range held perhaps another 2,500. The basement was used as a cachôt or "black hole" for the incarceration of recalcitrant prisoners while the upper floor is recorded in local tradition to have been an autopsy room' (ibid.: 49).

Later phases included the 'metalling of the airing yard with a thick deposit of beach gravel . . . in anticipation of an influx of new prisoners' (ibid.: 29). This took place between 1810 and 1815 during the final throes of the Napoleonic era in Europe encompassing Napoleon's defeats in the Peninsular

Wars (1808–14) and Waterloo (1815). After this, the castle was used as a prison for deserters, though this is archaeologically invisible.

Life at Portchester might not have been too dissimilar to barrack existence; conditions were rudimentary and far from comfortable. Boredom would have been a further problem and the French prisoners helped to alleviate this situation by crafting items from materials available to them. Such 'Prisoner of War Art' is now much sought after on the antiques market.

> Animal bones were extensively used by the prisoners to manufacture a wide range of items some for their own personal use, others to be sold to the local populace or to dealers. Bone shop models and bone boxes made in the prison camps were much appreciated at the time . . . As might be expected the excavations at Portchester have produced a number of bone artefacts and bone-working debris . . . (Cunliffe and Garratt, 1994: 110)

Similar prisoner-made objects were crafted at Norman Cross and are preserved in the nearby Peterborough Museum. As we have seen, much work was put not only into making boxes and models, but also into manufacturing bone gaming pieces. The results of this activity would have given the bored prisoner a further outlet for his energies.

Soldiers who were taken prisoner did not necessarily survive internment. The memorial to the 1770 French and Dutch soldiers of the Grand Armée on the Great North Road near Peterborough bears testament to this (see Plate 18). A pillar with a bronze eagle perched on its top was located at this point, close to the prison camp of Norman Cross (Yaxley barracks), which had opened at the end of the eighteenth century. The camp has gone and the bronze eagle was stolen (it was replaced in April 2005), but traces of the camp are still visible.

Andersonville Prison

For the infantryman, prison was not always an alternative to death, sometimes it simply meant that he died at a different location. One of the most notorious prison camps, as far as nineteenth-century soldiers were concerned, was Andersonville. This American Civil War site was the place of captivity for Union troops: 'At least 12,920 of the roughly 45,000 prisoners who entered its gates died as a result of malnutrition, exposure, dysentery, smallpox, scurvy, and various other diseases and sheer brutality' (Prentice and Prentice, 2003: 175). The camp commandant, Captain Henry A. Wirz, was later hanged for the goings-on in the camp. Substantial archaeological work has since been carried out at Andersonville, revealing much about the form of the prison and elements of life within its confines.

The original stockade had been built by slaves and had squared posts as shown by the excavations. Prisoners were made to build extensions to the camp and this, too, has been investigated: 'The 1987 SEAC Field investigations at the prison's northeast corner uncovered roughly 216 linear feet of stockade wall that was part of the 10 acre northern extension added in late June 1864.' In parts 'preservation of the stockade posts . . . was very good so it was possible to determine the placement and size of posts exposed in the trench . . . the prisoners had used unhewn pine logs rather than hand-hewn square posts used by the earlier slave gangs' (ibid.: 177).

Many of the objects recovered by these investigations related to the construction of the site, including an iron axe head, and axe head fragment, one brass and one iron buckle, 19 cut nails, and a brass fiddle-shaped padlock cover stamped with a crown symbol and the letters GR (ibid.: 179–80). Personal touches were also visible in this most de-humanised environment. Finds included a 'silver filigreed band with intact eraser [which] was all that remained of a pencil probably used to write letters home or perhaps to make entries in a diary' (ibid.: 186).

Escape

Not surprisingly, given harsh conditions at many of these prisons, the inmates would frequently try to escape. At Portchester, non-French inmates – those who were German or Swiss but still served in the Grande Armée – were sometimes recruited into the British Army, the King's German Legion, for example, so ending their imprisonment. After a change of English law in 1794, it also became possible for French men to enlist into the British Army (Holmes, 2001: 50). French prisoners would often attempt to escape from prison, too:

> many escapes were attempted and some succeeded throughout this period and particularly during the year 1811. Various means of escape were favoured: tunnelling is mentioned several times, on one occasion a rope

was used to help the prisoners scale the wall and in August 1812 the possible complicity of the turnkey was investigated. Escapees, when caught, were confined to the 'Black Hole' on reduced rations . . . (Cunliffe and Garratt, 1994: 158)

The traces of an attempted escape were excavated at Andersonville. 'During the 1990 excavations, a failed prisoner escape tunnel was also discovered along the southern stockade wall . . . Within the excavated units, the widest section of the escape tunnel was about three feet. Based on profile map reconstructions, the tunnel was approximately 20 inches high, just big enough for a man to crawl through' (Prentice and Prentice, 2003: 185–6). The tunnel failed as it had been cut through sandy soil, which collapsed and brought stockade posts down just 1m past the stockade line.

MEMORIALS AND BURIALS

Although individual leaders had been commemorated in the past, it was a relatively new occurrence to create memorials to those individual soldiers of low rank who had died in the service of their country. It started in the nineteenth century, in the wars of the British Empire, the American Civil War and Napoleon's campaigns. Names of battles were immortalised by the country that emerged victorious. Central Paris, for example, has a number of memorials to the conquests of Napoleon, including the Arc de Triomphe, the Gare d'Austerlitz and the Avenue de la Grande Armée. America has its Gettysburg and Sherman Avenues, although a civil war is, perhaps, more difficult to commemorate. Britain has Waterloo Station and numerous Alma Roads.

Perhaps, in terms of nomenclature, one of the more poignant memorials of nineteenth-century wars occurs at British Football Grounds. The Anglo-Boer War of 1899–1902 was one of the bloodiest learning curves ever encountered by the British Army. The Boers, though small in number, fought for a cause in which their belief was unshakeable. They made use of the terrain in which their local knowledge was crucial, and utilised the accuracy of the most modern rifles to inflict several defeats on supposedly stronger British forces.

The Battle of Spion Kop is one of the most well known of these engagements. In January 1900 British troops were pinned down on the hill, in very shallow trenches, by Boers who commanded the heights above them. Casualties were very high and many hundreds were killed. A large number of men who served in this battle had come from Lancashire and it was later determined that areas of terracing at several football grounds in this area would pay tribute to the service of their countrymen at this engagement. Hence, the Spion Kop (later simply the Kop) end at Blackpool and, famously, the Kop end at Liverpool. Other clubs – such as Bradford City, Birmingham City and Coventry City – also followed in this tribute.

The deeds of nineteenth-century regiments were also remembered in their home town or city, or on the battlefield itself. Many of these were raised some time later, when wounds from the event had had time to heal both literally and metaphorically. The battlefield at Waterloo is a case in point with monuments to all sides being raised – Dutch, German, French and British. The farmhouse of Le Haye Sainte, pivotal to the battle, has plaques on its enclosing walls to the sacrifices made by both British and German defenders, and also to the men of the Grande Armée who had stormed it.

In the age of the British Empire, Imperial might was often thrown against indigenous warriors who were armed with spear or sword as opposed to rifle and artillery. Despite the casualties suffered, all too often those killed by British forces not only had no marked grave, but also no memorial. Isandlwana is an exception to the rule. There, alongside the memorial to the 24th Regiment, and the whitewashed stones that mark the place of burial cairns, is a large monument to the Zulu forces that fought in the 1879 war. In America, too, there are Civil War regimental memorials throughout the country, such as the Shaw monument in Boston on which infantrymen are depicted in relief. It is in the nineteenth century that, for the first time, individual soldiers of lowly rank, rather than the great army commanders, are recognised in memorials.

Soldiers who are not named, but who serve to represent the common fighting man, have been given the term 'unknown soldier'. The individual infantryman was seen as the epitome of the sacrifice and struggle of the nation or cause. Although sometimes in heroic pose, it is more common for depictions of an unknown infantryman to be mourning the loss of fallen comrades or lying wounded in similar style to classical sculptures (such as the *Dying Gaul* – an ancient copy of which is held by the Capitoline Museum in Rome).

Many conflicts have been commemorated – from the memorial in London to the Guards regiments in the Crimean War (which also serves to depict the nurse Florence Nightingale), to the Boer War troops on monuments at Bury St Edmunds (Suffolk) and Cheltenham (Gloucestershire), for example. America is no exception, with statues of the Union or Confederate soldiers on memorials being common. In Georgia, to mention one state, infantry privates are shown from Abbeville (Wilcox County) to Waycross (Ware County).

Men who died in combat are also named (for example, on the obelisk to those British killed at Rorke's Drift in 1879), indicating that it had become important to remember individual dead – especially as mass burial was often still the only realistic option for those killed on campaign. There was no such thing as an identity disc in the nineteenth century for the infantryman and remains were often unidentifiable, especially when one considers the destructive power of artillery. Furthermore, immediate burial was not always possible; the British failed to bury their dead from Isandlwana on 21 January 1879 until five months later (20 June 1879), by which time they were skeletal (Van Schalkwyk and Taylor, 1999: 13). Burials here were of several individuals in a cairn, many of which have since been looted (*ibid.*: 13). Corpses were also robbed of items that might have served to identify them after the battle, both by soldiers and local people, some of whom were employed to bury the victims (Howard, 2002: 61). Loot was, of course, deemed by many soldiers to be one of the perks of the job. The above being the case, it is not surprising that archaeologists have excavated the last resting place of a number of soldiers who fought in the great battles of the nineteenth century – men whose names are no longer known to us.

THE FALLEN: UNKNOWN WARRIOR 11

Kutuzov seemed preoccupied and did not listen to what the General was saying. He screwed up his eyes with displeasure as he gazed attentively and fixedly at the prisoners who made a particularly wretched spectacle. Most of them were disfigured by frost-bitten noses and cheeks, and nearly all of them had red, swollen and festering eyes.

(Tolstoy, *War and Peace*, 1988: 1288)

In a ditch in the Lithuanian capital of Vilnius, several thousand human skeletons have recently been discovered. On excavation it became clear that these were the bodies of the remnants of Napoleon's Grand Armée, which had retreated from Moscow in the disastrous campaign of 1812. Harassed by

Cossacks, the survivors of the army staggered through temperatures of −35°C to the gates of Vilnius, where they died in droves.

> From a total area of 766 square yards (640 square metres) and up to four layers of corpses, a stupefying density was recorded . . . More than 3,000 skeletons were extracted from the matrix of sand by the archaeologists . . . Some of the cases are quite distressing. Some of the men were so exhausted that they died in a crouching position, frozen on their heels. One officer was still wearing his shako on his head, decorated with a red, white and blue rosette. (Bahn, 2002: 74)

Professor Rimantas Jankauskas has undertaken a detailed study of around 600 of these *c.* 3,300 poor unfortunates and has revealed many fascinating insights into their demise (the information below was kindly provided to me by him in many discussions). Trauma on the skeletons was not due to combat wounds – thus immediately discounting accounts of Cossack massacres or a bloodbath; it had been caused by the rough handling of the dead bodies. Limbs were known to snap off from bodies, which had frozen as a result of the extreme temperatures; others were damaged as they were thrown into the makeshift grave: 'There were perimortal fractures of longbones due to twisting, bending and blows with blunt objects' (Jankauskas, pers. comm.). Death came through cold, starvation and exhaustion: 'Again and again I turned from one side to the other, and in the end I was frozen stiff with my clothing. Only by marching did I overcome freezing. November 26, 27, and 28' – Jakob Walter Infantry Conscript, Regiment of Romig, No. 4 (Walter, 1991: 87).

Although there do not appear to be traces of wounds treated by field surgeons, a common complaint seems to be Scheuermann's disease or 'march foot'. These are fatigue fractures of the metatarsal bones of young soldiers not used to such heavy marching (see Plate 20). The soldier would feel pain, but he would not be disabled; he could continue to attempt his desperate escape. Walter illuminates this in his diary: 'When in the night a little moonlight appeared, I set out upon the march again, for, on account of the cramps in my feet, I could not lie still for a quarter of an hour' (*ibid.*: 87).

The skeletal evidence also provides other details, which add to our knowledge of these last, catastrophic days of the retreat and of the conditions endured by the soldiers. For the most part, these were the remains of quite large robust individuals of 'prime' fighting age, in their 20s and 30s. It seems that several of these soldiers suffered from some type of venereal disease – be it gonorrhoea, syphilis or another. Although debilitating, this would not have prevented active military service. Tertiary syphilitic lesions were present on a number of skulls at Vilnius.

Venereal diseases could be widespread among an infantry regiment, as Holmes (2001: 300) points out: 'On one day in 1844 the 63rd Foot found itself with 27 per cent of its soldiers infected, 112 with primary and 15 with secondary syphilis, and 125 with gonorrhoea.'

The bodies were tightly packed in the 'grave' (up to seven individuals per square metre according to Jankauskas (pers. comm.)), and thus it was very difficult to associate any of the artefacts with a particular person. But it seems possible that detailed studies of the properties of the skeleton (and the person's dietary changes in life) might reveal the Pan-European nature of Napoleon's army. Jankauskas believes that studies of several femurs have shown that some of the men were from the Poland/Lithuania region, others were from northern central Europe, while others originally came from southern Europe.

Professor Jankauskas has provided details of one individual – presumably a member of the infantry of the defeated Grande Armée – chosen at random, who is representative of those who died at Vilnius in 1812 and were buried in the ditch.

UNKNOWN WARRIOR 11

A member of Napoleon's Grand Armée of 1812

Excavated in September 2002 from Area 3

Skeleton 26

This is a young man, aged around 25–30 years at his death, who was found lying prone in the burial pit with his head to the north (see Plates 19, 20, 21). Around 173.5cm (5ft 9in) in height, he had a healed fatigue of the right third metatarsal (see Plate 20) and 'march foot', thought to have been sustained on the long retreat from Moscow. Although not directly associated with Number 26, a shoe of an infantryman of the line was found in the area. It is unclear how this young man died, as no fatal trauma is evidenced on the pathology, but one might deduce that he froze to death – the fate of so many at Vilnius.

UNKNOWN WARRIOR 12

The weather is quite comfortable. I have paid a visit to the old Chantilly battle field, two miles from here, and in which engagement the noble Kearney [sic] and the gallant Stevens fell. In passing over the field, what horrible scenes were presented to my view; I pray to God that I may never witness the like again. Human bones lay in every direction, half covered bodies met my gaze, showing that no pains had been taken in their burial, and revealing the horrors of a battle field, stamping indelibly upon my mind impressions that time can never eradicate.

> (J.C. Williams, Corporal, B Company, 14th Vermont Regiment, Fairfax Courthouse, 27 December 1862; Mario Espinola, pers. comm.)

The battle of Ox Hill (Chantilly) was fought as one of the engagements of the American Civil War on 1 September 1862. Unusually, it took place in a violent thunderstorm, which rendered much of the powder required by firearms useless. Greatly outnumbered, the Union troops under the command of Generals Stevens and Kearny, both of whom were killed during the battle, prevented the Confederates under 'Stonewall' Jackson from cutting off the Union Army's retreat to Washington. This was a bloody action in which the bayonet was liberally used in desperate hand-to-hand fighting, resulting in 2,100 casualties in just two hours. The bodies of many of the soldiers lay on the field for several days, and, in some cases – as Williams's letter reveals – cursory burial attempts led to bodies still being visible some months later.

Excavations in January 1997 recovered the remains of six unknown soldiers next to the main field hospital in Centreville, where a significant number of the wounded from the Battles of Second Manassas and Ox Hill had been treated. Victims from these battles would not normally have been buried in coffins – a shallow grave at their point of death being more efficacious for a hard-pressed army. The individuals here seem to have been buried in a coffin (as evidenced by the nails in the burial) – and had perhaps died sometime after the engagement, possibly in hospital. It is most likely that the burials occurred when the rescue party from Washington used the main hospital in Centreville as their base of operations to treat the wounded who had been abandoned on both battlefields. Espinola believes their presence in hospital would account for their varied state of undress and that Union civilians, who were part of the rescue effort, may well have made these coffins for the rank and file who had died while under their care (M. Espinola, pers. comm.).

The boys are gradually getting over the terrible Battle of Chantilly. It was a scene I shall never forget. It was wholesale murder to stand at the muzzle of the enemies' guns and have a volley poured into us. I had a very narrow escape of my life and being taken prisoner. A ball passed through my collar. (Private Henry Brown, F Company, 21st Massachusetts Volunteers. Leesboro, 8 September 1862; Last Salute, 2005)

UNKNOWN WARRIOR 12

A Union soldier from the Battle of Ox Hill, 1862

Civil War Burials, Centreville, Virginia

Site Number: 44FX1791-CW-300

Burial No. 3

A great deal of valuable work on the Battle of Ox Hill (American Civil War, 1 September 1862) has been undertaken by Mario Espinola, who found much historical and artefactual evidence for the struggle. Douglas Owsley, of the Smithsonian Museum of Natural History, examined Burial 3 from land adjacent to the location of the main field hospital in Centreville, Virginia. He found that the individual was a Caucasian male of medium build, around 1.65m (5ft 5in) in height and 28 35 years of age when he died. Fragments of uniform were present on the body, and the man had suffered a fractured jaw some months before he died.

This soldier had died from a gunshot wound to the head – as evidenced not only by both entry and exit wounds on the skull, but also by pieces of lead fragments from the projectile in and around the cranium. The buttons found with the individual were of brass and depicted an eagle with a shield (1854 design), showing that he was a member of the Union forces that died either in Ox Hill or perhaps in the preceding Second Manassas, as many men from the latter engagement were treated at this site (Mario Espinola, pers. comm.; also Archeological Recovery Report Civil War Burials, Centreville, Virginia. Site Number 44FX1791, Michael F. Johnson, Fairfax County Archeological Services).

SEVEN

Marching to Hell:
The Poor Bloody Infantry in
the First World War

Military Definitions: Infantryman . . . An animal of weird habits, whose peculiarities have only just been discovered. It displays a strange aversion to light, and lives in holes in the earth during the day, coming out at night seeking whom it may devour. In colour it assimilates itself to the ground in which it lives.

(*Wipers Times*, IV, 2, 20 March 1916, in Beaver, 1973: 44)

Archaeology of the First World War (1914–18) is a relatively new phenomenon. The conflict has generally been considered too recent and too well documented, and, because of unexploded munitions, the sites too dangerous for archaeologists to study in any depth. Huge swathes of France and Belgium suffered from the ravages of the First World War and an enormous quantity of ordnance was expended. Every year, the 'iron harvest' sees French and Belgian farmers ploughing up artillery rounds, Mills bombs, bullets and even gas shells. All this serves to ensure that any risk assessments written by field archaeologists working on sites with First World War elements have to be considered and that extreme care is taken during excavation.

Many of the sites have been and continue to be subject to development for roads, railways, housing and industry. Nowadays, archaeologists often have the opportunity to become involved before the land is disturbed, and, as a result, a wealth of information on the First World War is coming to light. In addition, examination of Gallo-Roman or prehistoric sites sometimes uncovers vestiges of the war through evidence from deposits cutting the earlier sites and from aerial photographs.

This chapter examines some of the finds that have come to light in recent years along the Western Front, the region of the conflict that, to date, has been the subject of most of the archaeological investigations. The battles that took place around a system of static trenches stretching from the Belgian coast to Switzerland resulted in the deaths of hundreds of thousands of men. Herein lies another deterrent to archaeological investigation, the macabre finding of human remains. One has only to consider the large number of men for whom there is no known grave, such as those recorded at the Menin Gate in Ypres, to realise that discoveries of this nature will continue for many years to come.

The fact that the First World War ended relatively recently has resulted in the excellent preservation of much of its related artefacts, although, as with all sites, this varies depending on the geology of the region. The waterlogged nature of many of the Flanders battlefields, due in part to the high water-table, has allowed organic deposits to survive that might not have done on drier sites. This level of artefactual information also helps to justify, should it be needed, our archaeological study. Such work is not simply the handmaiden of history; it can be a powerful tool in its own right and is especially useful when used in conjunction with historical documentation, oral testimonies and photographic images. After all, many of those who would have been able to tell the tale of the infantry were killed in action, and their story – how they lived and how they died – can be derived only through archaeology.

By concentrating on the troops in formalised infantry regiments, the examples featured in this chapter are almost exclusively male. This is not to say that women were not involved in the fighting on the Western Front – indeed, a French woman, Émilienne Moreau, was awarded the Croix de Guerre by her government for killing two German snipers when she was in the front line at the Battle of Loos in April 1915 (Jones, 1997: 199). In addition, some women disguised themselves as men in order to travel to the front. Although contradicting almost every contemporary military edict and social taboo, 'a few individual British women nonetheless managed to serve in the armed forces. Dorothy Lawrence, an aspiring journalist, disguised herself as Private Denis Smith. She was able to spend ten days on the Western Front with the Tunnelling Company of the British Expeditionary Force before she confessed her true status to her superior officer' (Grayzel, 2002: 54).

WEAPONRY

Given the close historic proximity of the First World War and the plethora of war museums, film footage of troops and photographs of participants, one might think that archaeology could add little to our knowledge, certainly in terms of weaponry and its usage. Before looking at the items that were indisputably used in combat, we must consider the conundrum that soldiers at the front were liable to improvise in an attempt to survive. Artefacts viewed as humdrum in the archaeological record by those who excavate them might have been used for an altogether more deadly purpose by those who fought in the trenches.

> Our greatest trial was the German canister – a two gallon drum with a cylinder containing about two pounds of an explosive called ammonal that looked like salmon paste, smelled like marzipan, and, when it went off, sounded like the Day of Judgement. The hollow around the cylinder contained scrap metal, apparently collected by French villagers behind the German lines: rusty nails, fragments of British and French shells, spent bullets, and the screws, nuts, and bolts that heavy lorries leave behind on the road. We dissected one unexploded canister, and found in it, among other things, the cog wheels of a clock and half a set of false teeth. (Graves, 1960: 1361)

Here lies one of the major problems confronting archaeologists as they try to interpret the battlefield. The sheer quantity of munitions expended over a relatively small area by forces that were relatively static over a long period renders an analysis of troop movements through a ballistics study very difficult, though it is possible to denote the presence of particular armies. The situation is not rendered any easier by the redepositing of artefacts such as in the example above of British and French shell case fragments and spent bullets. An analysis of the material record, without access to accounts, would lead the archaeologist to conclude that these items were just that – part of a set of false teeth (these are, on occasion, located with the remains of fallen soldiers) and part of a clock.

> Trench warfare was nothing new – what was new was the sheer range of weaponry available to those in the trenches and this swung the advantage back from attacker to defender. Industrialisation at last applied to war . . . [This included] bolt action machine-fed rifle, machine gun, breach-loading artillery with axial recoil, elongated shell with shrapnel bullets and high explosive in selective delivery. (Prior and Wilson, 2002: 8–9)

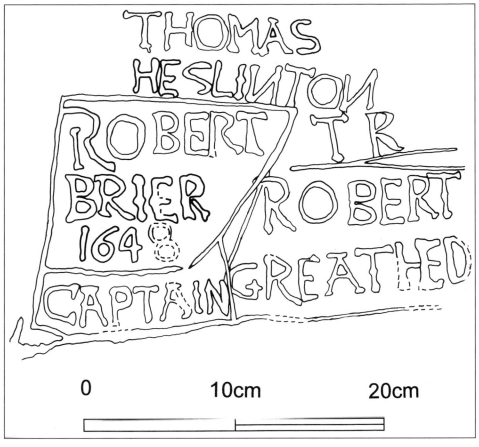

THOMAS
HESLINTON
ROBERT TR
BRIER ROBERT
1648
CAPTAINGREATHED

0   10cm   20cm

16. Civil War graffiti found at Pontefract Castle, Yorkshire.
(After Roberts, 2002: 299)

17. The forearm bones of Unknown Warrior 9 showing
'parry' fractures, Sandal Castle, Yorkshire. *(Photo courtesy of
Wakefield Historical Publications)*

18. The Norman Cross, a memorial to French prisoners of war in the Napoleonic period, who were held at this site near Peterborough, next to what is today the A1 road. The pillar was once topped by an Imperial Eagle, which was subsequently stolen (since the taking of this photograph, a replacement has been installed). *(Author's collection)*

19. The remains of Unknown Warrior 11, Vilnius, Lithuania, undergoing analysis. He was one of the soldiers of the Grande Armée who died on the retreat from Moscow in 1812. *(Photo courtesy of Professor Rimantas Jankauskas)*

20. Toe bones of Unknown Warrior 11 from Vilnius, Lithuania. The bulges indicate healing stress fractures commensurate with having marched long distances, probably in the retreat from Moscow in 1812. *(Photo courtesy of Professor Rimantas Jankauskas)*

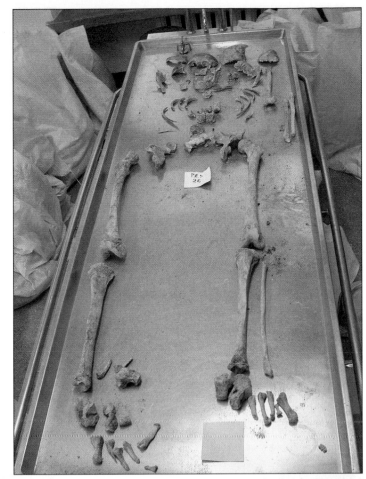

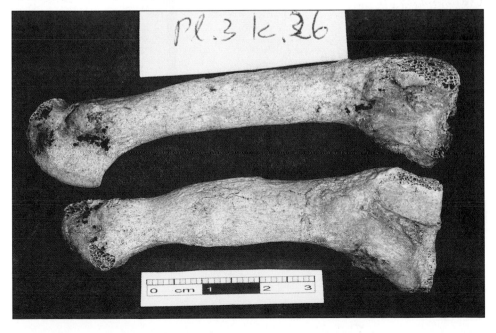

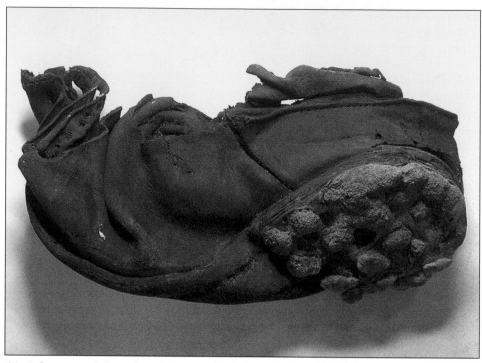

21. Infantryman's boot found close to the body of Unknown Warrior 11 in the burial pit at Vilnius, Lithuania. *(Photo courtesy of Professor Rimantas Jankauskas)*

22. Remains of a First World War gas mask excavated by The Diggers in Flanders. *(Copyright The Diggers, courtesy of Aurel Sercu)*

23. Australian troops cutting practice trenches in 1916 while training at Broadmeadows, now a western suburb of Melbourne. The soldier below the cross mark is Adolph Christensen, who was killed in the First World War in April 1918 and is buried at the Warloy-Baillon cemetery. *(Photo courtesy of Peter and Sandra Beckett)*

24. A First World War chalk carving in the Noyon region of France depicting the head of a French soldier in the form of a Zouave from North Africa. *(Moulage et photographie S. Ramond, Musée de Verneuil-en-Halatte, Oise)*

25. A kiwi carved in chalk at Bulford on Salisbury Plain by First World War soldiers from New Zealand. The carving serves as a memorial both to the presence of the troops in the area and to the sacrifices made by New Zealand forces during the war. Many New Zealand troops succumbed to the influenza pandemic at the end of the war. *(Author's collection)*

26. Souvenirs of the First World War, such as these 'trench art' tanks fashioned from the brass of shell cases, were often made by troops and were wide-ranging in form. *(Photo by courtesy of Richard Petty)*

27. An iodine ampoule, given to First World War infantrymen for first aid in the field, excavated by The Diggers at Auchonvillers, France. *(Copyright The Diggers, courtesy of Aurel Sercu)*

28. The Mourning Comrades, Langemark Cemetery, Belgium. The statue represents four individuals (two of whom are pictured) looking over the graves of many of their German comrades who fell in the First World War. Large numbers of the graves are provided with a simple dedication: to *Unbekannte Deutsche Soldaten* (Unknown German Soldiers). *(Author's collection)*

29. The coffin of the British Unknown Warrior from the First World War standing in a *chapelle ardente* in Boulogne with a French guard, November 1920. The coffin was later taken to Westminster Abbey, where it lies in state. *(Copyright Imperial War Museum: Photograph Q70592)*

30. The War Memorial at Royston in Hertfordshire, England, depicting unknown infantrymen from the Medieval period to the twentieth century. *(Author's collection)*

The excavation of a communication trench at Auchonvillers (also known, in true Tommy fashion, as the Anglicised 'Ocean Villas'), in use during the Somme campaign in France, located several items pertaining to weaponry, including numerous, mostly unfired, rounds of .303 rifle ammunition and the foil from an ammunition box (Fraser, 2003: 11). Throughout the Somme region, a vast range of munitions is brought to the surface every year when the land is ploughed, supporting what we already know about the panoply of arms of the First World War infantryman.

In Flanders, a group of amateur archaeologists known as The Diggers, in their excavations of the trench systems of Boezinge, have recovered a vast array of weaponry, including British rifles with bayonet still attached, British, French and German ammunition and various grenades and projectiles (ranging from British Mills bombs to German disc grenades, known as 'toads'). Trench mortar projectiles ('plum puddings') were recovered, and there was a large quantity of shrapnel. There was also the discovery of a battery of Livens projectors used to fire gas shells (Aurel Sercu, pers. comm.). Live grenades have also been excavated at Beaumont-Hamel by a Canadian and French team, 'requiring the intervention of bomb disposal personnel' (Saunders, 2002: 106).

All these weapons, combined with strong dugouts, barbed wire and the fact that attacking troops were frequently burdened with large quantities of equipment, ensured that head-on daylight attacks often proved costly. British casualties amounted to around 57,000 on the first day of the Battle of the Somme, of which 19,000 were killed. When raids of enemy positions took place, or on the occasions that major assaults were successful, the rifle with fixed bayonet was often too cumbersome to be functional in the messy business of trench clearance. Grenades were far more practical, though the zig-zag or crenulated design of trenches meant that these had to be thrown at each bend.

As the infantry hero of *All Quiet on the Western Front*, Paul Bäumer, commented: 'In any case, the bayonet isn't as important as it used to be. It is more normal now to go into the attack with hand-grenades and your entrenching tool. The sharpened spade is a lighter and more versatile weapon – not only can you get a man under the chin, but, more to the point, you can strike a blow with a lot more force behind it' (Remarque, 1996: 74).

For all the technical innovations and the mass-production that went with industrialisation, some of the most effective weapons for hand-to-hand combat would not have seemed out of place in earlier periods in history: knives, cudgels and clubs. This was certainly the case at Boezinge. Excavators on this site uncovered several clubs, one with a lead head and another that could almost have been a Medieval mace. This wooden club was around 50cm in length with a bulb at one end covered with iron studs with a spike at the top (Aurel Sercu, pers. comm.). Fighting at close quarters was still visceral.

ARMOUR AND UNIFORM

We were shot down like rabbits because you know for them we were a real target as we had red trousers on. When we were fired at we were like sitting ducks in the field, you see.

(Private Frank Dolbau, in Arthur, 2002: 25–6)

The French had not had the benefit of the British, whose bitter experiences in the Boer War had shown them the need to use a more sober colour scheme for their uniforms in combat – so, whereas the British soldier wore 'khaki' and his German adversary *feldgrau* (field grey), the French *poilu* (hairy ones) went to war in bright red trousers and blue coat, a situation rectified only when front-line units were supposedly issued with the new 'horizon blue' uniform in the spring of 1915. This was too late for the twenty-one soldiers of the 288th Infantry Regiment who were killed at Saint-Rémy-la-Calonne (see pages 199–200). When the bodies of the men were excavated, including that of the author Alain-Fournier, 'tattered traces of red and blue material were recovered' (Boura, 2000: 30).

Bales of pre-1915 blue-dyed Belgian army uniforms were uncovered in excavations in Flanders (Hooge) in 2003. Here the preservation conditions had ensured the fabric's survival, although the cotton thread had decayed. Leather belts were also present, as were woollen socks and a Belgian army 1896 pattern rucksack (Rob Janaway, pers. comm.). The Belgian army also started with uniforms that would not have seemed too out of place on the battlefields of the nineteenth century – even wearing the shako as headgear, the type of tall, cylindrical, plumed hat that had been worn by Wellington's riflemen.

One particular item of uniform that is found more often than other elements in archaeological investigations and can often provide a striking image is the soldier's boot. On several excavation sites human skeletons have been uncovered, which, if given a cursory glance, could be thought to be from a Medieval hospital, plague pit or Victorian cemetery – that is until one sees the boots, still on the feet of the deceased and made of sturdy leather and steel-shod. The remains of the soldiers of the 288th Infantry Regiment at Saint-Rémy-la-Calonne are a case in point (see photo by F. Adam in Krumeich, 1999: 88–9; and photo by H. Paitier in Boura, 2000: 30).

Just as powerful were the results of the work of French archaeologists near the A26 Calais–Paris motorway at Le Point du Jour, Arras. Excavations here prior to the construction of a factory uncovered a mass burial of British soldiers. Twenty unknown troops were found lying on their backs with their elbows overlapping. As with the French soldiers, they were wearing their boots when they were buried, and these have survived. Although it wasn't possible to identify any of the men, regimental insignia were discovered, and it seems that these troops may have been from the Grimsby Chums – a 'Pals' Battalion (10th Lincolns) that had lost half of its number of *c.* 1,000 officers and men on the first day of the Somme, 1 July 1916. They had probably been killed in the spring of 1917 when the unit again experienced crushing losses (see, e.g., Briet, 2002: 20).

As with nineteenth-century sites, archaeologists have recovered insignia that are unit- or regiment-specific, denoting the presence of certain troops at a location. At the Auchonvillers trench excavations, items were retrieved relating to the uniforms of individuals and their webbing. These included a Royal Irish Fusiliers' cap badge, 'probably dropped by a member of the 4th Division from July 1915 until early 1916' (Fraser, 2003: 11).

> Then, as we looked further away we saw this green cloud come slowly across the terrain. It was the first gas that anybody had seen or heard of, and one of our boys, evidently a chemist, passed the word along that this was chlorine. And he said, 'If you urinate on your handkerchiefs it will save your lungs anyway.' So most of us did that, and we tied handkerchiefs, plus pieces of putty or anything else we could find, around our faces, and it did save us from being gassed. (Private W. Underwood, 1st Canadian Division. 2nd Battle of Ypres, 1915, in Arthur, 2002: 79)

The First World War saw the first use of chemical weapons and their horrific effects. Poison gas (including phosgene, chlorine and 'mustard' variants) was used by the Germans on the Ypres salient in 1915 to great effect. It could induce blindness, blistering and severe oedema of the lungs, which would lead to death through asphyxiation. One of the most moving depictions of the effects of this weapon occurs in Wilfred Owen's poem 'Dulce Et Decorum Est' (Day Lewis, 1963: 55).

Poison gas was released through containers in the front line, or through shells and trench mortars. The British Livens projector battery found at Boezinge was one such method of weapon delivery (Aurel Sercu, pers. comm.). Although an effective countermeasure for mustard gas was not discovered in the First World War, many attempts were made to fight off the effects. An initial response, as seen above, was to place cloth soaked in urine across the nose and mouth. Soon, a gas hood was developed, which contained a small mica plate to enable the soldier to see while wearing it. One such plate from a first pattern British smoke hood was found by the excavators on the brick floor of the trench at Auchonvillers (Fraser, n.d.: 17).

Remnants of later gas mask types were found with the remains of two Royal Welch Fusiliers (see pages 207–8). A more striking example was uncovered in no man's land at Boezinge (see Plate 22). It was composed of rubber with two glass ocular pieces, c. 8cm in diameter (Aurel Sercu, pers. comm.). Excavation work at the Beecham dugout, at the foot of the Passchendaele Ridge in Flanders, yielded a number of interesting artefacts, including a British small box respirator (Barton et al., 2004: 286). By the end of the war, gas protection had become an important accessory to the infantryman's uniform.

For infantry, body armour appears to have been rendered obsolete by the use of firearms. Pikemen in the English Civil War ultimately stopped using the tasseted back- and breastplates, and by the nineteenth century armoured headgear was no longer worn by footsoldiers. This situation changed again in the First World War. In 1915, the French and Belgians adopted a steel helmet known as the 'Adrian' helmet after its designer, while the British helmet, known by some as the 'Brodie' after its designer, was patented in 1915 and adopted by Commonwealth troops in 1916. The latter helmets have been found in various excavations – their presence helping to provide a date for the deposits.

The Germans and Austrians also adopted a steel helmet – the 'Stahlhelm', or M16 – in 1916, replacing the spiked helmet (*Pickelhaube*). This headgear could be painted in camouflage patterns and had ventilation lugs on the side, which would also allow the attachment of a further armoured plate (*Stirnpanzer*), possibly for use by snipers. One well-known German infantryman, Ernst Jünger, felt that, rather than the introduction of armour being a retrograde step, it heralded a new, modern phase in the war. On moving to the town of Combles during the Battle of the Somme in August 1916, he saw an infantryman using the Stahlhelm for the first time and wrote: 'He was the first German soldier I saw in a steel helmet, and he straightaway struck me as the denizen of a new and far harsher world' (Jünger, 2003: 92).

In addition to the helmet, body protection was used. One extraordinary case from the Allied side was recounted by Captain Hugh Kinred of the 14th Gloucesters (Bristol Bantams). Kinred won the Military Cross following his actions on seeing a bomb drop beside seven sleeping comrades: 'In a moment, I saw the danger they were in, and that no time could be lost in picking it up: so I decided to smother it by lying on it. No sooner had I lain on it than it exploded, blowing me from the corner of the trench at an angle of about 30 degrees on to its top, and I should doubtless have been killed but for the lucky chance that I was wearing a Whitfield Steel waistcoat' (*Daily Mirror*, 22 August 1916; Bulmer, 1999: 29). The Germans also introduced full trench body armour (Fosten and Marrion, 1978: 21), not dissimilar to some of the plate armour from Visby (see Chapter 4) or the pikeman's protection from the 1640s – again for snipers or those in exposed positions. This was deemed to be very heavy and cumbersome and thus was soon discarded for similar reasons as it had been in the seventeenth century.

The construction of the A29 Amiens–Saint Quentin road and TGV Nord railway lines in northern France crossed the sites of much fighting of 1915–18, including the German spring offensive of 1918. Archaeologists working on the site of Gavrelle, Pas de Calais, uncovered a communal grave of twelve German soldiers. Although they lacked personal effects, some identity tags enabled the researchers to tell that these men were part of the 6th and 7th Companies of the 152nd Infantry Regiments, 48th Division, which had taken part in the great offensive of the Germans in March 1918 (Desfossés *et al.*, 2000: 35). The men had been hurriedly buried in a shell hole, and some were still wearing their steel helmets, which had been cracked and were not reusable. Steel helmets were not designed to protect against bullet strikes to the front or side of the helmet, though it was hoped they would afford some cover from shrapnel.

Another example of a German helmet, in this case a *Pickelhaube*, can be seen in the Pitt Rivers Museum in Oxford and serves to illustrate the distant forces on which the British Empire could call. At some point after the First

World War, James Mills visited the Naga Hills in north-eastern India and returned with a dance trophy with a difference. Unlike the traditional headhunting trophies of the region – human skulls with horns attached to the sides – this was constructed from a German spiked helmet, which had undergone the same treatment of attaching horns to the side. Presumably this object was imbued with great significance beyond that of a casual souvenir, and had been brought home by a Chan member of the Naga Labour Corps (Pitt Rivers Museum Accession Number 1928.69.308). Indeed, Saunders (2003: 183) believes that this item, brought back from the Western Front, was a 'symbolic substitute of a captured enemy head and proof of valour in battle'.

PRACTICE

Among the vast number of troops who took part in the First World War, many had little or no experience of combat or military life prior to 1914. An element of training for what they were about to do was essential if the infantryman was to have any chance of survival on the Western Front – and even then only with a great deal of fortune.

Men across the world in different armies cut practice trenches in an attempt to learn the basic necessities of this static form of warfare. Several examples of practice trenches in Britain have been recorded by the Council for British Archaeology's 'Defence of Britain Project' (Lowry, 1995), a study of the monuments connected to warfare, including the Duke of York's School trench system (Kent Sites and Monuments Record Number TR 34 SW 521 – KE17128), which was constructed in 1916, but no longer exists; Archers Court Hill (Kent Sites and Monuments Record Number TR 34 SW 518 – KE17125), 1916; and Whinless Down (Kent Sites and Monuments Record Number TR 24 SE 65 – KE17116), dug in 1916 and with traces still surviving.

Some of the most complete surviving First World War practice trenches are located on Salisbury Plain, a region that is still the main training area of the British Army. Here, examples of front-line, communication and even reserve trenches can be found at Shrewton Folly, Market Lavington, Slay Down and Perham.

Shrewton Folly, used by the Australian 3rd Division from 1916 onwards, prior to moving to northern France and Belgium, emphasised the importance of redigging existing areas of trenches, rather than creating new systems, and of creating proper machine-gun emplacements. Aerial photography by

O.G.S. Crawford in the 1920s reveals that some trenches were, at that point, still extant, but were later filled in. Today, they can be picked up by geophysics and excavation.

At Beacon Hill, on Salisbury Plain, training trenches are still extant and have been the subject of several archaeological recording techniques: plotted from aerial photographs, surveyed by English Heritage, and laser-plotted by Wessex Archaeology. With island traverses, communication trenches, bombing pits and reserve trenches, this extensive system would have provided valuable practice. It also made use of existing monuments, such as round barrows and Bronze Age linear ditches, as happened in actuality in the trench systems of the Western Front, such as the Butte de Warlencourt.

An admirable survey of the region (McOmish *et al.*, 2002) identified sites at Compton Down and New Copse Down, which still retained 'obstacles such as wire entanglements secured by screw pickets' (*ibid.*: 140). Other training elements can still be traced on land owned by the Ministry of Defence – these include tunnel systems below trenches in Colchester and North Wales. Archaeological work at Colchester revealed evidence for bombing practice – however the artefacts included champagne bottles as well as grenades (Brown, 2004: 58).

Practice trenches have also been located at Silloans in Northumberland (Hammond, 2004: 24), Clipstone Forest in Nottinghamshire (Grid Reference SK 615 635), Shipton Bellinger in Hampshire (Grid Reference SU 245 462), the Downs south of Blatchington in Sussex (Grid Reference TV 498983) and those connected to Stobs Camp at Penchrise Pen in the Scottish Borders (Grid Reference NT 4890 0650). Several good extant trench systems survive in Wales, of which those in the park of Bodelwyddam Castle and at Penally are especially impressive. The latter was the subject of an archaeological study, which revealed the presence of saps, extensive trenches with both parapet and parados, and communication trenches (Wessex Archaeology, 2004a).

Rifle practice formed part of the training, and the remains of First World War rifle ranges are still extant at Maelor Saesneg, near Wrexham, and at Cannock Chase, Staffordshire. The latter is close to a First World War hospital, German prisoner-of-war camps and a subsequent German war cemetery. Bayonet practice was also instilled and areas were set up in France to expose new troops to such fighting techniques. Among the most infamous of these was the so-called Bull-ring at Étaples in France, where men trained in sand dunes and woodland close to the town.

Recent archaeological field recording by the Institute of Lifelong Learning at Sheffield University has examined a series of zig-zag regular depressions associated with earthen banks around Redmires and Ash Cabin Flat on Hallam Moors to the west of Sheffield. These were the training areas of the Sheffield City Battalion, known as 'Hill 60'. 'Training here lasted only eight or nine months before the Battalion left for overseas service as part of the Yorks. and Lancs. Regiment. Several [men] died in the process of training and approximately two-thirds of the men eventually lost their lives at the Battle of the Somme' (Sidebottom, n.d.: 1).

The survey located 'sinuous depressions running around the top of the hills to the south, west and north. Some small mounds and dugouts were located on the eastern side of the hill and there appeared to be a possible machine-gun emplacement near the summit' (ibid.: 1). Oxford Archaeology has also carried out fieldwork on practice trenches at Whiteleaf Hill in Buckinghamshire. At the point examined, the trench was only around 0.6m deep and around 1m wide – perhaps indicating the practice of digging the specific shapes of trenches; there were also covering banks and the possibility of 'firing steps'. The overall layout was zig-zag (Edmund Simons, pers. comm.).

The Sites and Monuments Record for the former county of Avon in the south-west of Britain noted the presence of such workings at Lansdown, just to the north of the city of Bath (SMR refs. 9646 + 1991). These were cut through Roman and Saxon remains in 1915 by parties of around 100 men of the North Somerset Yeomanry, under Major A.H. Gibbs. The workings occurred within a relatively short distance of the monument commemorating the death of the Royalist infantry commander, Sir Bevil Grenville, who had been killed in the 1643 Battle of Lansdown. In cutting these practice trenches, the soldiers were accidentally undertaking their own archaeological work with several stone columns – presumed to be Roman – being found.

On this side of the road are many mounds, extending over a considerable area, that had evidently been thrown up at a remote period when quarrying to obtain stone for building the many walls on the Down. Here the work consisted of making a bomb-proof shelter with trenches leading up to it, outer trenches and dugout. On September 9th, when digging to construct one of the last named, at 3½ feet below the surface, was discovered two parts of columns, each about 18 inches high . . . (Bush, 1914–18: 127–8)

Photographs of these columns were sent to Professor Haverfield at Oxford University, who declared them to be 'Tuscan-Doric' style and Roman, if they were not from one of the many Georgian buildings of Bath (*ibid.*: 128). Initial recruits into the North Somerset Yeomanry were trained in musketry at the nearby Box rifle range and the 1/1st saw tough action at Ypres in 1915 in the 'never-to-be-forgotten defence of the shattered trenches' (Fisher, 1924: 168) – the trenches at Lansdown were clearly cut later than this event.

With so much soil disturbance on the Western Front, much of it in archaeologically rich areas, it is not surprising that many monuments and artefacts were uncovered by troops. Modern aerial photography serves to highlight this with some striking images of zig-zag trench systems crossing circular marks and complex circles attributable to Bronze Age monuments at Berry-au-Bac (Delétang, 1999: 137). A prehistoric burial mound, the Butte de Warlencourt, was incorporated into defences on the Somme, commanding the road to Bapaume. The mound was covered in barbed wire and honeycombed with dugouts, which saw much heavy fighting. In advance of the construction of the A29 *autoroute*, excavations at Ablaincourt-Pressoir (Le Chemin Blanc de Bouvent) found the remains of two Prussian soldiers alongside separate Iron Age deposits, including a brooch and coins (Lemaire, 1998), while the site at Villeneuve-Saint-Germain (les Etomelles) was of Bronze Age, Iron Age and Gallo-Roman deposits cut by First World War trench systems (Boulen, 1998).

Although soldiers have long been known for collecting items (Talbot-Rice and Harding, 1989), it seems that the infantry themselves were interested in archaeology. Evidence for this was provided by recent excavations at the corner of the Heidenkopf (Quadrilateral) at Serre on the Somme, where the remains of a German soldier with a prehistoric flint scraper in his bread bag have been discovered (Brown, 2005: 31). A Neolithic axe was also recovered by troops digging trenches at Harponville on the Somme (Saunders, 2002: 102).

For the infantryman interested in geology, sectors of the Western Front provided ample opportunity for obtaining samples for the collection – Jünger (2003: 181) noted that the rock at Côte Lorraine was 'full of fossils, especially of a flattish, bun-shaped sea urchin, which one could see literally thousands of along the trench walls. Each time I walked along the sector, I returned to my dugout with pockets full of shells, sea urchins and ammonites.'

In terms of practice digging, soldiers quickly learned that no training manual could fully prepare them for trench warfare – much had to be 'unlearnt' and their adaptability under pressure was put to the test. Methods to strengthen trenches were experimented with and 'new' modes of close-quarter combat were adopted. As an officer in the Coldstream Guards on the Western Front wrote: 'I suppose there is nothing in the world where theory differs from practice so much as in war. Contrast the practice trenches in Windsor Park with the trenches here' (Fielding, 2001: 31). By necessity war becomes the 'mother of invention', and indeed improvisation.

Training for Commonwealth troops also took place far from theatres of conflict around the world; the largest of the Canadian training areas was at Valcartier, a site with huge numbers of tents and rifle ranges, about 16 miles to the west of Quebec City. A fine example of training in Australia is shown by the image of trenches being cut at Broadmeadows (see Plate 23).

The experience of soldiers was hugely important for them to adapt to the battlefield conditions of the First World War. One of the most interesting finds at Saint-Rémy-la-Calonne was a purse containing numerous coins. These coins had been separated from one another by pieces of cardboard so that they would not jingle around in the pocket (Adam, 1999: 32).

THE LIFE OF THE SOLDIER

The Zeitgeist of the Western soldier, probably from the time it arrived in Europe, was tobacco, in an enduring partnership with alcohol. As we have seen from excavations of sites of the English Civil War onwards, pipes and bottles are far from rare on sites that had witnessed the marching of soldiers' feet. This holds, of course, for the First World War. Ferguson (1998: 351) went so far as to state that,

> without alcohol, and perhaps also without tobacco, the First World War could not have been fought. When Sergeant Harry Finch of the Royal Sussex Regiment advanced into no man's land on the eve of the Passchendaele offensive (31st July 1917), he was struck by the fact that most of the men in his section 'fell fast asleep' as they lay waiting to attack. That was the effect of the rum issue as much as tiredness.

The provision of 'Dutch courage' was perhaps not always conducive to instilling optimum fighting condition in the men, though it might have helped to take the edge off some of the fear.

> we went back rejoicing to have our rum ration . . . but one poor chap with us, he took a first sip of the rum and gave a shriek and dropped the jar because some fellow back in the rear had stolen the rum and filled the jar with brown Condy's fluid, a powerful disinfectant. This poor fellow had taken a mouthful and it went down into his stomach. We heard he died later. (Rifleman Henry Williamson, London Rifle Brigade, in Arthur, 2002: 54)

Rum jars have been recovered from several excavations on the Western Front, in addition to being found as fragments in plough soil. One such jar was found by the archaeologists working at Auchonvillers and they also retrieved beer bottles manufactured in Leeds (Fraser, 2003: 11). Others have been found in Flanders in the work of The Diggers around Boezinge (Aurel Sercu, pers. comm.).

> But beyond the last entanglement,
> Out of it all, on the firm road,
> Met together, with no delays,
> In the glow of the first pipes lit,
> Then, mates, O lucky winners,
> Then what stumbling voluble joy!
> (Charles Vildrac, from 'Relief' in Silkin, 1979: 234)

Uniquely in our study we have the surviving remnants of some of the tobacco of the period in archaeological contexts. Excavations in Flanders in 1999 by The Diggers recovered several pipe bowls, but most poignant was a small tin box filled with tobacco found with the body of a Royal Welch Fusilier and a series of matches in a rubber cloth stamped 1915 (Aurel Sercu, pers. comm.). Pipes have been found during fieldwork associated with the armies of the Central Powers, too, such as in the mass grave of the twelve German soldiers in a shell hole at Gavrelle, Pas de Calais (Desfossés *et al.*, 2000, 35). A pipe and box of matches were also present with the burials of three Germans found during rescue excavations at Thélus (Vimy), to the north of Arras (Nils Fabiansson, pers. comm.; see Archaeology of the

Western Front, 2003). As far as the French correspondent of *L'Independence* was concerned in late 1914, smoking was one of the characteristics of the British soldier: 'Tommy loves to laugh, he has clear eyes and smokes almost continuously a cigarette or pipe' (Laffin, 2003: 205). Richard Holmes (2004: 326) went as far as to say: 'The British army marched less on its stomach than in a haze of smoke.'

Eating

And then they brought us 'Princess Mary's gift box'. And in this box was cigarettes, tobacco and a bar of chocolate, which was very much appreciated. And then we had what the English newspapers called Christmas Dinner. This consisted of cold bully beef and a cold lump of Christmas pudding, that was our Christmas dinner. The English newspapers said that the British troops in the front 'enjoyed' their Christmas dinner.

(Private Clifford Lane, 1st Battalion Hertfordshire Regiment, in Arthur, 2002: 55)

The Auchonvillers work has recovered items relating to the food consumed by the soldiers, including a 'bully beef' tin (from the French *boeuf bouilli*, meaning boiled beef), butchered animal bones, which were found in the sump cut into the trench, and a 1lb tin of butterscotch made by Parkins of Doncaster. Cutlery has also been excavated – vital for consuming hot food from a mess tin (Fraser, 2003: 11). After the war, the trench was backfilled with the surrounding detritus of conflict, including food and mess tins and latrine buckets.

'Bully' tins have been excavated at Boezinge in Flanders, where it appears that additional flavouring for the meat was considered important by the men in these trenches as a bottle of HP Sauce was also found (Aurel Sercu, pers. comm.). The ability to eat canned food was vital for the front-line troops, enabling longer preservation of foodstuffs and easier storage. The provision of bully seems to have been in some ways comforting to the troops, judging by the comments of relatives of the author, who served in the First or Second World War and who were fond of eating it in peacetime.

The culinary tastes of the Gallic and Anglo-Saxon elements of the Allied armies on the Western Front differed somewhat. Laffin (2003: 215) quotes General Spears on the views of the 'Tommy' and the *poilu* when it came to food:

They disliked each other's cuisine. When the French commissariat fed some of our men . . . complaints were endless . . . Our people could do nothing with the vegetables from which they were expected to devise soups and savoury messes. They hated the coffee and threw away in disgust the inordinate quantities of bread served up . . . In short Tommy Atkins, like his civilian counterpart, was rigidly hidebound in his tastes.

At least food was getting to the troops. The German spring offensive of 1918 was held up not simply by Allied troops, but also because advancing German troops had stopped to loot Allied supply depots, including food stores. By this time, Germany was badly affected by a blockade, resulting in much ersatz material and small rations. It would have been a most demoralising discovery for the front-line German troops to see the comparatively lavish lifestyle of their opponents. 'Nearly all war memoirs make it clear that morale was heavily dependent on good rations. It is, in many ways, the central leitmotif of *All Quiet [on the Western Front* – Remarque, 1996]. The smell of bacon in the morning cheered men on both sides . . .' (Ferguson, 1998: 350).

Infantry, when not in the front line, could try to catch up on sleep, write letters to relatives, continue their relationship with alcohol or visit the many other ranks' brothels that sprang up to meet the demand. When not under attack in the trenches, time-honoured pastimes were more the order of the day. Mouth organs have been found in the archaeological work at Auchonvillers (Fraser, 2003: 11) and, in 1999, The Diggers retrieved a set of playing cards from one of the trenches (Aurel Sercu, pers. comm.).

Despite the squalor of the trenches, men fought what must surely have been a losing battle against personal hygiene; the remnants of toothbrushes, a comb, razors and even a shoe brush have been found in the excavations at Boezinge (Aurel Sercu, pers. comm.).

Accommodation

The men are quite wonderful, always cheerful under the most trying conditions; sleeping, when not in the trenches, crowded in such accommodation as can be got in a barn, or a cow-stall, or a loft.

(Fielding, 2001: 9)

For those at the front, accommodation meant the trenches. These were often elaborate, zig-zag or crenulated in plan to avoid blast from shell or bomb carrying too far along a single stretch, and with saps cut forward as advanced positions. These could have wooden planks or 'duckboards' along the floor under which drainage sumps were to be cut. All this with a protective mantle of a deadly spider's web of barbed wire to the fore. 'It would, I suppose, be an exaggeration to say that the parapets at this place [trenches opposite the Hohenzollern redoubt] are built up with dead bodies, but it is true to say that they are dovetailed with them, and everywhere arms, legs and heads protrude' (Fielding, 2001: 31).

Ideally the trenches would be strengthened and heightened with sandbags and revetted with iron, though the soldier often had to rebuild shell-damaged trenches while under fire and could use anything to improve his lot. At such times, the training manual was shelved and archaeology helps to reveal the ingenuity of those who fought.

In these 'barracks' men could face the elements for many days, sharing their billets with lice and rats, the latter soon becoming very large, as carrion became plentiful. There have been few excavations of trench systems to date, other than the Auchonvillers communication trench. This trench was initially dug by the French, but was then occupied by the British when they took over the village in 1915. The unit that took over was from the 4th Division – a regular formation that had suffered heavy casualties at the 2nd Battle of Ypres (Fraser, n.d.: 4). Rather than the typical view of a trench with duckboards at the bottom, this system was floored, in places, with brick and had a drain running down the side. This trench was reinforced by angle-irons, sandbags and with rabbit wire – all of which were recovered in the excavation work. Two sumps were found: one containing animal bones and kit items, the other flouting standard procedures by being cut into the side of the trench. As project historian Alistair Fraser (2003: 11) wrote, this highlights the fact that 'soldiers did not always follow the manuals', and thus the value of archaeology.

A further find from Auchonvillers highlights human nature in quite a powerful fashion. In the fill of the trench was a white tile on which, in chinagraph pencil, the legend 'In case of Fire Only' was written. 'This was presumably placed near the cellar [connected to the trench and used, in part to shelter troops] entrance and was intended to warn against improper use of fire buckets and their contents' (Fraser, n.d.: 16). Laffin describes the day-to-day conditions in the trenches in stark terms:

Life in the trenches was vile. True, in the better-disciplined units trench house-keeping was taken seriously. No rubbish was allowed and latrine buckets were situated down a short sap to the rear. Tools, bombs and ammunition were all neatly stacked. Mostly an officer would have a dugout into which he could crawl. The men would sprawl on the firestep shivering in the bitter cold, up to their knees in mud, with rain driving into their faces. In summer the heat in a trench was intense. Large rats ran over the men as they slept; everybody knew on what these rats fed. (Laffin, 2003: 212)

As we have seen, geological considerations are important in determining the extent to which artefacts survive. They were also fundamental in determining aspects of the Battle of the Somme. As Doyle (2001: 249) points out, British trenches were 'mostly cut through the limon complex which cap the plateau top above the 130m contour (reported as "reddish earth" by Masefield, 1917). These trenches were often waterlogged during the heavy summer rain or later in the campaign when the good weather of summer 1916 had broken. This demonstrates their local penetration into the clay with flints overlying the chalk, beneath the limon complex.'

By contrast, the German trenches followed the line of Beaumont Valley and were cut into chalk. This ensured that 'dry, deep dugouts were possible, and were constructed for maximum effect into the steep scarp slopes of the incised Y-Ravine. Masefield (1917) in his contemporary survey of the newly captured German ground reports that German dugouts were extensive, with long shafts, galleries, barrack rooms and other underground shelters, all supported by timber baulks, iron girders and concrete' (*ibid.*: 249). The well-drained chalk enabled sophisticated defensive systems to be created, allowing the German trenches to withstand the huge artillery bombardment that preceded the attacks on 1 July 1916.

Some of the most enduring images of the First World War are of the flooded battlefields of Flanders, especially from the 3rd Battle of Ypres, the hellish battle known as Passchendaele. It is this flooding that has ensured the remarkable survival of organic remains. The fact that the water-table is so high in this region means that The Diggers have been able to examine British and German front-line trenches with a remarkable degree of structural preservation, although under tricky excavation conditions. At Boezinge, the 'Yorkshire' Trench (a name derived from the 1917 trench map) was seen to have been constructed with inverted 'A-frames' of wood, which supported slatted wooden boarding (duckboards) on which the troops walked. Beneath this a drainage channel had been cut, hopefully alleviating to an extent the necessity of walking through liquid mud. The sides of the trench were reinforced with corrugated iron and the plan of the site was, as one would expect, zig-zag in layout to minimise blast risk. Other elements from this site included a wooden reel to hold telephone wire in the trench – so vital for communications – and even a wooden sledgehammer used in the construction of the trenches (Aurel Sercu, pers. comm.). Conditions in the trenches could, quite simply, be ghastly. As Ferguson (1998: 446) wrote: 'In addition to the pain of being "hit", men felt fear, horror, grief, fatigue and discomfort: the trenches were damper, dirtier, and more vermin-infested than the worst slum.'

As with the Somme, in the trenches of Flanders troops created dugouts as shelters to protect them from the bombardment of the enemy. These took the form of small scoops in the trench walls, or hollows covered with corrugated iron and then soil and sandbags, or the most desirable of all, the deep-mined dugout.

As Doyle *et al.* (2001) have shown, the methodology behind the construction of such shelters was heavily dependent on the geology of the region. The Association for Battlefield Archaeology in Flanders (ABAF) excavated the 'Beecham' dugout (Bostyn, 1999). This dugout, which was perhaps occupied by the Germans in the early part of the war and, judging by the artefacts recovered, by the British in the final stage (Doyle *et al.*, 2001: 269), had 1.2–2m of overhead cover and an overall depth of 4m. The dugout was lined with timber throughout and seemingly the bunks within 'provided accommodation for 66 men and three officers . . . Stepped, inclined entrances and gallery junctions were equipped with inclined frames enabling blankets to be rolled down and dampened as a precaution against gas attack' (*ibid.*: 269). Some of the bunks within these dugouts still hold traces of the chicken wire supports, which would have helped to keep the soldier in his bed (Barton *et al.*, 2004, 284). Even with these precautions, it is unlikely that the dugout would have withstood a direct hit from heavier forms of artillery such as howitzers.

Trench systems were not the only places that housed infantrymen. According to the archaeologist Alain Jacques, the British reused a series of Medieval stone quarries in Arras – an area known as 'Thompson's Cave'.

The ingenuity of British soldiers is shown by the fact that they converted these quarries into a 'billet capable of accommodating more than 24,000 men – the equivalent of the population of Arras at the start of the Great War' (Alain Jacques, pers. comm.). In addition, houses behind the lines also served as barracks, and barns provided shelter, too.

Soldiers also slept in tents and, as these items were fairly portable, they were present close to the front. Indeed, traces of tents have been found in a couple of excavations; the mass grave of French troops at Saint-Rémy-la-Calonne, while not containing much by way of material culture, yielded the rivets from a canvas tent (Adam, 1999: 32). The excavations of the German mass grave of twelve soldiers in a shell hole at Gavrelle seemed to indicate that tent canvases might also have served as makeshift shrouds on occasion – with aluminium eyelets from such an item being recovered (Desfossés *et al.*, 2000: 35).

Away from the areas of conflict, large camps were required to house those troops being trained prior to being cast into the maelstrom. In Britain, Salisbury Plain performed this role to a major extent. Not only were British troops put through their paces here, but soldiers from New Zealand, Canada and Australia as well. Little remains of these camps today, but archaeological techniques can highlight the presence of former hut sites. A geophysical survey in the vicinity of the prehistoric henge monument of Durrington Walls, as part of the Stonehenge Rivers project, revealed the location of Camp 1 at Larkhill, home to, among others, the Australian 3rd Division. Although the corrugated iron and wood no longer remain extant above ground, the camp perimeters and hut footings can still be seen in traces in the soil.

Writings

By 1914 large numbers of infantrymen were able to read and write. Consequently, many letters from front-line soldiers survive. Of more interest to us in this study are the traces of literacy in the archaeological record and the information they can give us.

As shown in previous chapters, graffiti is something that the soldier often leaves behind. Carved into the walls of barracks or prisons, it offers hints as to an area's function or the units that were present. For example, a cellar connected to the trench excavated at Auchonvillers had a large amount of graffiti, comprising initials (such as J.C.) and names of individual soldiers, including that of Private John Edward Hargreaves of the 7th Border Regiment, 17th Division (present in this sector from 1917). Fraser (2003: 11) noted that these scribblings were 'entirely done by infantrymen which seems to indicate that it was used to shelter part of the garrison of Auchonvillers'. Writing has also been found in a more utilitarian mode in First World War excavations in the form of signage denoting particular locations and room functions, such as in the Arras hospital (see page 197).

The limestone and chalk geology of the Somme region was of great significance to those who fought there. The presence of caves and quarries cut through the stone enabled soldiers to leave their own mark: to carve images into it, scratch their names over it and paint motifs onto it. Annette Becker, of the University of Lille, believes that the presence of initials, soldiers' names and their regiments, is significant beyond simply being a form of vandalism. For her, 'Soldiers' trench graffiti and sculptures demonstrate a strong need to leave some trace before the attack, before death, to tell of experiences or dreams before disappearing' (Becker, 1999: 116). Soldiers also drew doodles or wrote verse when incarcerated (see page 202).

Writings that are visible in the caves of the Soissons and Noyon regions are frequently patriotic, proclaiming divine backing of the campaign of one side or the other. German writings were often 'outlined with black paint and typically adorned with a black-painted cross, a date and the inevitable *Gott mit Uns* ["God with us"]' (Saunders, 2003: 122). The presence of troops in the French army who spoke Breton is also indicated by the writings of a soldier in the 262nd Infantry Regiment in one of the caves: 'DOUE HAG ER VRO, 262°RI, NOV 1916' (Becker, 1999: 125). Work in the dugouts of Flanders has also revealed traces of units that fought in the mud. In addition to the names of the Sappers of 227 Field Company Royal Engineers who constructed the dugout known as 'Gordon House' – W. Spalding, D. Erwin, F. Lamb[..]y and F. McLaughan – there are carvings relating to the 117 and 118 Machine Gun Companies (Barton *et al.*, 2004: 270).

Letters from the front, although censored by officers, were permissible and the paraphernalia associated with this activity is visible in the archaeological record. Pencils have been found by The Diggers (Aurel Sercu, pers. comm.) and a number of ink pens were found in the French mass grave at Saint-Rémy-la-Calonne, Meuse (Adam, 1999: 32). The German bodies at Gavrelle, Pas de Calais, were also associated with writing materials – a phial of ink and a fountain pen (Desfossés *et al.*, 2000, 35). Perhaps the

English–French/French–English dictionary excavated by The Diggers (Aurel Sercu, pers. comm.) had been used not simply to talk with local civilians and French troops, but also in an attempt to write something in a foreign language.

Although a naval site, recent discoveries at Scapa Flow in Orkney may well prove an exciting dataset, too. In 1919, the seized German High Seas Fleet was scuttled at Scapa Flow by the ships' own German sailors. In 2003, divers discovered material drifting from the wrecks. A series of postcards have since been retrieved from SMS *Karlsruhe*. Not only do these depict ships, but an example of a wounded infantryman with an attending nurse has been recovered. Once the cards have been fully conserved, they may provide interesting written information, which may also have some facets relating to the infantry of the age (Clydesdale, 2005: 42–3).

The First World War was noted for its poetry and also its biting satire, composed by the men who fought, frequently at the expense of those whom they considered responsible for the war, its privations and huge death toll. The same men who scratched their names into their billets, or carved images of women and regimental badges into caves, may also have come across the writings of their comrades in so-called trench newspapers such as the *Wipers Times*:

Building land for sale

—

Build that House on Hill 60.
Bright – Breezy and Invigorating
Commands an Excellent View of the Historic Town of Ypres.
For Particulars of Sale Apply :–
BOSCH and CO. MENIN
(*Wipers Times* or *Salient News*, I, 1, 12 February 1916, in Beaver, 1973: 11)

Art

Our present trenches are largely in Chalk – the most fascinating stuff to carve with a jack-knife – and it is like visiting an art gallery to walk through them. Model prayer books and hymn books and slabs of chalk carved with the Regimental crest.

(Fielding, 2001: 9 – written on 22 May 1915)

The carvings found in caves and trenches such as those mentioned above are dramatic, perhaps none more so than in the Chemin des Dames, Soissons, which present a view of the world of the soldier and his culture – of weapons, the desire for women, regimental honours, calls for victory and even religious shrines (Becker, 1999: 118). The quarries changed hands from one army to the other and motifs dear to both German and French soldiers have been found in close proximity. The imperial Prussian eagle, painted red after its carving at Les Cinq Piliers, near Dreslincort, sits in almost direct challenge to a nearby bright Gallic cockerel (Saunders, 2003: 124).

The work of the Durand Group has been important in uncovering much information pertaining to the underground battles of the First World War – in tunnels, mines and dugouts. Their techniques, using ground-penetrating radar, have shown several major tunnel complexes. In addition, standard surveys have located the presence of artistic depictions by British soldiers of their comrades, including a Scottish soldier accompanied by the phrase 'Stand Easy' (Durand Group, n.d.: 13).

For the French, images of soldiers were also popular and their infantry – poilus and North African Zouave troops (see Plate 24) – are depicted in the Soissonais and Noyonais cave carvings. Parisian skylines also feature, and the depiction of 'Marianne', symbol of the Revolution and French womanhood, was a popular subject – Joan of Arc being the other French female depicted to escape the more lascivious portrayal afforded to the female subject of the 'poilu's dream' (Becker, 1999: 124; Saunders, 2003: 123).

Chalk was not only a suitable material to carve in relief, it was also cut into blocks and shaped as free-standing objects – some of the more unusual examples being the carved and painted chalk dragons made by members of the Chinese Labour Corps (now held in the Imperial War Museum in London). Art could also be on a grand scale. Moving through the landscape in Wiltshire, one cannot help but notice the impressive white horses cut into the chalk bedrock of the otherwise lush green hills. These can be hundreds, or in the case of the Uffington White Horse, Oxfordshire, thousands of years old, but chalk motifs can also be more recent. Anzac troops training in and around Salisbury Plain left permanent testaments to their presence in the shape of the Australian Commonwealth forces badges at Codford and Fovant, and the huge chalk kiwi carved into the hill at Bulford, overlooking the rifle ranges (see Plate 25).

The type of art from the First World War that is perhaps best known, and was produced in many cases by the front-line troops themselves, is the so-called 'trench-art'. Detritus of the battles was turned into souvenirs both during and after the war (Briet, 2002: 20). Saunders's (2003) excellent work draws much of this together and reveals a vast array of works of art: smoking equipment (lighters, tobacco boxes) made from bullets and scrap metal; writing equipment (letter openers and inkwells); shell cases decorated to make vases, sometimes with places and dates depicted; rings or bracelets made from the copper driving bands of shells; miniature tanks (see Plate 26) fashioned from shell cases; and even photo frames decorated with army issue biscuits (*ibid.*: 39–40). The construction of these artefacts was not without its risk to the troops – especially when trying to remove the copper driving bands from shells: 'Even when the men were only chipping off the copper rings from the shells to work them into paperknives or bracelets, there were incidents' (Jünger, 2003: 61).

An example of trench art found *in situ* at Auchonvillers was a 'bullet pencil' (Saunders, 2002: 106), and there seems to have been a workshop for these products close to Arras (see page 201). Much of what we regard as archaeological, material that has remained *in situ* on the battlefield, has been reused, which is perhaps not surprising given the huge quantity of material expended in the conflict and discarded.

Religion

From a practical point of view there was no religion in the front line, although our unit padre used to come and visit us quite a lot. But he was never allowed to stay in one place too long because he got in the way.

(Private Norman Demuth, 1/5th Battalion London Regiment, in Arthur, 2002: 165–6)

For some, amid all the slaughter of the Western Front, it was well nigh impossible to have religious faith; for others it was all that the individual held on to – trusting to their God rather than simply to chance. With so many different nationalities serving in this theatre, inevitably there was a range of religious belief: Sikh, Muslim, Hindu, Buddhist, Catholic and Protestant were all represented within the armies of the British Empire alone.

In terms of archaeological evidence to date, the traces seem to be predominantly Christian. The frequent invocation to God to back their cause or at least to look over and protect the individual soldier can be seen both at micro and macro level. Remains of soldiers have been found with religious icons ranging from a small white porcelain figurine of Christ on the cross uncovered in fieldwork at Boezinge (Aurel Sercu, pers. comm.) to rosary beads and religious medals found in the excavation of the French mass grave of 1914 at Saint-Rémy-la-Calonne, Meuse (Adam, 1999: 32).

At a grander level, there are many religious carvings and shrines in the caves of the Soissons and Noyon areas. These include inscriptions such as the ubiquitous German *Gott mit Uns* (Saunders, 2003: 122) and the French *Vive le Christ qui aime les Francs* at Pierre (Becker, 1999: 125), or *Dieu protège la France* in the Chapel of Father Doncoeur at Confrécourt (Saunders, 2003: 124). French Catholic soldiers carved altars into the chalk and these are often supported by battle honours of the various infantry regiments. At Pierre, a relief of a crucifix sits upon a carved altar composed of an image of a castle's wall and turret. Below this, within a circle surrounded by what appears to be a laurel wreath, a chi-rho (an early Christian symbol) is depicted, only in this case it is formed by the crossing of three swords – perhaps a strange juxtaposition of the sacred and profane, but inexorably appropriate in the context of soldiers asking to survive, to be remembered or for salvation. To the left of the altar are escutcheons of the 97th and 264th Infantry Regiments, and to the right, the 98th and the 265th Regiments. Their honours contain memorials to the Crimean and Franco-Prussian Wars as well as the Somme.

For some, chance or fate was still the abiding force. The central character of *All Quiet on the Western Front*, Paul Bäumer, voices this feeling eloquently: 'It is simply a matter of chance whether I am hit or whether I go on living. I can be squashed flat in a bomb-proof dugout, and I can survive ten hours in the open under heavy barrage without a scratch. Every soldier owes the fact that he is still alive to a thousand lucky chances and nothing else. And every soldier believes in and trusts to luck' (Remarque, 1996: 72).

Casualties, Hospitals and Medical Care

About saving the lives of enemy wounded there was disagreement; the convention varied with the division. Some divisions, like the Canadians and a division of Lowland Territorials, who claimed that they had

atrocities to avenge, would not only avoid taking risks to rescue enemy
wounded, but go out of their way to finish them off.

(Graves, 1960: 112)

Keegan (1991: 305) compared the casualty rates of two of the biggest battles
in the history of the British Army: Waterloo and the Somme. As an example,
he found that, 'In the two battles the 1st Battalion, Inniskilling Fusiliers,
suffered 427 and 568 casualties, out of 698 and 801 soldiers engaged:
casualty rates of 61 and 70 per cent respectively. But at Waterloo . . . the
infliction of casualties was spread out over three hours; on the Somme, the
losses were probably suffered in the first thirty minutes.' Such vast numbers
of wounded placed huge strains on the medical services, who were detailed to
deal with them both at the front line and also in hospitals.

> There's a stench of blood, pus, shit and sweat.
> Bandages ooze away underneath torn uniforms.
> Clammy trembling hands and wasted faces.
> Bodies stay propped up as their dying heads slump down.
> (Wilhelm Klemm, 1914, from 'Clearing Station', in Silkin, 1979: 226)

A couple of recent excavations have located medical facilities relating to the
First World War, both in the trenches and also behind the lines. During
pipeline work in Arras, France, workmen discovered a series of steps going
down into a basement. What they had found proved to be a British military
hospital from the First World War. Alain Jacques surveyed the site and found
it to be both large and self-contained. Painted signs on the walls pointed out
directions, TO OPERATING THEATRE or EXIT RUE ST QUENTIN, while other graffiti
was inscribed by the wounded and by medical staff. The hospital was just
800m from the front line and had room for 700 wounded. According to
Jacques, all logistical rooms were present, including an operating theatre,
kitchens and billets. Signs such as 'Iceland Street' and 'Hunter Street' were
displayed for the benefit of stretcher bearers on their way back to the front
(Desfossés et al., 2000: 37–8). Much of the tunnelling had been undertaken
by New Zealand miners, hence an inscription by a Maori Sapper, no. 20680
Toi. Karini, among others, also found in the entrance to the tunnels (Giradet
et al., 2003: 67). The hospital did not have a long working life; it was
partially destroyed by shell fire on the third day of its existence, 11 April

1917, during the Battle of Arras, and the wounded were rehoused in two other sites in Arras (*ibid.*: 38).

Work at Auchonvillers examined this village, which was used by medical units. 'An Advanced Dressing Station had initially been set up in the station building just to the west of the village but was shifted at some unspecified time in the winter of 1915/16 to the large farmhouse on the western edge of Auchonvillers.' Graffiti in the cellar connected to the trench that has been excavated, 'indicate[s] that the French army used the cellar as a medical post. The British graffiti dates from 1915 and 1916 and includes an inscription written by a member of the 48th Division Field Ambulance, which can be dated to August 1916' (Fraser, n.d.: 6). Further excavation pertaining to a medical function included the presence of six glass ampoules. They contained iodine, which was issued to infantrymen as a form of field treatment of wounds. In the First World War, the wounds suffered by infantrymen were from a variety of sources. Keegan (1991: 264) stated that, on the Somme, combat wounds were accounted for by bullets (around 30 per cent), bayonet (a fraction of 1 per cent), and the vast majority by shells and bombs (around 70 per cent).

Such ampoules and a bottle of iodine in a German fire pit were also found at Boezinge, Belgium (see Plate 27). The latter was located next to some scissors, which might perhaps have been used for cutting field dressings. Indeed, the excavators have also discovered belts from stretchers and a bottle bearing the legend 'Boots the Chemist' – the well-known British chain of chemist shops. Furthermore, in 2001, excavation work revealed a small underground construction with two rooms close to light-railway tracks serving the trenches. In it was the remains of a stretcher, some 2.2m in length, this may well have been a small dressing station (Aurel Sercu, pers. comm.).

Medical treatment and immediate first aid was available to troops. In the British Army, members of the Royal Army Medical Corps (RAMC) frequently risked their lives to help wounded soldiers. In the history of the highest gallantry award available to the British soldier, the Victoria Cross, only three soldiers have been awarded it twice. Their acts of bravery have meant that two of these men belonged to the RAMC (Laffin, 2003: 212). Infantry casualties could be removed from the field of battle by medical orderlies and then treated in hospitals behind the lines prior to their rejoining their units or being taken to one of the many military hospitals in Britain, if they had not died of their wounds. This is not to say that medical treatment was immediately available at all times; there are countless anecdotes of soldiers being stranded for very long periods in no man's land following a failed offensive, their screams pervading the night. At times the belligerent parties observed local ceasefires so that an army could retrieve its dead and wounded after such an attack (see, e.g., Graves, 1960: 134).

Biological anthropological studies of the remains of the French individuals excavated from the mass grave at Saint-Rémy-la-Calonne have revealed interesting facts about the general health of the troops – although the set of twenty-one soldiers is, perhaps, too small to draw any overall conclusions about health in the French army as a whole. Duday (1999: 103) noted some interesting features among the fallen of the 288th Infantry Regiment. In one sample, he commented, it was perhaps unsurprising to see degenerative conditions such as arthritis. What was more interesting was that, in a scene reminiscent of the French troops some hundred years before at Vilnius, one of the individuals (number 17) had suffered an injury some time prior to death that would have made a life of marching in an infantry regiment most awkward. The man's right leg, at its joint with the ankle, showed signs of a double fracture, a wound that had reshaped the limb when reset.

With the majority of soldiers in the grave wearing identity discs it was possible to detect a hierarchy of burial with differentiation between the officers and the men (see Memorials and Burials, page 205). Boura (1999: 81) also noted a discrepancy in the height of the two groups:

> There is a marked contrast in the stature of the officers and rankers in the mass grave at Saint-Rémy. The latter ranged between 1.54m and 1.68m (5ft 1in–5ft 7in) in height, the average being 1.60m (5ft 4in), whilst the officers were 1.7m (5ft 8in), 1.75m (5ft 10in) and 1.88m (6ft 3in) tall. The infantrymen were from Gers and, for the most part, were artisans and farmers. Their skeletons had traces of a physical lifestyle with healed fractures and initial stages of arthritis – the general state of the teeth was also poor.

This study is among the first to differentiate between officers and other ranks, allowing archaeologists to discern important differences between the medical health of the two. Had years of poorer diet restricted the growth of the men?

THE PRISONER

Soldier Fahlenstein of the 34th Fusiliers recorded in his diary that orders were carried out on 28 August 1914 to kill wounded French prisoners. At around the same time NCO Göttsche of the 85th Infantry Regiment was told by his captain near the fort of Kessel, near Antwerp, that no English prisoners were to be taken. According to the diary of a German doctor, French wounded were bayoneted to death by a company of German sappers on 31 August. A Silesian newspaper even reported (under the heading 'A Day of Honour for our Regiment') that French prisoners were finished off in late September.

(Ferguson, 1998: 373; see also Holmes, 1999: 178–9, on the killing of prisoners)

The option of being made a prisoner, even when wounded, was not always open to the defeated infantryman. There were times when, following capture, there remained the possibility of being killed behind the lines. This was thought to have been the case with the incidents surrounding one of the most comprehensively excavated First World War sites. On 21 September 1914, twenty-one soldiers of the French 288th Infantry Regiment of Mirande (Gers) disappeared in a wood at Saint-Rémy-la-Calonne (see page 199). For some time it had been suggested that they had been executed by the German army – a war crime. About seventy years later the burial pit, measuring 5.2m by 2.6m, was excavated by the Lorraine archaeology service and a different story emerged. From the pathology, it was clear that wounds were random with impacts coming from several directions and at different angles and, although it was impossible to rule out the possibility that some of the wounds were of a *coups-de-grâce* nature, it seems more likely that the group was simply surrounded and eliminated (Adam, 1999: 35).

Information on prisoner-of-war camps is scarce. Although images of prisoners can be seen on postcards of the time, much of the documentary information relating to captives both in Britain and in Germany was destroyed during the Second World War. Furthermore, archaeological information about the camps is sparse.

First World War prisoners, like their Napoleonic and Boer War predecessors, engaged in trench art (see pages 163 and 195) with the manufacture of small artefacts. They made these to sell, as well as to alleviate boredom. As Saunders (2003: 42) said: 'In prisoner-of-war camps, trench-art objects were made primarily of wood, bone and textiles. The scrap metals associated with battlefields were not generally available, though bully-beef tins could substitute on many occasions, and occasionally brass and copper were available.' Snakes were made using beadwork and bearing legends such as 'Turkish Prisoner 1915' (*ibid.*, 42; see also fig. 7.6).

An account of this type of work appeared in the *Leigh Chronicle* on Friday 26 February 1915, in which the fascinated correspondent wrote of a

> huge shoulder-blade of a cow [that] is a work of great skill and penmanship. On one side are about sixteen four line verses, written in a legal hand, the coat-of-arms and flag of the Brandenburg Regiment, laurel wreaths denoting the battles the author has taken part in and at the bottom the words in German, 'The English are very brave, but nothing to be frightened of.' On the back are the names and regiments of the prisoner's friends who have fallen in battle. (L. Smith, 1986: 40).

As with the above example, some of this art is particularly illuminating in terms of illustrating the names of German prisoners, their units, dates and places of internment on a single item. One example of a carved bone was illustrated with an epaulette and the unit number 57, as well as the inscription '*Heinz Cremer Erinnerung An Meine Kriegsgefangenschaft*', followed by crossed flags, the date of 1915 and the camp name of 'Stobs' (Saunders, 2003: 117). Stobs held more than 5,000 German prisoners in 200 huts. The prisoners formed their own orchestra and ran a camp newspaper entitled *Stobsiade*. Little survives of the camp, although the remains of a cairn built to hold the bodies of two inmates who committed suicide are still visible. The bodies of the deceased were moved to Cannock Chase in Staffordshire where the 2,143 German prisoners of war who died in Britain are buried.

Non-commissioned prisoners could be made to work during their confinement on tasks that often required physical labour. German prisoners, for example, were used to reconstruct the Arras to Lens railway line between the armistice on 11 November 1918 and the peace treaty of 1919. Alain Jacques has excavated one of the gang's workshops and recovered the remains of a veritable craft industry. The soldiers had spent time fashioning shell cases and similar materials into matchbox covers, belt buckles and paper knives (Briet, 2002: 20).

Another pastime that is virtually untraceable archaeologically, but was popular in the prison camps of both the Allies and the Central Powers, was football. An account in the *Leigh Chronicle*, Friday 26 February 1915, stated:

A football correspondent in jocular mood writes that as he notices the prisoners of war are always playing football in the compounds at the camp he is hoping to raise a team of 'coalers' to play on the Mather-lane ground for the benefit of the Belgian Fund against a team of Germans. There must be no rules, referee or linesmen, and the team that comes off the playing pitch alive wins. There would be a bumper gate, he adds. (L. Smith, 1986: 42).

There are several written accounts of prisoner escapes from camps in the First World War (see, e.g., Warin, 1989, for British attempts, and L. Smith, 1986: 47, for a German version), but the limited amount of fieldwork related to such sites means that our archaeological evidence for these attempts is small. However, splendid photographs exist of failed escape tunnels at the prisoner-of-war camp at Holzminden, discovered and dug out in 1918 (Photo ID Number: Q 69484 6008-01 Imperial War Museum), and at Clausthal (Photo ID Number: Q 115193 8508-26 Imperial War Museum) in Germany.

In terms of imprisonment, it was not simply captured opponents that were interned; soldiers could be incarcerated by their own side for various breaches of military code, the ultimate sanction being execution by firing squad. In the Belgian town of Poperinge several British soldiers were shot for desertion, after having been imprisoned in one of four small cells in the town on the night before their execution. Conservation work to the walls of these cells has revealed graffiti scrawled by men held within during the First World War, often for smaller offences than those for which a capital sentence was handed down. Soldiers' names, verses, pictorial representations, and even downright salacious inscriptions were found. The miscreants of various nations are represented in these carvings and drawings, including doodles of an American soldier bayoneting a German soldier (somewhat erroneously wearing a *Pickelhaube* given the date of 1918, by which time German infantry were equipped with the familiar steel helmet) and a German officer (the Kaiser?), and an image of the Australian slouch hat. Names covering the walls include 609234 W. Finlay from 'Durham, South Shields', who was locked up for being '27 days Absent without Leave-Court Martial'. These writings are some of the best traces we can find archaeologically for a form of imprisonment in the First World War.

MEMORIALS AND BURIALS

Memorials to events in the First World War are to be found throughout the Western Front, both to regiments and to the individual soldiers themselves. Cities, towns and villages of the belligerent nations commemorated their own dead and rare was the place that did not have anyone to mourn. This was not the first war to see the common soldier remembered – indeed there were monuments to the fallen in the Boer War (see Chapter 6); however, this war, wherever possible, buried its dead together. Rows of white Portland stone headstones rising from the ground like so many teeth from a vast skull are to be found in Commonwealth cemeteries, while the French used simple plastic crosses and the Germans adapted their cemeteries to the landscape in which they were sited.

Holyoak (2004: 13) points out that attitudes to burial differed between the countries:

> despite families' entreaties, the [British] empire's dead were left where they were, for reasons of cost and equality. Repatriating only identified remains, it was argued, would discriminate against the families of the hundreds of thousands in graves marked only 'known unto God' or listed as missing . . . It was different elsewhere. In 1920 the French government caved in to pressure and allowed relatives to reclaim their war dead, at state expense. Within two years, in a remarkable exercise in logistics, some 300,000 fallen had been exhumed and returned to their home towns.

Most poignant of all are the memorials to those men who were either unidentifiable at the time of burial, or were simply never recovered. The names of the latter are generally recorded on the walls of cemeteries or huge monuments, such as the Menin Gate (Ypres), Thiepval (Somme), Le Mont-Kemmel (French) and Langemark (German; see Plate 28) in the Ypres Salient. Bodies that were found, but were unrecognisable, were buried in graves with as much information as possible, ranging from an 'Unknown Australian Soldier' to a 'Soldier of the Great War, known unto God'. In Britain's case, wooden battlefield crosses set up to denote the presence of a grave and the man it held were gradually replaced with headstones. Often the crosses were sent back to England, where they can be found in parish churches, such as at the Church of St Mary the Virgin, Hawkesbury, St Leonard's Church, Tortworth, South Gloucestershire, and Bromham Church in Wiltshire. There is even a wooden cross to an unknown soldier in Talbot House, Poperinge.

Some of the cemeteries are vast, such as Tyne Cot in Passchendaele, the largest Commonwealth cemetery. It contains 3,588 burials, and commemorates 34,872 missing servicemen. This graveyard preserved elements of the First World War within its very fabric, forever entwining the causes of the death of the men in their memorial. The large Cross of Sacrifice is built over one of the massive German concrete blockhouses, which is visible through a small gap in the Portland stone. Inscribed upon the cross are the words, 'This was the Tyne Cot blockhouse captured by the 3rd Australian Division 4th October 1917.' A further blockhouse is also visible within the grounds of the cemetery.

Units and nations are also commemorated, many with statues. As with the Boer War, soldiers are generally depicted in poses of remembrance and mourning and, given the huge loss of life in all armies, there is little triumphalism. Individual, unknown, low-ranking soldiers are often portrayed: an unknown 'Tommy' striding forward with fixed bayonet and rifle at Flers; an Australian 'Digger' carrying a wounded comrade back from danger at Fromelles; the French *poilu* at the Butte de Vauqois armed with rifle and grenade, looking towards Verdun. An even more muted representation is to be found at the German Langemark cemetery where four shadowy figures, bronze statues of mourning soldiers – unknown mourners for unknown dead – pay their respects to the mass German grave (see Plate 28). Here, more than 44,000 German dead are remembered, around 25,000 of whom were buried in a Kameraden Grab (Comrade's Grave) for unknown soldiers from all over Flanders. Mourning parents are also represented in the German cemetery at Vladslo, north of Ypres, where a kneeling man and woman are portrayed, sculpted by Käthe Kollwitz whose son Peter is interred in the cemetery.

Large sculptures of animals were also placed on the battlefields to commemorate regiments or nations that had fought in an area. There is an elk at Vimy Ridge for the Canadian forces, and a dragon for the Royal Welch Regiment at Mametz Wood.

War cemeteries are present not just in the countries of the conflict. At Cannock Chase, in England, there is a very large German cemetery containing graves marked by crosses of Belgian granite. These represent the final resting place for 2,143 German prisoners of war who died in British camps from their wounds, disease and suicide. They were brought to Cannock Chase after having been exhumed from the churchyards where they had been buried during the war and they are now accompanied by many of their countrymen who fell in the Second World War.

The work at the site of the mass burial at Saint-Rémy-la-Calonne indicated that there might have been a hierarchy of burial. Excavators believed that the captain was laid in first, followed by the other officers and finally the private soldiers, with all bodies laid head to toe (Adam, 1999: 32). Such a formalised mode of burial may have been possible early in the war (this incident was in 1914), but the sheer numbers of troops killed on the Western Front meant that such formalities were often impossible. Even when they were observed, artillery barrages frequently reopened the graves of those killed earlier in the war. The effects of artillery also ensured that some of those killed could not be buried as there was next to nothing left of them; at times only small portions of a man were laid to rest: 'The following day when I was given the job of going round with sandbags, collecting the pieces, we had to rescue some bits from telegraph wires where they'd been blown at great velocity, and we buried them in the common grave' (Private R. Richards, Royal Engineers, on the effects of a shell; Arthur, 2002: 106).

An example of the palimpsest of burial on this front is to be found at Monchy-le-Preux, Pas de Calais, as a result of rescue archaeology work. Here, the body of a British soldier (a subaltern of the Royal Scots Regiment) was found in a shell hole with his arms and legs spread wide apart indicating a lack of ceremony. Below his legs was the body of a German infantryman who had probably been killed some time before (Desfossés et al., 2000: 34). A similar situation was revealed in an evaluation excavation on the route of the A29 in France, at Monigny-les-Bains. The body of an unknown Australian soldier was intertwined with that of an Algerian (Olivier, 2000: 24). As we have noted (see Accommodation, page 191), a number of Germans were also buried in a shell hole at Gavrelle, and it seems to have been expedient to use these large holes for quick burial of the dead (ibid.: 35) and that mass burials were commonplace.

Some burials were placed next to the fallen of previous wars; according to Jünger (2003: 190), several German soldiers were interred 'in the military cemetery at Thiaucourt. In among the fallen of this war, there were also fighters from 1870 [the Franco-Prussian War]. One of those old graves was marked by a mossy stone with the inscription: "Distant to the eye, but to the heart forever nigh".'

As a postscript to this section, it could also be pertinent to mention the burial and memorial of soldiers who died and were buried in cemeteries together, yet who never came under fire. Cemeteries at places such as Durrington, Codford and Sutton Veny in Wiltshire reveal the fact that many men died as a result of disease in areas of training, many of them far from home – New Zealanders, Canadians and Australians.

THE FALLEN

The excavation of human remains from First World War battle sites is a sensitive issue. In many cases the deceased have surviving relatives and, at time of writing, there are even some surviving veterans. It is a conflict from which there are numerous photographs, film images and recorded testimonies of combatants and civilians. The recovery of human remains is imbued with a pathos unequalled on archaeological excavations. The vast number of men listed simply as 'missing' on the battlefields of Ypres, Verdun and the Somme ensures that recovery of human remains continues, whether by farmers, by those undertaking excavations in advance of development work, or even by walkers. Some of these remains, if excavated using archaeological techniques, can provide information on how the individual died, facets of his life in the trenches, and, on occasions, his name.

One such excavation, on the Heidenkopf at Serre on the Somme by No Man's Land Archaeological Team, is a case in point. In addition to the German soldier with the flint (see Practice, page 183), the team found another German soldier who, through careful analysis of a partial identity disc, and the pattern of his cuff buttons, they were able to identify as Jakob Hones. He was a farm labourer from Stuttgart who served in the 121 Reserve Infantry Regiment and had been killed in June 1915. A third body was that of a British man, found lying on top of chalk fill on the front edge of the Heidenkopf. The many small shell fragments among his bones and the fracture of his right femur illustrated the savage realities of death through shell burst (Brown, 2005: 30).

UNKNOWN WARRIOR 13

When part of the site of Boezinge, to the north of Ypres and east of the Ypres–Yser canal, was threatened by the development of an industrial estate, the Belgian government sanctioned the exploration of the area – the site of the first German gas attack in 1915 – by The Diggers, a group of amateur archaeologists. The group has been criticised for its use of metal detectors (Saunders, 2002: 103), but its efforts have yielded important information, which has been archived by the In Flanders Fields Museum in Ypres. Had it not been for The Diggers' work, much information might have been lost to developers (for The Diggers' reports, see The Diggers, 2005). The work confirmed that this area had covered British and German trench systems at a point where no man's land was far from wide. Excavations recovered both spent and live rifle rounds (British and German), a British rifle with fixed bayonet, barbed wire and wooden duckboards from the trenches, and a large amount of material relating to the lives and deaths of soldiers.

On 2 August 2001, the remains of two British soldiers were excavated at Boezinge. With one of the men, Burial 124, a number of items were found: a broken pipe, a shaving brush, a fragment of a toothbrush, a spoon, an iodine ampoule, remnants of a gas mask (by the individual's face), a pocket knife, a small mirror (perhaps a trench mirror for observation), several buckles, an entrenching tool, a blue water bottle, some broken pencils and two badges of the Royal Welch Fusiliers.

Close by was another man. He was found with a Mills bomb (hand grenade), the two eyeglasses of a gas mask, a brush, buckles, buttons, spoon, pipe, knife, cartridges, a tin box with tobacco snuff and (importantly for dating) a small leather purse with coins, some of which had a 1917 date. From his insignia he too was a Royal Welch Fusilier (Aurel Sercu, pers. comm.).

Some 2ft below the men were the remnants of a trench proper, including wooden duckboards. Given the fact that these two men were both Royal Welch Fusiliers and that coins of 1917 were found, it is possible to date their deaths to between January and July 1917 when the 38th (Welsh) Division with the Royal Welch Fusiliers was stationed at Boezinge. Both men were not interred as part of an established burial ritual; they were both battlefield casualties, buried by the same action that killed them.

UNKNOWN WARRIOR 13

A Royal Welch Fusilier, Burial 124 at Boezinge, Flanders

A soldier, killed in the first half of 1917 at Boezinge, close to Ypres, in Belgium (in the same year and region as the Battle of Passchendaele), was found in full kit complete with a steel helmet (see Colour Plate 12). Items of personal kit, such as his toothbrush, were discovered with him. What had killed this man? As he was later reburied in a nearby military cemetery there is no pathologist's report, but Paul Reed, a historian of the First World War, believes that we can make a plausible case for the mode of death of soldier 124 given his accoutrements, his location, and his position in death.

Reed hypothesises that this infantryman was in a forward sap undertaking observation duties (hence the trench mirror). He was killed by the effects of shell fire (either high explosive and/or shrapnel) while under a gas attack, indicated by the close presence of the gas mask (P. Reed, pers. comm.). Although death in an artillery barrage may seem an exceptionally violent end, such events need not always leave physical marks on the skeleton. 'Shell blast could create over-pressures or vacuums in the body's organs, rupturing the lungs and producing haemorrhages in the brain and spinal cord. It was the effects of this sort which killed three Welch Fusiliers [on the Somme] "sitting" in a shell hole . . . with no more visible mark on them than some singeing of their clothing' (Keegan, 1991: 264). Neither soldier 124 nor his comrade, soldier 125, was identifiable, although they were both Royal Welch Fusiliers. Their names will be on the Menin Gate in Ypres.

As Keegan (*ibid*.: 225) notes, the Royal Welch Fusiliers had among their numbers Siegfried Sassoon and Robert Graves and consequently referred to the 2nd Battalion as 'that extraordinary Battalion of poets'. Graves wrote a poem that is so apposite, it might have been composed for soldiers 124 and 125. Entitled 'Two Fusiliers', its final verse is:

> Show me two so closely bound
> As we, by the wet bond of blood,
> By friendship, blossoming from mud,
> By Death: we faced him, and we found
> Beauty in Death,
> In dead men breath.

> (Stallworthy, 1977: 252)

UNKNOWN WARRIOR 14

The Unknown Warrior, Westminster Abbey

The final unknown soldier in this volume is the source of its inspiration. Dedications have been made by other countries around the world in a similar fashion. This is the British Unknown Warrior (see Plate 29).

On 7 November 1920, one burial from Ypres, one from the Somme, one from Arras, and one from the Aisne were exhumed; they were the bodies of unknown British servicemen of unknown rank and unknown armed service. One of these bodies was chosen at random and was brought back to Britain on HMS *Verdun* in a coffin of English oak. (The other three bodies were buried in a military cemetery at St Pol.) On 11 November, the coffin was drawn past the cenotaph in London on a gun carriage and taken to Westminster Abbey where it passed through a guard of honour of 100 Victoria Cross holders (the highest honour bestowed on a British soldier; Gavaghan, 1995: 65). There, in the west nave, the warrior was laid to rest, buried in the abbey that holds the graves of kings and poets, scientists and musicians. On a slab of black Belgian marble, laid over the grave in 1921, the inscription on the tomb reads:

BENEATH THIS STONE RESTS THE BODY
OF A BRITISH WARRIOR
UNKNOWN BY NAME OR RANK
BROUGHT FROM FRANCE TO LIE AMONG
THE MOST ILLUSTRIOUS OF THE LAND
AND BURIED HERE ON ARMISTICE DAY
11 NOV: 1920, IN THE PRESENCE OF
HIS MAJESTY KING GEORGE V
HIS MINISTERS OF STATE
THE CHIEFS OF HIS FORCES
AND A VAST CONCOURSE OF THE NATION

THUS ARE COMMEMORATED THE MANY
MULTITUDES WHO DURING THE GREAT
WAR OF 1914–1918 GAVE THE MOST THAT
MAN CAN GIVE LIFE ITSELF
FOR GOD
FOR KING AND COUNTRY

FOR LOVED ONES HOME AND EMPIRE
FOR THE SACRED CAUSE OF JUSTICE AND
THE FREEDOM OF THE WORLD

THEY BURIED HIM AMONG THE KINGS BECAUSE HE
HAD DONE GOOD TOWARD GOD AND TOWARD
HIS HOUSE

In 1921 the Unknown Warrior was awarded the Congressional Medal of Honour of the United States of America (Gavaghan, 1995: 73).

John Laffin (2003: 222), in his book *Tommy Atkins: the Story of the English Soldier*, rather mournfully concluded:

Colonel John McCrae, a distinguished Canadian doctor, who died of pneumonia at Wimereux, France, in January 1918, movingly crystallized in his poem, 'In Flanders Fields', the loss of so many British and Commonwealth soldiers. One stanza reads:

We are the dead. Short days ago
We lived, felt dawn, saw sunset flow,
Loved and were loved, and now we lie
In Flanders fields.

I would make an addition to the last line:

In Flanders fields forgotten.

Despite, or perhaps as a result of, the scale of loss of life, this war more than any before it attempted to commemorate the common soldier – the private in the 'Poor Bloody Infantry'. As far as the living were concerned, campaign medals were issued to all soldiers, independent of rank. Fallen soldiers were buried, where possible, in cemeteries with individual headstones – cemeteries that are attended to this day. Where the body was not recovered, a name was entered on monuments such as the Menin Gate, the walls of Tyne Cot cemetery or the Thiepval monument (73,367 names of the missing on the Somme are carved on the latter – Laffin, 2003: 211). Cities, towns and villages produced their own memorials on which the names of the dead were carved.

Contrast the commemoration of the common soldier in the First World War with those of the Battle of Waterloo or flight from Moscow some 100 years earlier. Today, when remains of the dead and of the trenches in which they fought are uncovered through the progress of modern infrastructure, they are given due deference even when their names have long since been lost. Historians and archaeologists are constantly striving to understand more about the First World War and to uncover details of the lives of those who fought and died in it. Those who died on the Western Front are being remembered.

Conclusion

Pay heed to nourishing the troops; do not unnecessarily fatigue them.
Unite them in spirit; conserve their strength. Make unfathomable plans
for the movement of the army.

(Sun Tzu, *The Art of War*)

I have examined the presence of infantry from the Bronze Age to the First World
War, yet archaeological sites have revealed details of the lives of humans from
early in the prehistoric period. One of the elements that appears to be traceable
throughout most periods is the violent act. This is not a comment on the
predisposition of our species to fight, simply that such acts occur.

In each chapter I have emphasised the plethora of evidence available to
archaeologists in determining the presence of warfare and the lives of those who
fought. One must bear in mind a multitude of caveats when examining the
archaeology of violence. Were items really damaged in combat? Could those
individuals who were buried with weaponry be called 'warriors'? Were weapon
injuries combat-related or the result of judicial acts, murder, or accident?

We must also consider the limitations of the archaeological record. Clearly,
only a sample of evidence for combat survives (material left on the battlefield
could have been removed by the victors and later societies); death in combat
need not result in palaeopathological evidence and the suchlike. Carman
(1997a: 236) provides a useful discussion of these problems, but states, in a
paragraph worth quoting at length, that:

> Specific archaeologies can also emphasise the specifics of individual times and
> places to reveal the context of violent acts. These will reveal the circumstances
> (individual and social) of violence, the causes of it, and distinctions between
> victim, perpetrator and witness. At the same time, archaeology can
> demonstrate the different forms of violence apparent in varying contexts: war
> as opposed to individual assault, symbolic or symbolised/'non-violent' violence
> and sanctioned versus non-sanctioned violence.

An archaeological analysis of the material that *does* survive can provide a vivid illustration of the lives of the ordinary infantryman (and woman). This narrative is far less frequent in the historic resource, although some accounts of the lives of the private soldier do appear. Archaeology has the potential to speak without bias or overemphasis. Our dataset can show, for example, the victuals available to soldiers, how they spent periods of spare time, how and where they trained, whether this training was carried out to the exact textbook specifications in combat, and the weaponry that was actually used. By studying the remains of those who fought and fell, we can also uncover the illnesses from which they suffered, how they died, and what religion, if any, they looked to in their final moments.

Too many histories examine the lives of the commanders of armies, or their exaggeration of tactics and the outcomes of battles, yet all those who fought are equal in the archaeological record. Sometimes, archaeology will confirm historic tracts, on other occasions new theories will emerge as a result of these studies: perhaps troop dispositions differed from the official campaign histories; sometimes soldiers adopted tactics learned on campaign rather than at the depot (after all, digging a trench under artillery fire is somewhat different from performing a similar task on exercise).

This book looks at the 'common' soldier, the infantry private, as it is this individual who does the bulk of the fighting in most wars. These men and women need not be professional soldiers (as we have witnessed with the composition of forces in the First World War) and may not want to be a part of any military action. Yet our examination throws up much to illustrate the lives and deaths of such individuals, lives and deaths that are not written about, but which provide powerful, mute testament within an archaeological context. Some themes recur: the soldier's use of tobacco and of alcohol; the playing of games to alleviate boredom; the men's humour; their desire to leave a name or an image of themselves as a warrior as a permanent marker of their life.

The one element that is present in all periods is the burial of those about whom we know nothing other than their death in combat – soldiers who are 'unknown' (see Plate 30). We can tell much about their lives and deaths and yet, ultimately, we do not know who they were. It is to them that this book is dedicated.

Glossary

Ampoule glass container or phial containing medicine such as iodine, which was easy to administer in the front line

Antiquarian the earliest archaeologists – although many sites suffered from poor recording of the works they undertook, archaeological techniques and the discipline as a whole emerged as a result of their investigations

Arquebus early form of muzzle-loading firearm

Auxiliary non-citizen troops of the Roman army, supplementing the citizen-soldiers of the legions – these troops formed both cavalry and infantry units, with auxiliary troops frequently taken from the conquered regions

Basal looped type of spearhead that had loops at the bottom of the blade, which were either decorative or used to tie the spearhead to the shaft

Beaker ceramic drinking vessel that formed the essential element of the Beaker burial package of the Early Bronze Age

Blockhouse concrete fortification or strongpoint forming an essential component of First World War defence systems

Carp's tongue sword Late Bronze Age sword type found predominantly along the Atlantic coast; so called because it used a leaf-shaped blade for cutting, which tapered to a point – the 'Carp's tongue' – for stabbing

Chape metal attachment, sometimes hooked, to the end of the sword scabbard that enabled the removal of the blade from the sheath by a mounted warrior

Coif protective mail garment, hood-like in form, that covered the neck and head of the warrior

Cuirass body armour that protects the torso of a warrior, comprising back- and breastplate; frequently made of metal, but sometimes possibly of tough organic materials, such as leather, which rarely survive in the archaeological record

Excarnated exposure of the dead body in the open air before a later burial or ritual deposition of the defleshed bones

Gladius standard Roman infantry side arm; a blade weapon that was ideally suited to stabbing at close quarters

Jack Johnson British nickname for a type of German artillery shell; named after the US World Heavyweight boxing champion of 1908–15

Lamellar armour type composed of metal plates sewn into a fabric tunic

Legionary Roman infantryman

Longbarrow Neolithic burial mound, *c.* 4000 BC–2200 BC, often with separate chambers

Lorica hamata Roman mail armour composed of interlinked circles of iron or bronze

Lorica segmentata Roman legionary armour composed of a series of hinged plates; it would have had either a fabric or leather backing, or would have been worn over a tunic and was probably used for around 200 years from the first to the third centuries AD

Lorica squamata Roman armour composed of a series of metal scales (either bronze or iron) sewn onto a tunic, often of leather

Matchlock early form of muzzle-loading firearm, discharged when the priming pan of gunpowder was touched and ignited by a smouldering length of matchcord, held by the musketeer

Midden curated refuse dump; in the Bronze Age (*c.* 2200–700 BC) these appear to have had complex functions related to feasting and the deliberate deposition of waste materials

Minnie nickname for German trench mortars, derived from *Minenwerfer* mine thrower

Morion form of helmet of the sixteenth and early seventeenth centuries; there were several variants, including those with flat or peaked brims and coned or flattened body, and it could have a crest or a 'stalk' at the peak

Optical Stimulated Luminescence dating technique that measures ionised radiation, which is stimulated to produce measurable luminescence to calculate the time since the sample was buried

Palaeoenvironmental study of ancient environmental indicators

Palisade timber fence barrier used on hill forts and defended sites

Palstave bronze tool, similar in form to an axe, with the blade divided from the haft of the weapon by a ridge

Pike main pole-arm of the sixteenth and seventeenth centuries, composed of a long wooden shaft tipped with a metal blade or point; the blade often comprised arms of metal, which ran down the length of the pole to prevent it being lopped off by an enemy's blade in action (pike formations acted together to provide protection for each other and for the musketeers)

Pilum Roman infantryman's throwing weapon comprising a heavy wooden shaft and long slender metal neck and point; it was designed so that it could not be thrown back and would bend on impact to encumber any enemy unfortunate to be transfixed by it

Pugio Roman legionary dagger, probably used rarely in battle compared to the *pilum* or *gladius*

Radiocarbon scientific dating technique used to measure the level of carbon 14 isotopes

Rapier slender, tapering weapon used in a stabbing fashion; in the Bronze Age the rapier was replaced as the weapon of choice by the sword

Ricasso notch small notch below the handle of a Bronze Age sword, above the blade, which was used as part of the warrior's grip

Round barrow circular burial mound of the early Bronze Age period from around 2200 BC; often it would have central burials with later satellite depositions sometimes from different time periods, such as the Anglo-Saxon era

Rune form of writing script used by Norsemen

Samian Roman pottery form, red in colour, often with designs and motifs on the outside

Seax pointed, single-edged knife of Anglo-Saxon date, generally quite short

Spatha Roman sword, longer in form than the *gladius* and thought to have been used by cavalry

Sprue flash of waste lead left on the musket ball when removed from the mould; this lead was smoothed off by the musketeer before use

Stela (pl. stelae) upright stone which has been carved; these often had depictions of the warrior and their arms

Stratigraphy study of archaeological layers; by careful study of the stratigraphy, the archaeologist can evaluate a phase-plan of the site (in stratigraphic terms, the undisturbed site will have the earliest deposits as the bottom layers and the most recent as the upper layers)

Tassets articulated plates of armour attached to a breastplate, which cover the upper thighs of a pikeman

Trilithon combination of three stones as part of a henge monument, for example the combinations at Stonehenge with two uprights and a cross stone lintel

Umbo the metal shield boss of the Roman legionary shield – the *scutum*

Whizz-bang a term used by Allied troops (mainly British and Commonwealth) to describe, in onomatopoeic form, the sound of German field artillery shells – originally of 77mm calibre

Wristguard protective piece of equipment used by the archer to prevent the bowstring damaging the wrist; in the Bronze Age Beaker period, this appears at times to have been formed from stone, and from the Medieval periods there are surviving leather examples

References

Adam, F. (1999). 'L'Archéologie et La Grande Guerre'. In *L'Archéologie et La Grande Guerre. 14–18 Aujourd'hui – Today – Heute*. Revue Annuelle d'Histoire, 2. Paris, Éditions Noêsis, 28–35

Ager, B. (2001). 'Offensive Weapons'. In *Viking Weapons and Warfare*, http://www.bbc.co.uk/history/ancient/vikings/weapons_03.shtml (accessed 1 September 2005)

Allason-Jones, L., and Bishop, M.C. (1988). *Excavations at Roman Corbridge: The Hoard*. London, English Heritage

Allen, D., and Anderson, S. (1999). *Basing House Hampshire: Excavations 1978–1991*. Hampshire Field Club Monograph 10. Hampshire Field Club and Archaeological Society/Hampshire County Council

Allen, T. (1990). *Current Archaeology*, 121, XI/1 (September/October): 24–7

Ancient Sites Directory (2005). 'Maes Howe, Orkney', http://www.henge.org.uk/orkney/maeshowe.html (accessed 1 September 2005)

Archaeology of the Western Front (2003). 'Thélus / Vimy ("La Couture Baron"), Arras 2003', http://web.telia.com/~u86517080/BattlefieldArchaeology/ArkeologENG_3B.html#anchor993533 (accessed 1 September 2005)

Armitage, P. (2004). 'Berry Head Fort South'. *Council for British Archaeology (South-West)*, 12 (Winter): 5–6

Armitage, P., and Rouse, R. (2003). *Military and Other Buttons from the Berry Head Forts 1794 –1817*. Brixham, Brixham Heritage Museum

Arthur, M. (2002). *Forgotten Voices of the Great War: A New History of World War One in the Words of the Men and Women Who Were There*. London, Ebury Press

Atkin, M. (1987). 'Post Medieval Archaeology in Gloucester: A Review'. *Post Medieval Archaeology*, 21: 1–24

Atkin, M. (1989). 'Siege!' *British Archaeology*, 11 (January/February): 6–10

Aubrey, J., 'Monumenta Britannica'. Unpublished manuscript

Audoin-Rouzeau, S. (1999). 'Practiques et Objets de la Cruauté sur le Champ de Bataille'. In *L'Archéologie et La Grande Guerre. 14–18 Aujourd'hui – Today – Heute*. Revue Annuelle d'Histoire, 2. Paris, Éditions Noêsis, 104–15

Bahn, P. (2002) (ed.). *Written in Bones: How Human Remains Unlock the Secrets of the Dead*. Newton Abbot, David & Charles

Balicki, J. (2003). 'Defending the Capital: The Civil War Garrison at Fort C.F. Smith'. In Geier and Potter (2003), 125–47

Barclay, A., and Halpin, C. (1999). *Excavations at Barrow Hills, Radley, Oxfordshire*. Volume 1. *The Neolithic and Bronze Age Monument Complex*. Oxford Archaeological Unit, Thames Valley Landscapes, 2. Oxford, Oxford University Committee for Archaeology

Barnes, I. (2000). 'Magnetic Susceptibility and Viscocity'. In Dixon *et al.* (2000), 80

Bartlett, C. (2002). *English Longbowman 1330–1515*. London, Osprey Publishing

Bartlett, J.E., and Hawkes, C.F.C. (1965). 'A Barbed Bronze Spearhead from North Ferriby, Yorkshire'. *Proceedings of the Prehistoric Society*, 31: 370–3

Barton, P., Doyle, P., and Vandewalle, J. (2004). *Beneath Flanders Fields: The Tunnellers' War 1914–18*. Staplehurst, Spellmount

Battlefields Trust (2004). http://www.battlefieldstrust.com/ (accessed 1 September 2005)

BBC News (2004a). 'Romans Faced Head-to-Head Battle', http://news.bbc.co.uk/1/hi/england/cumbria/3582603.stm (accessed 1 September 2005)

BBC News (2004b). 'Medieval Surgeons were Advanced', http://news.bbc.co.uk/1/hi/health/3714992.stm (accessed 1 September 2005)

Beaver, P. (1973) (ed.). *The Wipers Times: A Complete Facsimile of the Famous World War One Trench Newspaper, Incorporating the 'New Church' Times, The Kemmel Times, The Somme Times, The B.E.F. Times, and the 'Better Times'*. London, Peter Davies

Becker, A. (1999). 'Graffiti et Sculptures de Soldats'. In *L'Archéologie et La Grande Guerre. 14–18 Aujourd'hui – Today – Heute*. Revue Annuelle d'Histoire, 2. Paris, Éditions Noêsis, 117–27

Bennike, P. (1985). *Palaeopathology of Danish Skeletons: A Comparative Study of Demography, Disease and Injury*. Copenhagen, Akademisk Forlag

Berry Head Archaeology (2000) http://www.brixhamheritage.org.uk/arch/berry_head_report2000.htm (accessed 1 September)

Bezeczky, T. (1996). 'Amphora Inscriptions: Legionary Supply?' *Britannia*, 27: 329–36

Biddle, M., and Kjølbye-Biddle, B. (1992). 'Repton and the Vikings'. *Antiquity*, 66: 36–51

Bidwell, P.T. (1979). *The Legionary Bath-house and Basilica and Forum at Exeter*. Exeter Archaeological Reports 1. Exeter, Exeter City Council

Birley, A. (2002). *Garrison Life at Vindolanda: A Band of Brothers*. Stroud, Tempus

Bishop, M.C. (2002). *Lorica Segmentata*. Volume 1: *A Handbook of Articulated Roman Plate Armour*. Journal of Roman Military Equipment Studies Monograph 1. Berwickshire, Armantura Press

Boardman, A. (2000). 'The Historical Background to the Battle and the Documentary Evidence'. In Fiorato *et al.* (2000), 15–28

Bostwick, D., and Roberts, I. (2002). 'Civil War Graffiti and Inscriptions'. In Roberts (2002), 293–9

Bostyn, F. (1999). *Beecham Dugout, Passchendaele 1914–1918*. Association for Battlefield Archaeology in Flanders, Studies 1. Zonnebeke, Association for Battlefield Archaeology in Flanders

Boulen, M. (1998). *Villeneuve-Saint-Germain: Les Étomelles*. Paris, Association pour les Fouilles Archéologiques Nationales

Boura, F. (1999). 'Une tombe de soldats á Saint-Rémy-la-Calonne'. In *L'Archéologie et La Grande Guerre. 14–18 Aujourd'hui – Today – Heute*. Revue Annuelle d'Histoire, 2. Paris, Éditions Noêsis, 70–83

Boura, F. (2000). 'L'Ecrivain, sa famille et les archéologues: Autour de la Tombe d'Alain-Fournier'. *Archéologia*, 367 (May): 28–31

Bowman, A.K. (2003). *Life and Letters of the Roman Frontier: Vindolanda and its People*. London, British Museum Press

Boylston, A., Holst, M., and Coughlan, J. (2000). 'Physical Anthropology'. In Fiorato *et al.* (2000), 45–59

Bradley, R., and Ellison, A. (1975). *Rams Hill: A Bronze Age Defended Settlement and its Landscape.* British Archaeological Reports 19. Oxford, Archaeopress

Brewer, R.J. (2000). *Caerleon and the Roman Army – Roman Legionary Museum: A Guide.* Cardiff, National Museum of Wales

Bridgford, S. (1997). 'Mightier than the Pen? An Edgewise Look at Irish Bronze Age Swords. In Carman (1997b), 95–115

Briet, S. (2002). 'La Grande Guerre à 400 mètres'. *Libération,* 6641 (Friday 20 September 2002): 20

British Archaeology News (1999). 'Medicines Identified from the *Mary Rose*'. *British Archaeology,* 43 (April); http://www.britarch.ac.uk/ba/ba43/ba43news.html (accessed 1 September 2005)

Brothwell, D. (1971). 'Forensic Aspects of the So-called Neolithic Skeleton Q1 from Maiden Castle, Dorset'. *World Archaeology,* 3/2: 233–41

Brown, M. (2003). 'Mighty was the Sword: Victims of the Battle of Lewes'. *Battlefields Review,* 25: 56–9

Brown, M. (2004). 'A Mirror of the Apocalypse: Great War Training Trenches'. *Sanctuary* (the Ministry of Defence conservation magazine), 33: 54–8

Brown, M. (2005). 'Journey Back to Hell: Excavations at Serre on the Somme'. *Current World Archaeology,* 10: 25–33

Bulmer, R.H. (1999) (ed.). *Frenchay – A Village at War: Extracts from the Parish Magazine of St John the Baptist, Frenchay, South Gloucestershire.* Frenchay, Frenchay Tuckett Society and Local History Museum

Bush, T.S. (1914–18). 'Discovery on Lansdown'. *The Somerset Archaeological and Natural History Society: Proceedings of the Bath and District Branch.* Bath, Herald Press: 127–8

Caesar, J. (1982). *The Conquest of Gaul,* trans. S.A. Handford. Harmondsworth, Penguin

Carauna, I. (1991). 'A Wooden Training Sword and the So-Called Practice Post from Carlisle. *Arma: Newsletter of the Roman Military Equipment Conference,* 3/1(June): 11–14

Carlton, C. (1991). 'The Impact of Fighting'. In Morrill (1991), 17–31

Carman, J. (1997a). 'Giving Archaeology a Moral Voice'. In Carman (1997b), 220–40

Carman, J. (1997b) (ed.). *Material Harm: Archaeological Studies of War and Violence.* Glasgow, Cruithne Press

Carman, J., and Harding, A. (1999) (eds). *Ancient Warfare.* Stroud, Sutton Publishing

Casey, P.J., and Davies, J.L., with Evans, J. (1993). *Excavations at Segontium (Caernarfon) Roman Fort, 1975–1979.* Council for British Archaeology Research Report 90. London, CBA

Clarke, D.V., Cowie, T.G., and Foxon, A. (1985). *Symbols of Power at the Time of Stonehenge.* Edinburgh (HMSO), National Museum of Antiquities

Clauss, M. (2001). *The Roman Cult of Mithras: The God and his Mysteries.* New York, Routledge

Clunn, T. (1999). *In Quest of the Lost Legions: The Varusschlacht.* London, Minerva Press

Clydesdale, A. (2005). 'Postcards from the First World War: Finds from Scapa Flow'. *Archaeologist* (magazine of the Institute of Field Archaeologists), 55 (Winter): 42–3

Coles, J.M. (1962). 'European Bronze Age Shields'. *Proceedings of the Prehistoric Society,* 28: 156–90

Coles, J.M., Leach, P., Minnitt, S.C., Tabor, R., and Wilson, A.S. (1999). 'A Later Bronze Age Shield from South Cadbury, Somerset, England'. *Antiquity*, 73/279: 33–48

Collingwood, R.G., and Wright, R.P. (1991). *Roman Inscriptions of Britain*. Volume II: *Instrumentum Domesticum Fascicule 3*, ed. S.S. Frere and R.S.O. Tomlin. Stroud, Alan Sutton

Constandse-Westermann, T.S. (1982). 'A Skeleton found in a Roman Well at Velsen'. *Helinium*, 22: 135–69

Cool, H.E.M. (2005). 'Pyromania'. *British Archaeology*, 80 (January/February): 30–5

Cornelison, Jr, J.E. (2003). *The Archaeology of Retreat: Systematic Metal Detector Survey and Information System Analysis at the Battlefield of Chickamauga, September 1863*. In Geier and Potter (2003), 289–304

Coughlan, J. and Holst, M. 2000. 'Health Status'. In Fiorato *et al.* (2000), 60–76

Courtney, P., and Courtney, Y. (1992). 'A Siege Examined: the Civil War Archaeology of Leicester'. *Post Medieval Archaeology*, 26: 47–90

Courville, C.B. (1965). 'War Wounds of the Cranium in the Middle Ages, 2. As Noted in the Skulls of the Sedlec Ossuary near Kuttenberg, Czechoslovakia'. *Bulletin of the Los Angeles Neurological Society*, 30: 34–44

Cowan, R. (2003a). *Roman Legionary, 58BC–AD 69*. Oxford, Osprey

Cowan, R. (2003b). *Imperial Roman Legionary, AD 161–284*. Oxford, Osprey

Credland, A.G. (1983). 'Military Finds'. In Mayes and Butler (1983), 259–66

Creighton, J.D., and Wilson, R.J.A. (1999) (eds). *Roman Germany: Studies in Cultural Interaction. Journal of Roman Archaeology Suplemenatary Series 32*. Portsmouth, RI

Cunha, E., and Silva, A.M. (1997). 'War Lesions from the Famous Portuguese Medieval Battle of Aljubarrota'. *International Journal of Osteoarchaeology*, 7: 595–9

Cunliffe, B.W. (1977). 'The Outer and Bailey and its Defences'. *Excavations at Portchester Castle*. Volume III: *Medieval*. London, Society of Antiquaries/Thames & Hudson

Cunliffe, B. W. (1984). *Roman Bath Discovered*. London, Routledge & Kegan Paul

Cunliffe, B.W. (1994). *The Oxford Illustrated Prehistory of Europe*. Oxford, Oxford University Press

Cunliffe, B.W. (2001). *Facing the Oceans: The Atlantic and its Peoples*. Oxford, Oxford University Press

Cunliffe, B.W., and Garratt, B. (1994). *Excavations at Portchester Castle*. Volume V: *Post Medieval, 1609–1819*. London, Society of Antiquaries/Thames and Hudson

Curle, J. (1911). *A Roman Frontier Post and its People: The Fort of Newstead in the Parish of Melrose*. Glasgow, Society of Antiquaries of Scotland

Dalland, M. (1992). 'Scar: A Viking Boat Burial'. *Current Archaeology*, 131 (October): 475–7

Daniell, C. (2001). 'Battle and Trial: Weapon Injury Burials of St Andrews Church, Fishergate, York'. *Medieval Archaeology*, 45: 220–26

Daniels, C.M., and Jones, C.D.B. (1969). 'The Roman Camps on Llandrindod Common'. *Archaeologia Cambrensis*, 118: 124–34

Davies, R.W. (1971). 'The Roman Military Diet'. *Britannia*, 2: 122–42

Dawson, T. (2004) (ed.). 'Archaeology'. *Medieval History Magazine*, 8 (April): 70–2

Day Lewis, C. (1963) (ed.). *The Collected Poems of Wilfred Owen*. London, Chatto & Windus

Deegan, M., and Rubin, S. (1988). 'Written in Bones: Palaeopathology and Anglo-Saxon Remedies'. *Archaeology Today*, 9/1 (January): 40–5

De la Bédoyère, G. (2001). *Eagles over Britannia: The Roman Army in Britain*. Stroud, Tempus

Delétang, H. (1999) (ed.). *L'Archéologie aérienne en France. Le Passé vu du ciel*. Paris, Éditions Errance

Denison, S. (2003) (ed.). 'News: Roman and Medival Inscriptions Found in Norfolk'. *British Archaeology*, 72 (September), 7

Desfossés, Y., Jacques, A., and Prilaux, G. (2000). 'Premières recherches sur la Grande Guerre dans le Nord-Pas-de-Calais'. *Archéologia*, 367 (May): 32–9

De Vries, K. (1998). *Infantry Warfare in the Early Fourteenth Century*. Woodbridge, Boydell Press

De Vries, K. (2003). 'Medieval Military Surgery'. *Medieval History Magazine*, 4 (December): 18–25

Dickson, C., and Dickson, J. (2000). *Plants and People in Ancient Scotland*. Stroud, Tempus

The Diggers (2005). http://www.diggers.be (accessed 1 September 2005)

Ditchfield, P.H., and Page, W. (1905) (eds). *The Victoria County History of Berkshire*, Volume 1. London, Archibald Constable & Co.

Dixon, P., O'Sullivan, J., and Rogers, I. (2000). *Archaeological Excavations at Jedburgh Friary 1983–1992*. AOC Archaeology Group Monograph 5. Edinburgh, Scottish Trust for Archaeological Research

Dore, J.N., and Wilkes, J.J. (1999). 'Excavations directed by J.D. Leach and J.J. Wilkes on the Site of the Roman Fortress at Carpow, Perthshire 1964–1979'. *Proceedings of the Society of Antiquaries of Scotland*, 129: 481–575

Dorutju, E. (1961). 'Some Observations on the Military Funeral Altar of Adamclisi, Dacia'. *Revue d'archéologie et d'histoire ancienne*, 5: 345–63

Doyle, P. (2001). 'Geology as an Interpreter of Great War Battle Sites'. In Freeman and Pollard (2001), 237–52

Doyle, P., Bostyn, F., Barton, P., and Vandewalle, J. (2001). 'The Underground War 1914–18: The Geology of the Beecham Dugout, Passchendaele, Belgium'. *Proceedings of the Geologists' Association*, 112: 263–74

Duday, H. (1999). 'Remarques sur L'Anthropologie de Terrain'. In *L'Archéologie et la Grande Guerre. 14–18 Aujourd'hui – Today – Heute*. Revue Annuelle d'Histoire, 2. Paris, Éditions Noêsis, 94–103

Durand Group (n.d.). *Durand Group Prospectus Version 1.2*

Eaves, I. (2002). 'Arms, Armour and Militaria'. In Roberts (2002), 324–54

Ede-Borrett, S.L. (1983) (ed.). *The Letters of Neremiah Wharton*. Wollaston, Northamptonshire, Tercio Publications

Ellis, P. (1987). 'Sea Mills, Bristol: The 1965–1968 Excavations in the Roman Town of Abonae. The Gloucester Roman Antefix'. *Transactions of the Bristol and Gloucestershire Archaeological Society*, 105: 15–108

Ellis, P. (1993) (comp. and ed.). *Beeston Castle, Cheshire. Excavations by Laurence Keen and Peter Hough 1968–85*. English Heritage Archaeology Report 23. London, English Heritage

Ellison, M., Finch, M., and Harbottle, B. (1979). 'The Excavation of a 17th Century Pit at the Black Gate, Newcastle-upon-Tyne, 1975'. *Post Medieval Archaeology*, 13: 153–81

Emery, F. (1977). *The Red Soldier: The Zulu War 1879*. London, Hodder & Stoughton

English Heritage (2004). 'The Norse Burial Ground at Cumwhitton', http://www.oxfordarch.co.uk/vikingburial/index.htm (accessed 1 September 2005)

Environment Agency (2005). http://www.environment-agency.gov.uk (accessed 1 September 2005)

Evans, D.R. (1988). 'Soldiers of Squalor?' *Archaeology Today*, 9/1 (January): 23–7

Evans, D.R., and Metcalf, V.M. (1992). *Roman Gates Caerleon*. Oxbow Monograph 15. Oxford, Oxbow/Glamorgan Gwent Archaeological Trust

Evans, J.G., with Atkinson, R.J.C., O'Connor, T., and Green, H.S. (1984). 'Stonehenge: The Environment in the Late Neolithic and Early Bronze Age *and* a Beaker-Age Burial'. *Wiltshire Archaeological and Natural History Magazine*, 78: 7–30

Farrer, M.P. (1862). *Notice of Runic Inscriptions Discovered during Recent Excavations in the Orkneys*. Printed for Private Circulation

Ferguson, N. (1998). *The Pity of War*. Harmondsworth, Penguin

Feugère, M. (2002). *Weapons of the Romans*. Stroud, Tempus

Fielding, R. (2001). *War Letters to a Wife*. Staplehurst, Spellmount

Fiorato, V. (2000). 'The Context of the Discovery'. In Fiorato *et al.* (2000), 1–14

Fiorato, V., Boylston, A., and Knüsel, C. (2000) (eds). *Blood Red Roses: The Archaeology of a Mass Grave from the Battle of Towton AD 1461*. Oxford, Oxbow

Fisher, W.G. (1924). *The History of the Somerset Yeomanry: Volunteer and Territorial Units*. Taunton, Goodman & Son

Flanagan, L. (1987). '400 Years on: The Spanish Armada of 1588'. *Archaeology Today*, 8/10 (November): 5–11

Foard, G. (2001). 'The Archaeology of Attack: Battles and Sieges of the English Civil War'. In Freeman and Pollard (2001), 87–104

Fosten, D.S.V., and Marrion, R.J. (1978). *The German Army 1914–1918*. London, Osprey

Fox, W.F. (1889). *Regimental Losses in the American Civil War 1861–1865: A Treatise on the Extent and Nature of the Mortuary Losses in the Union Regiments, with Full and Exhaustive Statistics Compiled from the Official Records on File in the State Military Bureaus and at Washington*. Albany, NY, Albany Publishing Company

Fraser, A. (2003). 'The "Ocean Villas" Project – Update: World War One Battlefield Archaeology on the Somme'. *Battlefields Review*, 28: 10–11

Fraser, A. (n.d.). *Auchonvillers Project: Auchonvillers 1914–1918*. Interim Report

Freeman, P.W.M., and Pollard, A. (2001) (eds). *Fields of Conflict: Progress and Prospect in Battlefield Archaeology*. Oxford, British Archaeological Report (International) Series, 958. Oxford, Archaeopress

Frere, S.S., Hassall, M.W.C., and Tomlin, R.S.O. (1984). 'Roman Britain in 1983'. *Britannia*, 15: 265–369

Gaimster, D., Boland, P., Linnane, S., and Cartwright, C. (1996). 'The Archaeology of Private Life: The Dudley Castle Condoms'. *Post Medieval Archaeology*, 30: 129–42

Gavaghan, M. (1995). *The Story of the Unknown Warrior*. Preston, M & L Publications

Geier, R., and Potter, S.R. (2003). *Archaeological Perspectives on the American Civil War*. Gainsville, FL, University of Florida Press

George Washington's Fredericksburg Foundation. 'Archaeology at Kenmore', http://www.kenmore.org/foundation/arch_kenmore.html (accessed 1 September 2005)

Giradet, J.M., Jacques, A., and Letho Duclos, J.-L. (2003). *Somewhere on the Western Front: Arras 1914–1918*. Documents d'archéologie et d'histoire du XXe siècle, No. 8. Arras

Goldsworthy, A. (2002). *Roman Warfare*. London, Cassell & Co.

Goldsworthy, A. (2003). *The Complete Roman Army*. London, Thames & Hudson

Gore, R. (1984). 'The Dead Do Tell Tales'. *National Geographic*, 165/5 (May): 557–613

Graves, R. (1960). *Goodbye to All That*. London, Penguin

Gravett, C. (1999). *Hastings – 1066: The Fall of Saxon England*. Oxford, Osprey Publishing

Grayzel, S.R. (2002). *Women and the First World War*. London, Longman

Greaves, Adrian (2002). *Rorke's Drift*. London, Cassell

Greaves, Adrian (2003) (ed.). *Journal of the Anglo-Zulu War Historical Society*, 13. Tenterden, Debinair

Greaves, Andrew (2000). 'Fieldwork Report: Isandlwana 2000' (KwaZulu Natal, South Africa). *Journal of the Anglo-Zulu War Historical Society*, 8: 1–5

Greep, S.J. (1992). *Objects of Worked Bones and Antler*. In Evans and Metcalf (1992), 188–90

Guzzo, P.G. (2003) (ed.). *Da Pompei a Roma. Histoires d'une eruption. Pompéi, Herculaneum, Oplontis*. Milan/Ghent, Electra/Snoeck

Haines, C., and Sumner, G., with Naylor, J. (2000). 'Recreating the World of the Roman Soldier: The Work of the Ermine Street Guard'. *Journal of Roman Military Equipment Studies*, 11: 119–27

Hammond, N. (2004). '2000 Years of Military History'. *Archaeology in Northumberland*. Northumberland County Council, 14: 24

Harding, A.F. (1999a). 'Swords, Shields and Scholars: Bronze Age Warfare, Past and Present'. In Harding (1999), 87–93

Harding, A.F. (1999b) (ed.). *Experiment and Design: Archaeological Studies in Honour of John Coles*. Oxford, Oxbow

Harrington, P. (1992). *Archaeology of the English Civil War*. Princes Risborough, Shire

Harrington, P. (2004). *English Civil War Archaeology*. London, B.T. Batsford

Harrison, R. (2004). *Symbols and Warriors: Images of the European Bronze Age*. Oxford, Western Academic and Specialist Press

Hawkes, S.C. (1989) (ed.). *Weapons and Warfare in Anglo-Saxon England*. Oxford University Committee for Archaeology Monograph 21. Oxford, Oxbow

Heaney, S. (1999). *Beowulf*. London, Faber & Faber

Hibbert, C. (1998). *Agincourt*. Moreton-in-Marsh, Windrush Press

Hibbert, C. (2000) (ed). *The Recollections of Rifleman Harris*. Moreton-in-Marsh, Windrush Press

Hinton, D.A. (1977). 'Objects of Iron'. In Cunliffe, B.W. (1977), 192–204

Holbrook, N., and Bidwell, P.T. (1991). *Roman Finds from Exeter*. Exeter Archaeological Reports Volume 4. Exeter, Exeter City Council and University of Exeter

Holmes, R. (1999). *The Western Front*. London, BBC

Holmes, R. (2001). *Redcoat: The British Soldier in the Age of Horse and Musket*. London, HarperCollins

Holmes, R. (2004). *Tommy: The British Soldier on the Western Front 1914–1918*. London, HarperCollins

Holst, M., and Coughlan, J. (2000). 'Dental Health and Disease'. In Fiorato *et al.* (2000), 77–89

Holst, M., Coughlan, J., and Boylston, A. (2000). 'Catalogue of the Palaeopathology (Appendix C)'. In Fiorato *et al.* (2000), 201–10

Holyoak, V. (2004). 'Who Owns our Dead?' *British Archaeology*, 75 (March): 10–14

Hope, V.M. (2003). 'Trophies and Tombstones: Commemorating the Roman soldier'. *World Archaeology*, 35/1: 79–97

Howard, M. (2002). *Wellington's Doctors: The British Army Medical Services in the Napoleonic Wars*. Staplehurst, Spellmount

Ingelmark, B. (2001). 'The Skeletons'. In Thordeman (2001), 149–209

Jackson, R. (1990). 'Roman Doctors and their Instruments: Recent Research into Ancient Practice'. *Journal of Roman Archaeology*, 3: 5–27

James, S. (2004). *Excavations at Dura Europos 1928–1937. Final Report VII. The Arms and Armour and other Military Equipment*. London, British Museum Press

Johnston, D.E., with Powers, R., and Wheeler, A. (1980). 'The Excavation of a Bell-Barrow at Sutton Veny, Wiltshire'. *Wiltshire Archaeological and Natural History Magazine*, 72/73: 29–50

Jones, D.E. (1997). *Women Warriors: A History*. Washington, Brasseys

Jones, J., and Watson, J. (2003). 'Conservation of a Spectacular Assemblage: Roman armour and leather from Carlisle'. In Wilmot (2003), 10–12

Jünger, E. (2003). *Storm of Steel*. London, Allen Lane (Penguin)

Keegan, J. (1991). *The Face of Battle: A Study of Agincourt, Waterloo and the Somme*. London, Pimlico

Kennett, D.H. (1973). 'Seventh Century Cemeteries in the Ouse Valley'. *Bedfordshire Archaeological Journal*, 8: 99–108

King, A. (1990). *Roman Gaul and Germany*. London, British Museum Press

Kjellström, A. (2005). 'A Sixteenth-Century Warrior Grave from Uppsala, Sweden: The Battle of Good Friday'. *International Journal of Osteoarchaeology*, 15: 23–50

Knight, I.J. (1987) (ed.). *There will be an Awful Row at Home about This*. Shoreham-by-Sea, Zulu Study Group, Victorian Military Society

Knight, R.W., Browne, C., and Grinsell, L.V. (1972). 'Prehistoric Skeletons from Tormarton'. *Transactions of the Bristol and Gloucester Archaeological Society*, 91: 14–17

Knüsel, C. (2000). 'Activity-Related Skeletal Change. In Fiorato *et al.* (2000), 103–18

Knüsel, C., and Boylston, A. (2000). 'How Has the Towton Project Contributed to our Knowledge of Medieval and Later Warfare?' In Fiorato *et al.* (2000), 169–88

Kos, M.S. (1978). 'A Latin Epitaph of a Roman Legionary from Corinth'. *Journal of Roman Studies*, 68: 21–5

Krumeich, G. (1999). 'L'Archéologie: Des sources allemandes'. In *L'Archéologie et la Grande Guerre. 14–18 Aujourd'hui – Today – Heute*. Revue Annuelle d'Histoire, 2. Paris, Éditions Noêsis, 84–93

Laband, J.P.C. (1985). *Fight Us in the Open: The Anglo-Zulu War through Zulu Eyes*. Pietermarizburg/Ulundi, KwaZulu Monuments Council/Shuter and Shooter

Laband, J.P.C. (1987). 'The Battle of Khambula, 29 March 1879: A Re-Examination from the Zulu Perspective'. In Knight (1987), 20–9

Laffin, J. (2003). *Tommy Atkins: The Story of the English Soldier*. Stroud, Sutton Publishing

Last Salute (2005). 'The Battle of Ox Hill (Chantilly)', http://www.espd.com (accessed 10 September 2005)

Laurance, J. (1997). 'Ancient Arts of Anesthesia are Unlocked.' *Independent*, http://www.healthy.net/library/newsletters/update/anethesia.htm

Lemaire, F. (1998). *Ablaincourt-Pressoir: Le Chemin Blanc de Bouvent*. Paris, Association pour Les Fouilles Archéologiques Nationales

Leonard, T. (2001). 'Viking Skeleton Shows Anglo-Saxons' Thirst for Blood'. *News. Telegraph*, http://portal.telegraph.co.uk/news/main.jhtml?xml=/news/2001/11/06 (filed 6 November 2001, accessed 17 April 2005)

Löndahl, V., Price, N., and Robins, G. (2001). *Bomarsund: Archaeology and Heritage Management at the Site of a Crimean War Siege*. In Freeman and Pollard (2001), 207–28

Lowry, B. (1995) (ed.). *Twentieth Century Defences in Britain: An Introductory Guide*. York, Council for British Archaeology

Lucy, S. (2000). *The Anglo-Saxon Way of Death*. Stroud, Sutton Publishing

Lucy, S., and Reynolds, A. (2002) (eds). *Burial in Early Medieval England and Wales*. The Society for Medieval Archaeology Monograph Series 17. London, Society for Medieval Archaeology

McBride, W.S., Andrews, S.C., and Coughlin, S.P. (2003). 'For the Convenience and Comforts of the Soldiers and Employees at the Depot: Archaeology of the Owen's House/ Post Office Complex, Camp Nelson, Kentucky'. In Geier and Potter (2003), 99–124

McKinley, J.I., and Boylston, A. (2002). 'The Skeleton'. In Pitts *et al.* (2002), 136–7

McOmish, D., Field, D. and Brown, G. (2002). *The Field Archaeology of the Salisbury Plain Training Area*. London, English Heritage

Manchester, K. (1983a). *The Archaeology of Disease*. Bradford, University of Bradford Press (3rd edn, C. Roberts and K. Manchester, Stroud, Sutton Publishing, 2005)

Manchester, K. (1983b). 'Human Remains'. In Mayes and Butler (1983), 337–9

Manning, W.H. (1964). 'The Excavation of a Mound near Caesar's Camp, Easthampstead'. *Berkshire Archaeological Journal*, 61: 92–4

Manning, W.H. (1989) (with assistance of I.R. Scott). *Report on the Excavations at Usk 1965–1976. The Fortress Excavations 1972–1974 and Minor Excavations on the Fortress and Flavian Fort*. Cardiff, University of Wales Press

Manning, W.H., with Price, J., and Webster, J. (1995). *Report on the Excavations at Usk 1965–1976. The Roman Small Finds*. Cardiff, University of Wales Press

Martin, C. (2001). 'Before the Battle: Undeployed Battlefield Weaponry from the Spanish Armada, 1588'. In Freeman and Pollard (2001), 73–85

Mary Rose (2005). http://www.maryrose.org (accessed 1 September 2005)

Masefield, J. (1917). *The Old Front Line*. London, Heinemann

Matthews, C.L., and Hawkes, S.C. (1985). 'Early Anglo-Saxon Settlements and Burials on Puddlehill, near Dunstable, Bedfordshire'. *Anglo-Saxon Studies in Archaeology and History*, 4: 59–115

Maude, K. (1987). 'The Search for Quentovic'. *Archaeology Today*, 8/10 (November): 40–5

Mayes, P., and Butler, L.A.S. (1983). *Sandal Castle Excavations 1964–1973*. Wakefield, Wakefield Historical Publications

Mercer, R. (1999). 'The Origins of Warfare in the British Isles'. In Carman and Harding (1999), 143–56

Mitchell, P.D. (2004). *Medicine in the Crusades: Warfare Wounds and the Medieval Surgeon*. Cambridge, Cambridge University Press

Moffat, B. (1988a). 'An Investigation of Medieval Medical Treatments'. *Soutra Hospital Archaeoethnopharmacological Research Report. Proceedings of the Royal College of Physicians of Edinburgh*, 18: 80–6

Moffat, B. (1988b) (ed.). 'SHARP Practice 2: Second Report on Researches into the Medieval Hospital at Soutra, Lothian Region Scotland'. *Soutra Hospital Archaeoethnopharmacological Research Report*, 2

Moffat, B. (1992) (ed.). 'SHARP Practice 4: Fourth Report on Researches into the Medieval Hospital at Soutra, Lothain/Borders Region Scotland'. *Soutra Hospital Archaeoethnopharmacological Research Report*, 4

Moffat, B. (1995) (ed.). 'SHARP Practice 2: Second Report on Researches into the Medieval Hospital at Soutra, Lothian Region Scotland'. *Soutra Hospital Archaeoethnopharmacological Research Report*, 5

MOLAS (2004). *The Prittlewell Prince: The Discovery of a Rich Anglo-Saxon Burial in Essex*. London, Museum of London Archaeology Service

Moorhouse, S. (1971). 'Finds from Basing House, Hampshire (*c.* 1540–1645): Part Two'. *Post Medieval Archaeology*, 5: 35–76

Morel, J.-M.A.W., and Bosman, A.V.A.J. (1989). 'An Early Roman Burial in Velsen I'. In Van Driel-Murray (1989),167–91

Morrill, J. (1991) (ed.). *The Impact of the English Civil War*. London, Collins & Brown

Nash, S. (2004). 'Battles over Battlefields'. *Archaeology*, 57/5: 24–9

Nash-Williams, V.E. (1969). *The Roman Frontier in Wales*. Cardiff, University of Wales Press

Needham, S. (1979). 'Two Recent British Shield Finds and their Continental Parallels'. *Proceedings of the Prehistoric Society*, 45: 111–34

Newark, T. (1993). *Celtic Warriors: 400 BC – AD 1600*. London, Blandford

Nicholson, R. (2002). 'The Fish Bones'. In Roberts, 2002: 390–4

Nicolle, D. (1984). *Arthur and the Anglo-Saxon Wars*. Oxford, Osprey Publishing

Noake, P. (1993). 'The Post Medieval Pottery'. In Ellis (1993), 191–210

Novak, S.A. (2000a). 'Battle-Related Trauma'. In Fiorato *et al.* (2000), 90–102

Novak, S.A. (2000b). 'Case Studies'. In Fiorato *et al.* (2000), 240–68

Olivier, L. (2000). 'Pour une archéologe du passé recent'. *Archéologia*, 367 (May): 24–7

Ortner, D.J., and Aufderheide, A.C. (1991) (eds). *Human Palaeopathology: Current Syntheses and Future Options*. Washington, Smithsonian Institution Press

Osgood, R.H. (1995). 'Three Bronze Phalerae from the River Avon, near Melksham'. *Wiltshire Archaeological and Natural History Magazine*, 88: 50–9

Osgood, R.H. (1998). *Warfare in the Late Bronze Age of North Europe*. British Archaeological Reports (International Series), 694. Oxford, Archaeopress

Osgood, R.H. (1999a). 'The Unknown Warrior? The Re-Evaluation of a Skeleton from a Bell Barrow at Sutton Veny, Wiltshire'. *Wiltshire Archaeological and Natural History Magazine*, 92: 120–32

Osgood, R.H. (1999b). 'Britain in the Age of Warrior Heroes'. *British Archaeology*, 46 (July): 8–9

Osgood, R.H., and Bell, T.W. (forthcoming). *Violent Deaths in the Middle Bronze Age: Excavations at Tormarton, South Gloucestershire*

Osgood, R.H., and Monks, S., with Toms, J. (2000). *Bronze Age Warfare*. Stroud, Sutton Publishing

Page, R.I. (1990). *Norse Myths*. London, British Museum Press

Patscher, S., and Moosbauer, G. (2003). 'Nichts ist, das ewig sei, kein Erz, kein Marmorstein . . .'. *Varus Kurier*, 9 (April): 4–5

Peake, H. (1906). 'Ancient Earthworks'. In Ditchfield and Page (1905), 251–84

Peirce, I. (2002). *Swords of the Vikings*. Woodbridge, Boydell Press

Pericoli, U. (1973). *1815: The Armies at Waterloo*. New York, Charles Scribner's Sons

Pienaar, A. (2002). 'Boer War Fort Dump Excavated and Analysed'. *Beeld Newspaper*, Monday 21 October

Pitts, M., Bayliss, M., McKinley, J., Boylston, A., Budd, P., Evans, J., Chenery, C., Reynolds, A., and Semple, S. (2002). 'An Anglo-Saxon Decapitation and Burial at Stonehenge'. *Wiltshire Archaeologial and Natural History Society*, 95: 131–46

Pollard, A. (2001). '"Place Ekowe in a State of Defence": The Archaeological Investigation of a British Fort at KwaMondi, Eshowe, Zululand'. In Freeman and Pollard (2001), 229–36

Pollard, A., and Oliver, T. (2002). *Two Men in a Trench. Battlefield Archaeology: The Key to Unlocking the Past*. London, Michael Joseph (Penguin)

Pollard, A., and Oliver, T. (2003). *Two Men in a Trench II: Uncovering the Secrets of British Battlefields*. London, Michael Joseph (Penguin)

Potter, S.R., and Owsley, D.W. (2003). *An Irishman Dies at Antietam: An Archaeology of the Battlefield*. In Geier and Potter (2003), 56–72

Potter, S.R., Sonderman, R.C., Creveling, M.C., and Dean, S.L. (2003). '"No Maneuvering and Very Little Tactics": Archaeology and the Battle of Brawner Farm'. In Geier and Potter (2003), 3–28

Prentice, G., and Prentice, M.C. (2003). *Far from the Battlefield: Archaeology at Andersonville, Prison*. In Geier and Potter (2003), 166–87

Prior, R. and Wilson, T. (2002). *Passchendaele: The Untold Story*. Yale, CT, Yale Nota Bene

Pryor, F. (1991). *Flag Fen Prehistoric Fenland Centre*. London, Batsford/English Heritage

RCHME. (1964). *Newark on Trent: The Civil War Siegeworks*. London, HMSO

Remarque, E.M. (1996). *All Quiet on the Western Front*. London, Vintage (first published 1929)

Reynolds, A. (2002a). *Later Anglo-Saxon England: Life and Landcape*. Stroud, Tempus

Reynolds, A. (2002b). *Burials, Boundaries and Charters in Anglo-Saxon England: A Reassessment*. In Lucy and Reynolds (2002) (eds), 171–94

Richards, J. (2001). *Blood of the Vikings*. London, BBC

Richardson, J. (2002). 'Mammal Bones'. In Roberts (2002): 363–84

Richardson, T. (2000). 'Armour'. In Fiorato *et al.* (2000), 137–47

Roberts, I. (2002). *Pontefract Castle: Archaeological Excavations 1982–86*. Yorkshire Archaeology 8. Leeds, West Yorkshire Archaeology Service

Robinson, H.R. (1975). *The Armour of Imperial Rome*. London, Arms and Armour Press

Robinson, J. (2004). *The Lewis Chessmen*. London, British Museum Press

Robinson, M. (2000). 'A Preliminary Investigation of Waterlogged Sediments from the Early Fort Ditches at Alchester for Environmental Evidence'. In Sauer (2000), 157: 64–5

Robinson, P. (2001). 'The Rey Cross Camp'. In Vyner (2001), 76–85

Roman Hideout (2002). 'Roman Garrison Gourmets Revealed in Carlisle Dig', http:www.romanhideout.com/news/2002/engheritage20020708.asp (accessed 1 September 2005)

Rule, M. (1989). 'From Grave to Cradle'. *Yesterday's World*, 2 (November/December): 16–23

Russell Robinson, H. (1977). 'The Armour Fragments'. In Cunliffe (1977), 194–6

Salvatore, J.P. (2001). 'Three Roman Military Cremation Burials from Holloway Street, Exeter'. *Proceedings of the Devon Archaeological Society*, 59: 125–39

Sauer, E.W. (2000). 'Alchester, a Claudian "Vexillation Fortress" near the Western Boundary of the Catuvellauni: New Light on the Roman Invasion of Britain'. *Archaeological Journal*, 157: 1–78

Saunders, N.J. (2002). 'Excavating Memories: Archaeology and the Great War, 1914–2001'. *Antiquity*, 76: 101–8

Saunders, N.J. (2003). *Trench Art: Materialities and Memories of War*. Oxford, Berg

Schlüter, W. (1999). 'The Battle of Teutoburg Forest: Archaeological Research at Kalkriese near Osnabrück'. In Creighton and Wilson (1999), 125–59

Scott, D.D., Fox, Jr, R.A., Connor, M.A., and Harmon, D. (1989). *Archaeological Perspectives on the Battle of the Little Bighorn*. Norman, OK, University of Oklahoma Press

Scott, I.R. (1991). 'The Military Equipment'. In Holbrook and Bidwell (1991), 263–5

Selzer, W. (1988). *Römische Steindenkmäler: Mainz in Römischer Zeit*. Mainz, Philipp von Zabern

Shaw, P. (2003) (ed.). 'Archaeology'. *Medieval History Magazine*, 4 (December): 7

Shepherd, D.J. (1999). 'The Elusive Warrior Maiden Tradition: Bearing Weapons in Anglo-Saxon Society'. In Carman and Harding (1999), 219–43

Sherratt, A.G. (1994). 'The Emergence of Elites: Earlier Bronze Age Europe, 2500–1300 BC'. In Cunliffe (1994), 167–201

Siddorn, J.K. (2000). *Viking Weapons and Warfare*. Stroud, Tempus

Sidebottom, P. (n.d.). *Uncovering the Secrets of Hill 60* (May 2003)

Silkin, J. (1979) (ed.). *The Penguin Book of First World War Poetry*. Harmondsworth, Penguin

Smith, L. (1986). *The German Prisoner of War Camp at Leigh 1914–1919*. Radcliffe, Neil Richardson

Smith, N. (1995). 'Military Training Earthworks in Crowthorne Wood Berkshire: A Survey by the Royal Commission on the Historical Monuments of England'. *Archaeological Journal*, 152: 422–40

Smith, V.T.C. (1995). 'Brimstone Hill Fortress, St Kitts, West Indies. Part Two: Description'. *Post Medieval Archaeology*, 29: 77–106

Stallworthy, J. (1977). *Wilfred Owen*. Oxford, Oxford University Press

Stead, I.M. (1991). *Iron Age Cemeteries in East Yorkshire*. London, English Heritage

Sterling, B.B. (2003). 'Archaeological Interpretations of the Battle of Antietam through Analysis of Small Arms Projectiles'. In Geier and Potter (2003), 323–47

Stirland, A.J. (2000). *Raising the Dead: The Skeleton Crew of King Henry VIII's Great Ship, the Mary Rose*. Chichester, Wiley

Strickland, M., and Hardy, R. (2005). *The Great Warbow: From Hastings to the Mary Rose*. Stroud, Sutton Publishing

Sumner, G. (2003). *Roman Military Clothing (2) AD 200–400*. Oxford, Osprey

Sun Tzu (1971). *The Art of War*. Oxford, Oxford University Press

Sutherland, T. (2000a). 'Recording the Grave'. In Fiorato *et al.* (2000), 36–44

Sutherland, T. (2000b). 'The Archaeological Investigation of the Towton Battlefield'. In Fiorato *et al.* (2000), 155–68

Tacitus (1970). *The Agricola and Germania*, trans. H. Mattingly and S.A. Handford. Harmondsworth, Penguin

Tacitus (1989). *Annals IV*, ed. and trans. D.C.A. Shotter. Oxford, Aris & Phillips

Talbot-Rice, E., and Harding, M. (1989). *Butterflies and Bayonets: The Soldier as Collector*. Chelsea, National Army Museum

Thordeman, B. (2001). *Armour from the Battle of Visby 1361*. Facsimile of the 1939 Original. Highland Hill, TX, Chivalry Bookshelf

Tolstoy, L. (1988). *War and Peace*. Harmondsworth, Penguin

Tweddle, D. (1992). 'The Anglian Helmet from Coppergate'. *The Archaeology of York: The Small Finds*. York, York Archaeological Trust/Council for British Archaeology

Underwood, R. (1999). *Anglo-Saxon Weapons and Warfare*. Stroud, Tempus

Van Driel-Murray, C. (1989) (ed.). *Roman Military Equipment: The Sources of Evidence*. British Archaeological Reports (International Series) 476. Oxford, Archaeopress

Van Driel-Murray, C. (1995) (ed.). *Journal of Roman Military Equipment Studies*, 6

Van Schalkwyk, L., and Taylor, M. (1999). 'The Excavation and Re-interment of Mortal Remains from Cairn 27, Isandlwana Battlefield, South Africa'. *Journal of the Anglo-Zulu War Historical Society*, 6: 12–14

Von Clausewitz, C. (1997). *On War*. Ware, Wordsworth

Vyner, B. (2001). *Stainmore: The Archaeology of a North Pennine Pass*. Hartlepool, Tees Archaeology/English Heritage

Waller, J. (2000). 'Archery'. In Fiorato *et al.* (2000), 130–6

Walter, J. (1991). *The Diary of a Napoleonic Foot Soldier*, ed. and intro. Marc Raeff. Moreton-in-Marsh, Windrush Press

Warin, A. (1989) (ed.). *Dear Girl, I Escaped . . . Experiences of the Great War 1914–1918*. Bristol, Redcliffe Press

Wason, D. (2003). *Battlefield Detectives*. London, Granada

Watts, K., and Mahrer, N. (2004). 'Brothers in Arms? Exhibition Catalogue'. *Medieval History Magazine*, 8 (April): 50–9

Webster, G. (2002). *The Legionary Fortress at Wroxeter: Excavations by Graham Webster, 1955–85*, ed. J. Chadderton. London, English Heritage

Wells, P.S. (2003). *The Battle that Stopped Rome: Emperor Augustus, Arminius, and the Slaughter of the Legions in the Teutoburg Forest*. New York, Norton

Wenham, S.J. (1989). 'Anatomical Interpretations of Anglo-Saxon Weapon Injuries'. In Hawkes (1989), 123–39

Wessex Archaeology (2004a). 'Penally Training Area, ATE Pembroke, Pembroke, Pembrokeshire'. Archaeological Desk-Based Assessment and Condition Survey. Ref 53268.02: January 2004. Unpublished

Wessex Archaeology (2004b). 'The Amesbury Archer', http://www.wessexarch.co.uk/projects/amesbury/archer.html (accessed 1 September 2005)

Wheeler, W. (1999). *The Letter of Private Wheeler 1809–1928*, ed. and foreword by G.H. Liddell Hart. Moreton-in-Marsh, Windrush Press

Whitehorne, J.W.A., Geier, C.R., and Hofstra, W.R. (2003). 'The Sheridan Field Hospital, Winchester, Virginia, 1864'. In Geier and Potter (2003), 148–65

Wiegels, R. (1997). 'Es war das tapferste Heer von allen . . .'. *Varus-Kurier Zeitung für Freunde und Förderer des Projekts Kalkriese*, 3/2 (November): 6–10

Wiegels, R. (2000). '"Vae Victis". Zum Problem des Sterbens und kollektiven Tötens im Krieg in römischer Zeit'. *Varus-Kurier Zeitung für Freunde und Förderer des Projekts Kalkriese*, 6/1(December): 7–10

Wilbers-Rost, S. (1997). 'Aus der Forschung: Naturwissenschaftliche Untersuchungen zu den bisherigen Grabungen auf dem Oberesch'. *Varus-Kurier Zeitung für Freunde und Förderer des Projekts Kalkriese,* 3/2 (November): 15–16

Wilbers-Rost, S. (1999). 'Grabungen auf dem Timpen und dem Oberesch: Erste Ergebnisse und neue Erkenntnisse'. *Varus-Kurier Zeitung für Freunde und Förderer des Projekts Kalkriese,* 5/1 (December): 3–4

Wilbers-Rost, S. (2000). 'Die Grabungen auf dem Oberesch im Jahr 2000'. *Varus-Kurier Zeitung für Freunde und Förderer des Projekts Kalkriese,* 6/1 (December): 2–4

Wilbers-Rost, S. (2003a). 'Die Befunde auf dem "Oberesch" in Kalkriese und die Varusschlact'. *Archäologie in Niedersachsen,* Volume 6. Oldenburg, Isensee Verlag: 30–6

Wilbers-Rost, S. (2003b). 'Der Hinterhalt gegen Varus; zu Konstruktion und Funktion der germanischen Wallanlage auf dem "Oberesch" in Kalkriese: Archäologische Forschungen in Niedersachsen 1987–2002'. In *Festschrift für Günter Wegener,* Volume 2: *Die Kunde: Zeitschrift für niedersächsische Archäologie,* Neue Folge 54: 123–42

Wild, J.P. (1981). 'A Find of Roman Scale Armour from Carpow'. *Britannia,* 12: 305–6

Wilmot, T. (1997). *Birdoswald: Excavations of a Roman Fort on Hadrian's Wall and its Successor Settlements 1987–92.* London, English Heritage

Wilmot, T. (2003) (ed.). *CFA News: Newsletter of the Centre for Archaeology,* 6 (Summer). London, English Heritage

Wilson, P.R. (2002). *Cataractonium: Roman Catterick and its Hinterland. Excavations and Research 1958–1977. Part II.* Council for British Archaeology Research Report 129. London, CBA

Wood, M. (1982). *In Search of the Dark Ages.* London, Ariel Books/BBC

Wood, M. (1986). *Domesday: A Search for the Roots of England.* London, Guild Publishing

Wright, G. (2002). 'Civil War Siege Coinage'. In Roberts (2002), 282–6

Wroughton, J. (1999). *An Unhappy Civil War: The Experiences of Ordinary People in Gloucestershire, Somerset and Wiltshire 1642–1646.* Bath, Lansdown Press

York Archaeological Trust (2005). http://www.yorkarchaeology.co.uk/ (accessed 1 September 2005)

Zienkiewicz, J.D. (1986a). *The Legionary Fortress Baths at Caerleon.* Volume I: *The Buildings.* Cardiff, National Museum of Wales/Cadw

Zienkiewicz, J.D. (1986b). *The Legionary Fortress Baths at Caerleon.* Volume II: *The Finds.* Cardiff, National Museum of Wales/Cadw

Zylla, I.-M., and Tolksdorf-Lienemann, E. (2000). 'Unter die Lupe Genommen: Die Knochenfunde von Kalkriese'. *Varus-Kurier Zeitung für Freunde und Förderer des Projekts Kalkriese,* 6/1 (December): 5–7

Recommended Websites

Although their longevity cannot be guaranteed, the following websites were invaluable in the preparation of this work (all accessed 1 September 2005)

Chapter One
Archaeoptics work on the Stonehenge carvings
   http://www.wessexarch.co.uk/press/stonehenge_lasers.html
   http://minotaur.archaeoptics.co.uk/index.php/2005/07/04/application-of-3d-laser-scanning/
Wessex Archaeology's Excavations of the Amesbury Archer
   http://www.wessexarch.co.uk/projects/amesbury/archer.html

Chapter Two
Guy de la Bédoyère's pages on the Roman army
   http://www.romanbritain.freeserve.co.uk/Legions.htm
General information on the legions
   http://www.morgue.demon.co.uk
Roman army and military equipment history pages
   http://www.armatura.connectfree.co.uk/arma.htm
A resource with maps of Roman military locations
   http://www.roman-britain.org
Discussion forum for all topics connected to the Roman armies
   http://www.romanarmy.com/rat.html
Database of Roman Army Tombstones
   http://www.romanarmy.com/imb/
Oxford Archaeology North and the Carlisle Armour
   http://www.carlislemillenniumdig.co.uk

Chapter Three
The British Museum, holder of the Lewis Chessmen and Sutton Hoo artefacts:
   http://www.thebritishmuseum.ac.uk/compass/index.html
The Prittlewell excavations
   http://www.molas.org.uk
The BBC website for the documentary series *The Blood of the Vikings*
   http://www.bbc.co.uk/history/programmes/bloodofthevikings/index.shtml
Oxford Archaeology's information on its excavations at Cumwhitton
   http://www.oxfordarch.co.uk/vikingburial/index.htm
Information on the Viking runes in the Neolithic tomb of Maes Howe
   http://www.henge.org.uk/orkney/maeshowe.html

A website that explores several Anglo-Saxon and Viking battle sites and has links to archaeology
    http://www.battlefieldstrust.com/resource-centre/viking

Chapter Four
Skeletons from the Battle of Towton
    http://www.brad.ac.uk/acad/archsci/depart/report97/towton.shtm
Excavations at Visby
    http://www.historiska.se/exhibitions/korsbetningen/index.html
A resource on Medieval battlefields
  · http://www.battlefieldstrust.com/resource-centre/viking

Chapter Five
The *Mary Rose*
    http://www.maryrose.org
Civil War archaeology
    http://www.worcestershire.gov.uk/home/cs-archeo-info/cs-archeo-cwarch.htm
A resource on Civil War battlefields
    http://www.battlefieldstrust.com/resource-centre/viking/

Chapter Six
Zulu War
    http://www.kwazulu.co.uk/archaeology.htm
Napoleonic period
    http://www.brixhamheritage.org.uk/arch/berry_head_report2000.htm
Imperial War Museum:
    http://www.iwm.org.uk
American Civil War
    http://www.espd.com

Chapter Seven
Archaeology of the First World War
    http://w1.865.telia.com/%7Eu86517080/BattlefieldArchaeology/ArkeologENG.html
The Diggers
    http://www.diggers.be
Auchonvillers
    http://www.timetrav.force9.co.uk/Ocean/Ocean.htm
Western Front Association
    http://www.westernfrontassociation.com/
National Army Museum:
    http://www.national-army-museum.ac.uk/
Great War Cave Art
    http://www.abcollection.com/fr/musee/confrecourt.php
    http://perso.wanadoo.fr/memoiremurs/guerre1418.html#02
Arras Hospital
    http://news.bbc.co.uk/1/hi/world/europe/992293.stm

A prisoner-of-war camp in England
   http://members.aol.com/stobsmilitary
Commonwealth War Graves Commission
   http://www.cwgc.org
The Great War Forum (from the Long, Long, Trail)
   http://1914-1918.invisionzone.com/forums/index.php?
The Australian War Memorial
   http://www.awm.gov.au

Index